# IFIP Advances in Information and Communication Technology 579

## IFIP – The International Federation for Information Processing

IFIP was founded in 1960 under the auspices of UNESCO, following the first World Computer Congress held in Paris the previous year. A federation for societies working in information processing, IFIP's aim is two-fold: to support information processing in the countries of its members and to encourage technology transfer to developing nations. As its mission statement clearly states:

> *IFIP is the global non-profit federation of societies of ICT professionals that aims at achieving a worldwide professional and socially responsible development and application of information and communication technologies.*

IFIP is a non-profit-making organization, run almost solely by 2500 volunteers. It operates through a number of technical committees and working groups, which organize events and publications. IFIP's events range from large international open conferences to working conferences and local seminars.

The flagship event is the IFIP World Computer Congress, at which both invited and contributed papers are presented. Contributed papers are rigorously refereed and the rejection rate is high.

As with the Congress, participation in the open conferences is open to all and papers may be invited or submitted. Again, submitted papers are stringently refereed.

The working conferences are structured differently. They are usually run by a working group and attendance is generally smaller and occasionally by invitation only. Their purpose is to create an atmosphere conducive to innovation and development. Refereeing is also rigorous and papers are subjected to extensive group discussion.

Publications arising from IFIP events vary. The papers presented at the IFIP World Computer Congress and at open conferences are published as conference proceedings, while the results of the working conferences are often published as collections of selected and edited papers.

IFIP distinguishes three types of institutional membership: Country Representative Members, Members at Large, and Associate Members. The type of organization that can apply for membership is a wide variety and includes national or international societies of individual computer scientists/ICT professionals, associations or federations of such societies, government institutions/government related organizations, national or international research institutes or consortia, universities, academies of sciences, companies, national or international associations or federations of companies.

More information about this series at http://www.springer.com/series/6102

Lynette Drevin · Suné Von Solms ·
Marianthi Theocharidou (Eds.)

# Information Security Education

## Information Security in Action

13th IFIP WG 11.8 World Conference, WISE 13
Maribor, Slovenia, September 21–23, 2020
Proceedings

Springer

*Editors*
Lynette Drevin
North-West University
Potchefstroom, South Africa

Suné Von Solms
University of Johannesburg
Johannesburg, South Africa

Marianthi Theocharidou
EU Agency for Cybersecurity
Maroussi, Greece

ISSN 1868-4238 ISSN 1868-422X (electronic)
IFIP Advances in Information and Communication Technology
ISBN 978-3-030-59290-5 ISBN 978-3-030-59291-2 (eBook)
https://doi.org/10.1007/978-3-030-59291-2



This Springer imprint is published by the registered company Springer Nature Switzerland AG
The registered company address is: Gewerbestrasse 11, 6330 Cham, Switzerland

# Preface

This volume contains the papers presented at the 13th World Conference on Information Security Education (WISE 13) held during September 21–23, 2020. It was held in conjunction with the 35th IFIP TC-11 SEC 2020 International Information Security and Privacy Conference. It was initially planned to be held in May 2020 in Maribor, Slovenia, but due to the COVID-19 restrictions, it was rescheduled and successfully held online.

WISE 13 was organized by the IFIP Working Group 11.8, which is an international group of people from academia, government, and private organizations who volunteer their time and effort to increase knowledge in the very broad field of information security through education. WG11.8 has worked to increase information security education and awareness for almost two decades. This year, WG11.8 organized the 13th conference of a successful series under the theme "Information Security in Action." We have received 28 submissions from around the world. Each submission was blind reviewed by at least three International Program Committee members. The committee decided to accept 13 full papers. The acceptance rate for the conference was thus 46%.

This conference took place thanks to the support and commitment of many individuals. First, we would like to thank all TC-11 members for continually giving us the opportunity to serve the working group and organize the WISE conferences. Our sincere appreciation also goes to the members of the Program Committee, to the external reviewers, and to the authors who trusted us with their intellectual work. We are grateful for the support of WISE11.8 Officers: Lynn Futcher, Matt Bishop, Natalia Miloslavskaya, and Erik Moore. Finally, we would like to thank the IFIP SEC 2020 organizers for their support. As for the preparation of this volume, we sincerely thank Miriam Costales and our publisher Springer for their assistance.

August 2020

Lynette Drevin
Suné von Solms
Marianthi Theocharidou

# Organization

## WISE 13 Conference Chair

| | |
|---|---|
| Lynn Futcher | Nelson Mandela University, South Africa |

## WISE 13 Program Chairs

| | |
|---|---|
| Lynette Drevin | North-West University, South Africa |
| Suné von Solms | University of Johannesburg, South Africa |

## WISE 13 Conference Secretariat

| | |
|---|---|
| Matt Bishop | University of California, Davis, USA |

## WISE 13 Publications Chair

| | |
|---|---|
| Marianthi Theocharidou | European Union Agency for Cybersecurity, Greece |

## WISE 13 Logistics Chair

| | |
|---|---|
| Natalia Miloslavskaya | National Research Nuclear University, MEPhI, Russia |

## WISE 13 Web Chair

| | |
|---|---|
| Erik Moore | Regis University, USA |

## Program Committee

| | |
|---|---|
| Stefan Alfredsson | Karlstad University, Sweden |
| Maria Bada | University of Cambridge, UK |
| Matt Bishop | University of California, Davis, USA |
| Reinhardt Botha | Nelson Mandela University, South Africa |
| Jun Dai | California State University, Sacramento, USA |
| Melissa Dark | Purdue University, USA |
| Lynette Drevin | North-West University, South Africa |
| Simone Fischer-Hübner | Karlstad University, Sweden |
| Lothar Fritsch | Karlstad University, Sweden |
| Steven Furnell | Plymouth University, UK |
| Lynn Futcher | Nelson Mandela University, South Africa |
| Ram Herkanaidu | Plymouth University, UK |
| Lech Janczewski | The University of Auckland, New Zealand |
| Audun Josang | University of Oslo, Norway |

| | |
|---|---|
| Suresh Kalathur | Boston University, USA |
| Christos Kalloniatis | University of the Aegean, Greece |
| Sokratis Katsikas | Open University of Cyprus, Cyprus |
| Andrea Kolberger | University of Applied Sciences Upper Austria, Austria |
| Hennie Kruger | North-West University, South Africa |
| Costas Lambrinoudakis | University of Piraeus, Greece |
| Wai Sze Leung | University of Johannesburg, South Africa |
| Javier Lopez | University of Malaga, Spain |
| Leonardo Martucci | Karlstad University, Sweden |
| Vashek Matyas | Masaryk University, Czech Republic |
| Natalia Miloslavskaya | National Research Nuclear University, MEPhI, Russia |
| Stig Mjolsnes | Norwegian University of Science and Technology, Norway |
| Erik Moore | Regis University, USA |
| Ida Ngambeki | Purdue University, USA |
| Ruxandra F. Olimid | Norwegian University of Science and Technology, Norway, and University of Bucharest, Romania |
| Marianthi Theocharidou | European Union Agency for Cybersecurity, Greece |
| Alexander Tolstoy | National Research Nuclear University, MEPhI, Russia |
| Suné von Solms | University of Johannesburg, South Africa |

## Additional Reviewers

Ana Nieto
Rodrigo Roman

# Contents

# Teaching Methods and Tools

# Learning and Grading Cryptology via Automated Test Driven Software Development

Konstantin Knorr(✉)

Trier University of Applied Sciences, Trier, Germany
knorr@hochschule-trier.de

**Abstract.** Understanding common cryptological concepts like encryption, hashing, signatures, and certificates is a prerequisite when working as an IT security professional but it is also a major challenge in security education. Often students struggle with cryptology as sound previous mathematical knowledge is required and study time is limited. Teachers face the problem to fairly assess the students' knowledge and understanding of cryptology. The paper presents an approach to face these challenges by utilizing test driven software development techniques for students who have taken courses in programming and theoretical cryptology. The paper describes the practical experience gained in courses with $\sim 30$ students utilizing a specialized client-server system to automate the tests. We propose that this setup is beneficial for learning as it gives immediate feedback and allows students to focus on the erroneous parts of their software. The test cases can also be used to grade students' code by weighting the test cases e.g. in an exam setting.

**Keywords:** Cryptology · Java · JUnit tests · Test driven software development · Playfair cipher

## 1 Introduction

Students learning cryptology face the challenge to understand complex topics like number theory for asymmetric ciphers in a limited time frame. Cryptology is typically taught and exercised on a pen and paper basis in theory only due to an overloaded curriculum. This dilemma is additionally fostered by new developments in cryptology like elliptic curves and post quantum techniques which require even more theory and time.

We argue in this paper that learning cryptology in combination with test driven software development (TDSD) is beneficial for the students and also allows for a transparent grading system providing quality assessment of students. TDSD provides instant feedback, supports learning form failures, is programming language independent, and gives an immediate evaluation. Grading the student's source code by predefined test cases relieves the instructor from evaluating the code which is tedious, difficult, and error-prone. Software testing is also a major step towards the greater goal of software quality. Edwards and Perez-Quinones [1] argue that despite the importance


L. Drevin et al. (Eds.): WISE 2020, IFIP AICT 579, pp. 3–17, 2020.
https://doi.org/10.1007/978-3-030-59291-2_1

of the topic, most computer science curricula provide only minimal coverage of the topic, as it is poorly suited for the topic of a new course. Students therefore typically leave university unprepared for real world testing tasks upon graduation.

In many universities the curriculum for computer science encompasses courses for programming and for IT security which often includes theoretical cryptology. The scope is given in Europe following the Bologna reform in ECTS (European Credit Transfer System) credit points (CP), one CP equals ~30 working hours. In many computer science study programs, the IT security scope is limited to 5–10 CPs. This does not leave enough time for an in-depth coverage of cryptology. However, by creating a new course e.g. called "Implementing Cryptology", based on previous skills in cryptology and programming, the understanding in both areas can be improved.

Courses typically consist of lectures where the theoretical content is presented by the lecturer and exercises in which work assignments for the theoretical content have to be solved by the students (homework). Most modules need to be graded by the lecturer. The grade is typically the result of a written exam or an oral examination. Some universities' examination regulations allow for requiring students to have successfully solved a certain percentage of the assignments prior to taking the exam or oral examination. While the exam is typically in a highly supervised environment (cheating will lead to "failed"), the homework is typically done in an unsupervised environment e.g. at home. One of the major challenges for the lecturer is to find fair and transparent grades for the students while taking his time effort into consideration especially for courses with a large number of students.

The paper describes the LCJTC (Learning Cryptology with Java Test Cases) approach which has been applied to courses with 20–30 students. We argue that LCJTC allows students to better learn and understand cryptology and also provides a transparent and fair grading schema.

The remainder of the paper has the following structure: Sect. 2 gives the necessary background information on TDSD, JUnit tests, the system used to assess the students' code, and cryptology in Java. As an easy-to-understand example for a cryptological cipher we will use the Playfair cipher presented in Sect. 2.4 throughout the paper. Section 3 describes the LCJTC approach including grading. The paper closes in Sect. 4 with a discussion of LCJTC in practice including the topics cheating, privacy issues, and related work. Finally, a conclusion including future work is given.

# 2 Background

## 2.1 Tests Driven Software Development and JUnit Test

TDSD aka test-first coding stems from Beck [2] and is a subgroup of agile software development. The fundamental idea is to produce only code that passes predefined test cases. Coding first and then writing test cases could result in omitting important test cases. It encourages programmers to always have a running version of their code and to test features and code during implementation thereby avoiding integration problems typically encountered in other development models at the end of a project.

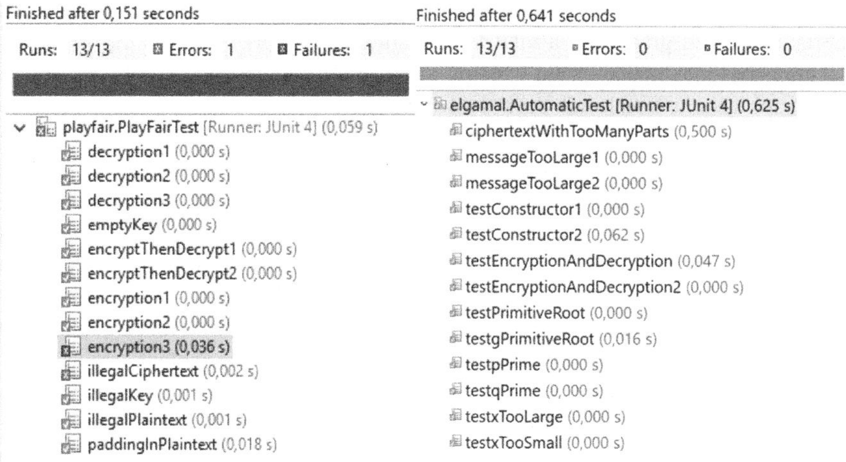


**Fig. 1.** JUnit test cases for Playfair (left) and Elgamal (right) ciphers and their run time in the Eclipse IDE. For Playfair 11 of 13 tests passed. Test `encryption3` produced a failure, as an incorrect ciphertext was calculated, test `illegalCiphertext` raised an unexpected exception. All Elgamal tests passed. (Color figure online)

A programmer writes a test and then the code that needs to be tested. The test is a piece of software, too and is typically written in the same IDE. When another programmer later wants to make changes to the code, he first executes all test cases to ensure that the code base is error free. He then changes or adds code, again executes all test cases, and makes sure they pass in order not to add any errors in this new code. In case tests do not pass, he knows that he introduced an error and can fix it. This cycle is repeated until all test cases pass. Summarized, the major steps in TDSD are: 1. add a test, 2. run all tests, 3. write some code, 4. run tests, 5. refactor code, 6. repeat from step 1.

TDSD is programming language independent. It is mainly applied to unit tests in comparison to the later and more complex integration, system, and acceptance tests. Several so called XUnit frameworks have been proposed for unit tests. For the Java programming language, the popular JUnit framework [3] implements the TDSD paradigm and allows for testing classes, methods, and exceptions. Major IDEs like Eclipse provide graphical user interfaces to visualize JUnit tests and their results (cf. Fig. 1). A JUnit test can have three different results:

- Passed (coloured green), e.g. test `decrpytion1` in Fig. 1.
- Error (coloured red): an unexpected exception has been thrown by the code.
- Failure (coloured blue): an incorrect result has been calculated for that test.

## 2.2 Automatic Software Evaluation System

Automatic assessment and grading of programming assignments has been in the focus of researchers and practitioners for many years. See [1, 4–6] for an introduction and overview of current systems. The main advantages of these systems are traceability of the programming progress, immediate feedback, and scalability. Especially for larger cohorts automated grading is a vital tool in study programs.

This paper makes use of the existing and long-running ASE (Automatic Software Evaluation) system which has been described in detail in [7, 8]. ASE has been in use since 2006 at the University of Applied Sciences in Trier, Germany. Its architecture is a web based client server system. Authentication of students and instructors is accomplished via Shibboleth login. ASE's kernel comprises web sockets for managing client-server communication and database and execution environments for selected programming languages like Java, C++, and Python. Each language can load plugins e.g. unit test runners or modules to check programming style.

The different tests can be configured using XML files. This includes maximal time lengths allowed for the tests. The result of the assessment of the student's code is stored in a database and written in an XML file which is then presented in the student's browser. The ability to assess graphical Java programs written in JavaFX even though the server has no desktop environment installed differentiates ASE from other systems. ASE uses the TestFX framework ("headless tests") for this purpose. ASE also uses TLS to protect all data in transit. A typical life cycle for ASE assignments is the following:

- The instructor presents theoretical teaching content in class and prepares corresponding assignments (s. Appendix A for an example), a time frame for the assignment, the test cases and uploads the test cases to the server.
- Students solve the assignments and submit the solution to ASE.
- ASE verifies the submission by executing the test cases on the submitted code and provides instantaneous feedback which parts are correct or wrong with error messages that are part of the test cases (e.g. line 6 in Listing 2). Also, peer-review is possible allowing students to review each other's code.
- After the deadline the instructor reviews assignment results and can comment on common errors in the next lecture and optionally makes adaptions to the test cases and assignment text.

### 2.3 Java and Cryptology

Java by Oracle is a popular object-oriented programming language especially in the academic world. It is based on classes with attributes and methods including constructors. Classes can be grouped into packages. Java also allows for an elaborate exception handling. The JCA (Java Cryptography Architecture) [9] encompasses hash functions, key generation, is part of the java.security package, and was introduced with JDK 1.1. JCE (Java Cryptography Extension) is the Java interface for encryption, decryption, and authentication and is included in the package javax.crypto [10]. It is part of Java since JDK 1.4. The Cipher class forms the core of the JCE framework, providing the functionality for encryption and decryption.

As encryption for symmetric key sizes larger 56 bit and for asymmetric key sizes larger 512 bit underlies export restrictions in the US, JCA does not contain any encryption operations and all encryption is handled in JCE allowing only "weak" keys in default installation. The local Java security policy needs to be replaced (for version pre 1.8.0_151) or edited (for newer versions) for larger key sizes, otherwise an InvalidKey exception is thrown. For many cryptological scenarios JCA and JCE are not sufficient and external cryptology providers like Bouncy Castle [11] are required. External providers typically have (1) more cipher suites and algorithms than the default JCA/JCE, (2) other helpful utilities e.g. for encoding and decoding or for reading arcane formats like PEM, and (3) are of non US origin and are therefore not subject to the rigid US export restrictions and possible legal consequences.

```
1.  import javax.crypto.Cipher;
2.  import javax.crypto.SecretKey;
3.  import javax.crypto.spec.*;
4.  import org.bouncycastle.util.Strings;
5.  import org.bouncycastle.util.encoders.Hex;
6.  public class gcmEncryptor {
7.  public static void main(String[] args) throws Exception{
8.  SecretKey aesKey = new SecretKeySpec(
        Hex.decode("000102030405060708090a0b0c0d0e0f"), "AES");
9.  byte[] iv = Hex.decode("00112233445566778899aabb");
10. byte[] msg = Strings.toByteArray("Hello Maribor!");
11. System.out.println("msg:   " + Hex.toHexString(msg));
12. Cipher cipher = Cipher.getInstance("AES/GCM/NoPadding", "BC");
13. GCMParameterSpec spec = new GCMParameterSpec(64, iv);
14. cipher.init(Cipher.ENCRYPT_MODE, aesKey, spec);
15. byte[] cText = cipher.doFinal(msg);
16. System.out.println("cText: " + Hex.toHexString(cText));}}
```

**Listing 1.** Java code to encrypt the string “Hello world!” with AES in GCM mode.

Listing 1 shows the most important steps when using modern symmetric ciphers with Java. It uses a hard-coded key which should never be done for productive code. This is done here only for the sake of simplicity. Also, the optional addition of authenticated data and the decryption is not shown.

The Cipher class is instantiated in line 12 with the symmetric cipher AES in GCM[1] mode which does not require padding. Note that the external crypto provider Bouncy Castle (“BC” in line 12) is used. The initialization of the encryption in line 14 requires an AES key which is generated in line 8 (hardcoded, 128 bit) using the SecretKey class and a specification object for GCM mode (cf. line 13, 64-bit tag and 96 bit initialization vector). Following these preparatory steps, the message is encrypted using the doFinal method in line 15 and printed to screen in line 16. Note that all cryptological functions operate on bytes in Java. Therefore, in order to encrypt a string in Java it needs to be

[1] Galois Counter Mode = modern block mode for symmetric ciphers like AES which allows for encryption and authentication of data.

converted into bytes (cf. line 10). To print bytes to screen the Bouncy Castle Hex class is used. Most of the objects can raise exceptions e.g. when an incorrect key length is used (cf. line 7).

Listing 1 shows the complexity of implementing modern cryptology in Java. Several classes need to be used together in a correct and safe way, e.g. Cipher, SecretKey, SecretKeySpec, and GCMParameterSpec. The complexity further increases when using asymmetric cryptology as two different keys (public and private) are used. JCE also offers so called factory classes – another complex topic typically not covered in introductory programming classes. This stresses the importance of teaching cryptology in combination with software engineering. Otherwise students can produce vulnerable code [12].

**Table 1.** Playfair square for the passphrase CRYPTOLOGY

| | | | | |
|---|---|---|---|---|
| C | R | Y | P | T |
| O | L | G | A | B |
| D | E | F | H | I |
| K | M | N | Q | S |
| U | V | W | X | Z |

## 2.4 Playfair Cipher

For illustration purposes we introduce the Playfair cipher. Playfair is a historic cipher and can easily be broken with computer aid e.g. by frequency analysis. Nevertheless, we use it here for didactic purposes as an easy to understand example.

The Playfair cipher is named after Lord Lyon Playfair and was invented by Sir Charles Wheatstone in 1854. It is a substitution cipher which was used in WWI [13] and uses the alphabet = {A, …, I, K, L, …, Z}. J is not used and is replaced by I in the plaintext and key. Double characters in the plaintext are separated by an X. If the length of the resulting plaintext is uneven, an additional X is added at the end (padding). The plaintext is then split in two character blocks ("bigrams"). For the plaintext EDUCATION the following bigrams are processed: ED, UC, AT, IO, NX. Based on the key which is a string a so called $5 \times 5$ Playfair square is generated. Assume the key equals CRYPTOLOGY. The key letters are written in the square starting top left continuing to the right. Double letters (like O and Y in our key) are omitted. The remaining letters are inserted in alphabetical order. The resulting Playfair square for our key is given in Table 1.

To encrypt, bigrams will be mapped to bigrams using the Playfair square. (1) If both plaintext letters are in the same row, replace them with their right neighbours (in the example: ED => FE). Start from left, when the right neighbour is outside the square. (2) If both plaintext letters are in the same column replace them with their lower neighbours (UC => CO). Take the top entry when leaving the square. (3) In all other cases replace them with the letters on the same row respectively but at the other pair of corners of the rectangle defined by the original pair (AT => BP). The resulting ciphertext is FECOBPDBQW. Note that the rules require different letters which is guaranteed by the padding.

Decryption is very similar to encryption. As Playfair is a symmetric cipher, the receiver needs the same key using a secure channel. To decrypt it, he first generates the same Playfair square using the key. Secondly, he takes bigrams of the ciphertext and applies the following three rules to them: in encryption rule (1) replace right by left, in (2) lower by upper. Rule (3) is identical. Decrypting the ciphertext yields EDUCATIONX. Note the terminal X which is due to padding.

## 3 Learning Cryptology with Java Test Cases

The combination of using JUnit test cases to teach students cryptology and also grade their code will be called LCJTC (Learning Cryptology with Java Test Cases) from now on. The approach has been used in practice in the Bachelor course "Applied Cryptology with Java" at Trier University of Applied Sciences, Germany. The course is worth 5 CPs and is an optional course in the computer science curriculum. The course was given in the winter semesters 2016/17 and 2018/19. In the first course 35 students participated in the assignments and 26 took the exam. In the second course 25 students worked on the assignments and 20 took the exam. The mandatory use of ASE (cf. Sect. 2.2) was introduced in 2018/19. As a prerequisite for participating in the course students had to pass classes in (1) IT security (5 CPs) including a theoretical introduction to cryptology and in (2) object oriented programming in Java (10 CPs). Classes were held on a weekly basis over a period of 14 weeks with 90 min of lecture and 90 min for the assignments per week.

### 3.1 Assignments and Their Selection

Table 2 shows the content of the lectures and the corresponding assignments. The Playfair assignment is given in Appendix A as a sample. The topics covered roughly follow standard cryptological text books like [14] for the theoretical part and [15, 16] for Java cryptology. The assignments were chosen based on the recommendations given in [12, 17, 18] and selected for didactical or practical purposes. The TLS assignment e.g. was chosen due to the paramount importance of the TLS protocol to protect TCP traffic. The PasswordSafe assignment illustrates the challenges to be tackled when generating and encrypting credentials. CryptoTimer illustrates that asymmetric ciphers encrypt much slower than symmetric ones (by a factor of 10–1000 in our setting). The BMPEncryptor e.g. illustrates the shortcoming of using the ECB mode when encrypting bitmap images.

Several assignments like CertValidator, CipherExceptor require an inverse way of thinking about cryptology. Contrary to other assignments where correct code must be developed these assignments require to deliberately raise exceptions, produce errors, or break encryption and provide test cases to illustrate this behaviour. This inverse way of thinking nicely illustrates typical problems in cryptological software and hopefully prevents students from making these errors in the future [12, 17].

**Table 2.** Topics of lectures and assignments

| | Content of lecture | Assignments |
|---|---|---|
| 1 | JUnit-Tests, exception handling, introduction to ASE, classical substitution and transposition ciphers | 1. Playfair cipher*, 2. Railfence cipher* |
| 2 | JCA & JCE, Bouncy Castle, modern symmetrical block ciphers including modes of operation and padding | 1. BMPEncryptor which shows differences of ECB vs. CTR encryption, 2. CipherExceptor raises all exceptions contained in Java's Cipher object |
| 3 | Stream ciphers, hash functions, MAC, PBKDF, pseudo random functions | 1. PasswordSafe, 2. PasswordHasher: hashing and storing passwords in /etc/shadow-style, 3. cracking a stream cipher via timing attack, 4. CBC-MAC |
| 4 | Java's BigInteger class, asymmetric cryptology: RSA, Rabin, Elgamal | 1. BigInteger, 2. RSA cipher*, 3. Rabin cipher* |
| 5 | Homomorphic Encryption, Paillier crypto system | 1. Elgamal cipher*, 2. Paillier cipher*, 3. CryptoTimer compares run times of ciphers |
| 6 | Digital Signatures incl. RSA, DSA, ECDSA, Merkle, and Lamport signatures | 1. JavaSigner: signing files with RSA, DSA or ECDSA, 2. Lamport signatures* |
| 7 | Java Keystore, X.509 certificates | 1. KeyStoreReader* (reading and using credentials from a given keystore), 2. X509Printer (printing X.509 details to screen), 3. CertValidator: create JUnit test cases for selected certificate exceptions |
| 8 | Transport layer security (TLS) protocol | 1. Build up a TLS connection using a given certificate chain and credentials |
| 9 | Elliptic curve cryptology | 1. MyFirstEllipticCurve*, 2. ECDH in Java |
| 10 | Shamir's secret sharing, selected advanced cryptological topics like post quantum ciphers, e-voting, e-cash, cryptological card games | 1. Shamir Secret Sharer* |

Assignments marked with * in Table 2 were assessed by ASE. The source code of the other assignments had to be turned in via an e-learning platform. For selected assignments the code had to be presented to the instructor during class. The last four weeks of the course were used for student projects where 1–3 students worked on self-selected projects, cf. Lecture 10 for sample topics. The projects were presented in class in the last two weeks of the course.

Implementing cryptological software is subtle, can easily lead to attackable code, and should be done by professionals. Notorious problems are side channel attacks e.g. when implementing RSA or insufficient pseudo randomness. Therefore, a central paradigm is to teach students not to code their own crypto code in practical settings but to use existing and well established code like OpenSSL or Bouncy Castle [11] for scenarios with more than low security requirements. Nevertheless, the assignments include cipher implementation like RSA, Elgamal, or Playfair for didactical purposes.

### 3.2 Cryptological JUnit Tests

Cryptological concepts comprise but are not limited to encryption/decryption, signature and signature verification, hashing, pseudo random number generation [14]. Each of these concepts can be further grouped into test categories, e.g. for symmetric encryption schemas like Playfair the following categories can be defined:

- C1: Correct encryption: Given a plaintext and key, check if the correct ciphertext is calculated.
- C2: Correct decryption: Given a ciphertext and key, check if the correct plaintext is calculated.
- C3: Decryption as inversion of encryption: Using the same key, is the encrypted and then decrypted plaintext equal to the original plaintext?[2]
- C4: Invalid inputs, parameters, and padding: (1) invalid input or encoding for keys, plaintext or ciphertext, (2) invalid parameters like wrong key length, wrong block size, wrong length of an initialization vector, and (3) invalid padding

```
public class PlayFairTest extends TestCase{
@Test
@TestOrder(10)
@TestDescription("Check correct encryption of Playfair cipher")
@DependsOnCorrectnessOf("SignatureTests.testSignature")
@TestFailureMsg("The correctly encrypted text should be" +
    "FECOBPDBQW")
public void encryption1() {
PlayFair pf = new PlayFair("CRYPTOLOGY", "EDUCATION", true);
String ciphertext = pf.getCiphertext();
Assert.assertEquals("Your implementation returns <code>" + cipher-
    text + "</code>.", "FECOBPDBQW", ciphertext);}
@Test
@TestOrder(11)
@TestDescription("Check illegal keys")
@DependsOnCorrectnessOf("SignatureTests.testSignature")
@TestFailureMsg("Only characters a-z or A-Z are allowed as keys.")
@Test(expected = IllegalCharacterException.class)
public void illegalKey() throws IllegalCharacterException {
new PlayFair("CRYPTO*LOGY", "SUPPER", true);}}
```

**Listing 2.** ASE Playfair test case `encryption1` checks the correct encryption of a given plaintext, test case `illegalKey` checks if an `IllegalCharacterException` is thrown when an illegal key is used.

[2] Note that some encryption schemes like Playfair in combination with certain padding schemas can yield different decrypted ciphertexts than the original plaintext.

For asymmetric ciphers and signature schemas additional categories exist. Typically, private and public keys need to fulfil certain number theoretical preconditions and are dependent upon each other. Private keys are used for different operations compared to public keys, see the Elgamal tests in Fig. 1 for examples. Implementing tests for categories C1–C3 is straightforward in Java. Test case `encryption1` defined in lines 2–10 in Listing 2 is an example for C1. These tests are implemented using assertions like `Assert.assertEquals` in line 10 provided by the JUnit framework. C4 tests require a different approach and can be tested by requiring a certain exception (cf. line 16 in Listing 2). Test `illegalKey` defined in lines 11–18 is an example. Note that no assertion is necessary. The constructor in line 18 raises the `IllegalCharacterException` required in line 16. The assignment in Appendix A requires this exception for characters different from A–Z. The key in line 18 contains the illegal character *.

Listing 2 contains several ASE features. The annotation `@TestOrder` allows to define a mandatory chronological order of test cases, `@TestDescription` allows to provide a description of the test case that will be presented in the ASE GUI to the students. `@DependsOnCorrectnessOf` is used to check if other tests have successfully passed before it. The signature tests listed in lines 5 and 14 check if the naming conventions for package, class, and methods required in the assignment have been followed by the students. Finally, `@TestFailureMsg` provides the opportunity to display a specific message in case of a failed test. See [7, 8] for more details.

### 3.3 Grading

Especially for larger cohorts automated and fair grading of student software code is desirable. Following the LCJTC approach this is done in the following way: Prior to be admitted to the exam, students had to (1) pass ~75% of the test cases in ASE, (2) present ~75% of the non-ASE assignments to their instructor, and (3) present and document their student projects. As students are used to JUnit test cases, these are also used in the exam setting. Depending on the complexity of the test case and the category, an additional weight factor is applied.

Table 3 illustrates the approach following the Playfair cipher. Test cases from all four categories C1–C4 are used. C3 test cases have weight 3, C1 and C2 ones have weight 2, and C4 tests have weight 1. The sample results of three students are shown. Test cases are rated on a 1/0 basis (pass => 1, fail => 0). The score of the Playfair assignment is the weighted sum of the rated test cases. Scores for the different exam assignments can be summed up to yield the final grade for the student. Student B in Table 3 passed all tests and got the best score, while student C only managed to solve C4 test cases.

**Table 3.** Grading students A, B and C with selected weighted Playfair test cases

| Playfair test cases | Category | Weight | Student A | Student B | Student C |
|---|---|---|---|---|---|
| encryption1 | C1 | 2 | 1 | 1 | 0 |
| encryption2 | C1 | 2 | 1 | 1 | 0 |
| decryption1 | C2 | 2 | 0 | 1 | 0 |
| decryption2 | C2 | 2 | 0 | 1 | 0 |
| emptyKey | C4 | 1 | 1 | 1 | 1 |
| illegalKey | C4 | 1 | 1 | 1 | 1 |
| illegalPlaintext | C4 | 1 | 1 | 1 | 1 |
| illegalCiphertext | C4 | 1 | 1 | 1 | 1 |
| encryptThenDecrypt1 | C3 | 3 | 0 | 1 | 0 |
| encryptThenDecrypt2 | C3 | 3 | 0 | 1 | 0 |
| paddingInPlaintext | C4 | 1 | 1 | 1 | 1 |
| Score | | | 9 | 19 | 5 |

# 4 Discussion and Conclusion

## 4.1 Discussion

Students typically spent several hours spread over 3–4 days on each assignment. They tended to prefer assignments which used existing Java ciphers over coding their own ciphers like Rabin. Most of the students were able to solve the assignments. Exam time had to be extended from 90 to 120 min as understanding the assignments took the students longer than expected. It is planned to hand out a skeleton implementation which includes some classes and methods to speed up the coding. The grading time of the exam is apart from smaller preparatory steps almost instantaneous.

Feedback on LCJTC by the students has been extremely positive, with students expressing clear appreciation for the practical benefits of TDSD. In the questionnaires filled out after the course, the students additionally indicated an increased interest in cryptology after the course. Several students however disliked coding their own ciphers (like Playfair and RSA) and preferred to use existing implementations. The difficulty of the assignments was rated OK by 75% and “Difficult” by the remaining 25%. Over 90% of the students liked the final student project. The main critique was to drop the final exam and generate the grade based on the weekly assignments. This is planned for future classes but requires changes to the examination regulations of the course.

JUnit tests have also been used for grading the exams of the students. The students were given only the assignments and not the test cases. The grades have been calculated as described in Sect. 3.3. Students had the opportunity to inspect their code after the exam. The test cases have been valuable in showing the students their errors. The transparency and fairness of the approach has been positively acknowledged.

Handing out the test cases also would allow a specific way of cheating for categories C1 and C2. As an example consider test case `encryption1` in Listing 2. The test case contains the plaintext and corresponding ciphertext. The student could easily write the following encryption method that passes this test without understanding the encryption rules of the Playfair cipher. Pseudocode: `If (plaintext == EDUCATION and key == CRYPTOLOGY) then ciphertext = FECOBPDBQW`. Of course, this is easily detected by manual review but not by an automatic assessment. In future exams two disjunct sets of test cases can be used: one for the exam, the second for grading. This calls for a test case generator.

Automatically testing student code on ASE raises several privacy related questions. Students need to authenticate to ASE and each of their commits and the corresponding results are stored in a central database. A lot of privacy related information is evident or can be deduced. Examples are the percentage of passed and failed tests, their preferred working time, and sociological aspects like with whom they work on their assignment. In Europe, the General Data Protection Regulation gives clear guidelines for personal data. The use of ASE is currently voluntary. Students not wanting to use ASE will be given the necessary test cases and can demonstrate the passing of the test cases directly to the instructor. A more complex legal issue arises when enforcing the use of ASE for assignments or exams and the student is not willing to give his consent.

When using ASE for the first time, students need to agree on the privacy notice which also explains the purpose and usage of the data collected, their rights (e.g. deletion of their data), and time frames for storing the data. ASE's only purpose is to check the committed code against the tests. Internally, pseudonyms instead of student names are used. After a course is finished all corresponding data is automatically erased.

### 4.2 Related Work

The idea of using TDSD in the classroom is not revolutionary. Desai et al. [19] provide statistical evidence proving the benefit of TDSD in academia. Especially automated grading has raised the interest of many researchers, see [1, 4–6] but not exclusively for cryptographic software. Isong [5] describes an approach typical of such grading systems. Her automated program checker focuses on compiling and executing student programs against instructor-provided test cases, and then assigns a grade based on the comparison of the actual output of the student program against expected results provided by the instructor – an approach very similar to ASE. Edwards and Perez-Quinones [1] propose to let students pass in their code plus their JUnit test cases. Grading can then be done by submitting the student code to all passed-in test cases complemented by master test cases provided by the instructor.

Braga et al. [20] use TDSD in the construction of cryptographic software. They argue that test cases can automate acceptance tests for cryptographic software. Cryptographic test cases are considered good acceptance tests as they meet halfway between cryptologists and developers. However, they do not use Java and use a non-educational setting.

Testing software with fuzzing is a well-established technique when testing the robustness of software. Fuzzing involves providing invalid, unexpected, or random data as inputs [21]. The software is then monitored for exceptions such as crashes or potential memory leaks which falls into category C4 defined above and does not take into account C1–C3. Fuzzing has found lots of cryptographic failures e.g. the notorious TLS heartbleed attack. A more recent example is given in [22].

To the best knowledge of the author this is the first application of TDSD techniques to learn and grade software for cryptography in an educational setting.

### 4.3 Conclusion and Future Work

Coding cryptology is beneficial for understanding and learning cryptology. Only when the concepts are fully understood, it can be implemented correctly. And only then the test cases will pass. Sticking to the test cases also helps to split a large assignment into smaller, more conquerable parts. In our Playfair example, the steps could e.g. be padding, input sanitization, creation of the Playfair square, encryption, and decryption (cf. Sect. 2.4 and Appendix A).

For instructors LCJTC represents a major time shift from correcting students' code ex post to creating sample solutions, test cases, and detailed assignments prior to classes. The positive effect of this approach is that it is scalable and can thereby be applied to larger cohorts and is also well-suited for distance learning. The time effort for instructors can be reduced by sharing resources with other instructors[3], thereby extending the range and number of assignments. Possible extensions include post-quantum ciphers [23] or side-channel and timing attacks.

As Listing 1 clearly indicates, using modern ciphers in Java is a complex task. As ASE already supports other programming languages like Python or C++ it is planned to explore crypto assignments in other languages. This approach can then be used to compare crypto implementations e.g. concerning the time needed for encryption.

For some assignments like CertValidator, CipherExceptor students are required to hand in their own test cases, following the classical TDSD paradigm as described in Sect. 2.1. However, in many assignments the instructor defines the test cases and codes a reference solution while the student tries to write code that passes the given test cases. This is due to ASE's current inability to test test cases, which should be addressed in future ASE versions.

## Appendix A: Playfair Assignment

In order to illustrate the LCJTC method, we will use the Playfair cipher introduced in Sect. 2.4 and show a corresponding assignment here:

Implement the Playfair cipher in Java like introduced in Sect. 2.4 with the following requirements:

- Package name = playfair
- Class name = PlayfairCipher

[3] If you are interested, please contact the author. Note that the material is currently only available in German.

- Attributes of class: `private char[][] charTable = new char[5][5]`. Contains the Playfair square, `String key`, `String plaintext`, `String ciphertext`
- Methods:
  - Constructor: `PlayfairCipher(String key, String text, boolean encrypt)`. Boolean encrypt indicates, if the text is encrypted (value = true) or decrypted (value = false). The constructor sets all attributes to their correct value.
  - `void createTable(String key)`. Generates the Playfair square given a key
  - `String encrypt(String plaintext)`. Encrypts plaintext.
  - `String decrypt(String ciphertext)`. Decrypt ciphertext.
  - `String prepareText(String text)`. Padding and replacing J with I.
- For plaintexts, ciphertexts and keys containing illegal characters an IllegalCharacter-Exception must be thrown.
- Test vector: plaintext = EDUCATION, key = CRYPTOLOGY, ciphertext = FECOBPDBQW.

## References

1. Edwards, S., Pérez-Quiñones, M.: Experiences using test-driven development with an automated grader. J. Comput. Sci. Coll. **22**(3), 44–50 (2007)
2. Beck, K.: Test-Driven Development: By Example. Addison Wesley, Boston (2002)
3. JUnit Homepage. https://junit.org. Accessed 29 Jan 2020
4. Iffländer, L., et al.: PABS – a programming assignment feedback system. In: Proceedings of the 2nd Workshop Automatische Bewertung von Programmieraufgaben (2015)
5. Isong, J.: Developing an automated program checker. J. Comput. Small Coll. **16**(3), 218–224 (2001)
6. Krusche, S., Seitz, A.: ArTEMiS - an automatic assessment management system for interactive learning. SIGCSE 2018, 21–24 February, Baltimore, MD, USA (2018)
7. Herres, B., Oechsle, R., Schuster, D.: Der Grader ASB. In: Herausgeber Oliver, J. et al. Automatisierte Bewertung in der Programmierausbildung, pp. 255–271. Waxmann-Verlag (2017)
8. Schuster, D., et al.: Automatische Bewertung von JavaFX-Anwendungen. In: Proceedings of the 3rd Workshop Automatische Bewertung von Programmieraufgaben (2017)
9. Knudsen, K.: Java Cryptography. O'Reilly, Sebastopol (1998)
10. Weiss, J.: Java Cryptography Extensions, 1st edn. Morgan Kaufmann, Burlington (2004)
11. Bouncy Castle. https://www.bouncycastle.org. Accessed 12 Mar 2020
12. Lazar, D., et al.: Why does cryptographic software fail? A case study and open problems. In: Proceedings of 5th Asia-Pacific Workshop on Systems, pp. 1–7 (2014)
13. Kahn, D.: The Codebreakers: The Comprehensive History of Secret Communication from Ancient Times to the Internet. Scribner, New York (1996)
14. Stinson, D., Paterson, M.: Cryptography: Theory and Practice, 4th edn. CRC, Boca Raton (2018)
15. Hook, D.: Beginning Cryptography with Java. Wrox, Birmingham (2005)

16. Hook, D., Eaves, J.: Java Cryptography: Tools and Techniques, ebook (2020). https://leanpub.com/javacryptotoolsandtech
17. Long, F., et al.: The CERT Oracle Secure Coding Standard for Java. Addison-Wesley, Boston (2011)
18. McGraw, G.: Software Security – Building Security. Addison-Wesley, Boston (2006)
19. Desai, C., Janzen, D.: Savage, K: A survey of evidence for test-driven development in academia. ACM SIGCSE Bull. **40**, 97–101 (2008)
20. Braga, A., Schwab, D., Vannucci, A.: The use of acceptance test-driven development in the construction of cryptographic software. In: 9th International Conference on Emerging Security Information, Systems and Technologies (2015)
21. Takanen, A., DeMott, J., Miller, C.: Fuzzing for Software Security Testing and Quality Assurance. Artech House, Norwood (2008)
22. Aumasson, J., Romaillerm, Y.: Automated testing of crypto software using differential fuzzing. In: Blackhat Conference, US (2017)
23. NIST homepage for post-quantum cryptography. https://csrc.nist.gov/Projects/Post-Quantum-Cryptography. Accessed 9 Feb 2020

# An Institutional Risk Reduction Model for Teaching Cybersecurity

Erik Moore[1(✉)], Daniel Likarish[1(✉)], Bobbie Bastian[2], and Michael Brooks[2]

[1] Regis University, Denver, CO 80221, USA
{emoore, dlikaris}@regis.edu
[2] Adams 12 Five Star Schools, Thornton, CO 80241, USA
{bobbie.r.bastian, michael.brooks}@adams12.org

**Abstract.** This work presents a model for reviewing the risks of institutions teaching cybersecurity. The work is based on efforts in this direction at Regis University and Adams 12 Five Star Schools in Colorado. These two institutions are described in a comparative case study reviewing the following four aspects of addressing risk: policy, adjudication, infrastructure protection, and curricular boundaries. The model is presented in a generalizable framework to facilitate risk analysis across the education of children in public schools, university level education, and professional development programs. This framework is not intended to supplement a traditional threat analysis program and not replace it. In addition to the specialized risks addressed here, institutions teaching cybersecurity are often perceived as potential targets for adversaries because of the schools as a pipeline to cyber defense activities, and because institutions teaching cybersecurity are part of societal long-term cyber defense strategies that confront criminal, nation state, and activist threats.

**Keywords:** Cybersecurity · Cybersecurity curriculum · Cybersecurity education · Ethical policy · Policy · Adjudication · Infrastructure · Risk management · Risk mitigation · Cyber defense · University cybersecurity program · K-12 cyber security · Threat analysis · Risk framework

## 1 Introduction

Cyber risk for an institution that teaches cybersecurity goes beyond baseline cybersecurity and includes behavioral risks that develop as student populations acquire and practice newfound cybersecurity skills. The study presented here covers two cases, a public school district where cybersecurity skills are taught to minors, and a university where cybersecurity is taught at the undergraduate, graduate, and professional development levels. This study reviews risk mitigation efforts across a broad range of education activities from extra-curricular risks with students starting at about 13 years old to the training of long-time cybersecurity professionals embedded in the industry. A multi-layered risk mitigation framework is used to methodically present the cases.

The sense of urgency that drove the formulation of this paper comes from many stories that the authors have heard over the last few years from peers at other


Published by Springer Nature Switzerland AG 2020
L. Drevin et al. (Eds.): WISE 2020, IFIP AICT 579, pp. 18–31, 2020.
https://doi.org/10.1007/978-3-030-59291-2_2

cybersecurity programs. A school's curricular WordPress websites end up hacked shortly after a cybersecurity teacher reviews the exploits with students. A cybersecurity competition encourages minors to actively practice red team activities without that competition organization addressing the inherent risks institutions face in developing those skills in students whose executive functions may not be mature enough to handle the habituated behavior. And minors are occasionally convicted of crimes after learning exploits in a high school environment [1].

While teachers and institutions may fall back on, "but we had them sign an ethical agreement" the authors see this as falling short of the full range of institutional responsibilities inherent in reducing the risks of teaching cybersecurity. These risks are not only to the institution, but to the parent, the student and the communities in which they hope to thrive. This paper provides an initial set of materials to open up greater discourse in this area, spurring questions like, "What should the limits be on curricular and extracurricular content for various groups of students?", "Can cybersecurity curricular content analysis spur coordinated work in the institution's risk mitigation strategy?" The work of Marquardson and Garmillion [2] presents clear description of risk and control categories in this area, acknowledging and addressing the risks of institutions teaching cybersecurity. In contrast, the work presented here analyzes two cases spanning the public education of children, through university level activities, and to ongoing professional development in cybersecurity, addressing each level. The cases presented describe the practices and formal efforts within the programs of Adams 12 Five Star Schools (Adams 12) and Regis University, both in the State of Colorado, USA.

At Regis, the practices that led to this policy was developed on the Academic Network run by the college faculty and the network's Project Scientist. At Adams 12 the program was spurred by the development of the first cybersecurity course. This paper is part of an effort to expand these initial practices and formulate policy. One challenge that spurred the work forward was the need to evaluate multiple cyber competitions for Kindergarten through $12^{th}$ grade appropriateness. While education institutions are subject to the same cyber attacks all institutions face, we designed this model to increase awareness in addition to general cybersecurity practice [3].

## 2 Research Methodology

The method used in this study is the presentation and comparison of two cases to analyze a range of practice, and develop models that can demonstrate coherence and usability across that range. The cases are presented in parallel structure, reviewing specific areas of risk and identifying variance in both risk and the practice of mitigating risk between the institutions. While some aspirational notes are made, the cases are based on actual institutional practice and efforts at risk mitigation. The risks addressed here are in regards to institutional and personal behavioral outcomes.

The work of Fujs, Mihelič and Vrhovec, suggest that the case study method is one of the more commonly used research methods in cybersecurity analysis [4]. Their observation that achieving credibility through triangulation is applied here in practice, using four lenses of observation across the two cases. In terms of the use of qualitative methods in general, Creswell and Creswell [5] suggest that a focused research question, based on the post-positivist perspective, can drive the analysis of the topic in question.

The analysis of this case attempts to answer the question, are there controls that can be added to social behavior that can assist in the mitigation of risk across a range of institutions teaching cybersecurity? We present two cases where current controls are used across both the public education of children and the adult education towards degrees and professional development. The analysis formulates both common and unique elements of these practices into a model. Analysis of the case attempts to understand whether, from an institutional level, can we form a coherent model that accommodates differentiators while maintaining a coherent framework. Then, we pose the question, could such a model support a risk mitigation strategy that might be applied across a broad range of education and training programs. This research does not collect data about individual learners, but focuses on the institutions, programs, and structures that contain the inherent risk. Data is gathered from the research team's interviews and experiences participating in the cases as members of those institutions.

## 3 A Layered Risk Mitigation Framework for Analyzing Cyber Education Risks

The four layers of risk mitigation work introduced here in Table 1 specifically address the cybersecurity challenges of institutions that teach or train in cybersecurity disciplines. The layers represent areas where the authors offer case analysis and methods being used at their institutions to mitigate risk. Following that, gap analysis suggests work yet to be done to address risks within the two cases. Then the authors reflect on the generalizability of the work and follow-on research on their roadmap that might support broader efforts to address the particular risks of institutions teaching cybersecurity.

**Table 1.** The framework for comparing layers of protection for schools teaching cybersecurity to children in public education and to adults at the college and professional level.

| Framework Comparing Layers of Protection of Institutions Teaching Cybersecurity | |
|---|---|
| **Adams 12 Five Star Schools** | **Regis University** |
| Limits on teaching risky content areas to minors in curricular and extracurricular contexts | Limits on teaching risky content areas to adult learners and institutional partner members |
| Technical cybersecurity controls | Technical cybersecurity controls |
| Ethical training and adjudication with student and parents | Ethical training and adjudication with adult learners and institutions |
| Ethical policy and agreements with students and parents | Ethical policy and agreements with adult learners and institutions |

The framework above was developed through a comparative review process of risk mitigating measures related to cybersecurity programs with the authors, who are the developers of each of these areas within their respective institutions. As individual controls were reviewed in an extended way, the authors extracted the pattern of this layered approach.

The authors chose a framework that spans public education of children and higher education because both institutions in this paper are already spanning that full range. Regis offers outreach programs to children in public and private education. Adams 12 is offering courses for college credit in association with a local college. Career pathways to higher education and articulation with higher education are even required to receive federal funding for computer science courses such as the Perkins grant. [6] The combined framework is designed to facilitate transparent collaboration between different types of institutions. By developing highly generalized structure, each institution has the freedom to evaluate their specific content and cybersecurity posture with local relevance.

Ethical policy and agreements lay the foundation of what is acceptable and unacceptable behavior for students, establishing boundaries for both ethical use of technology and specifically the appropriate use of institutional technology, learned skills, and access to resources and information. Ethical training and adjudication relates more to the curricular goals of helping students understand the personal and professional ethical standards, and intervening with guidance or punitive measures when necessary. Technical network containment is a widely used model for behavioral control in hands-on cybersecurity programs in terms of technical risks that addresses external risks and general student user behavior. As a basic control, network compartmentalization is still very necessary and is based on a strong foundation of policy that has generally been outward-facing towards hackers and the Internet. These controls could apply to students studying a variety of laboratory-based information technology programs and extracurricular activities where some malicious behavior occasionally occurs on institutional systems.

## 4 A Case of Cybersecurity Coursework, Competitions, and Professional Training for Adults

Adams 12 needed to address three use cases to reduce institutional risk while providing cybersecurity education training infrastructure. Regis serves college students from freshman through graduate programs where autonomous choices and career readiness is required. Regis also provides cybersecurity training that includes technical physical exercises for active cyber defense teams and cyber security professionals. In addition to these core services, Regis offers community outreach workshops of a few hours each to children in public schools.

Regis has delivered these hands-on cybersecurity training resources to support a variety of modalities over the past twenty years. The risk reduction measures presented below were developed during the period when the authors developed expertise in the protecting following:

- Online and classroom delivery of cybersecurity labs using modern network and data centers structures.
- Cybersecurity laboratory environment where development, experimentation, and analysis can take place. Classroom-based learning using user interface, compute cycles, data storage, virtual machines, laptops, etc.
- Cyber range environment for a variety of competitions including the Rocky Mountain Front Range CANVAS exercise and the Rocky Mountain region of the Collegiate Cyber Defense Challenge (RMCCDC).
- Agilely deployable "Cyber Gymnasium" where various challenges and components can be rapidly deployed to meet the training needs of various partners, user groups, etc.

The college-level laboratory instructional design, including coursework associated laboratory assignments and graduate research programs, was developed utilizing Malcom Knowles principles, enriching the adult learner experience [7]. For Regis, class-associated laboratory work and academic research facilities have been closely integrated into the day-to-day functions of the Regis Cyber Range. This network facility sits separate from the production networks of Regis University Network and is primarily controlled by a Project Scientist and the faculty of the College of Computer & Information Sciences.

Groups coming in for training that use ready-made modules from the "Cyber Gymnasium" are provisioned with resources the same way that new classes are brought online. Guest participants included contexts like ISSA, ISACA, and ISC.

Cyber competitions like CANVAS and the RMCCDC require major reconfiguration of the Cyber Range to accommodate large numbers of participant teams, vigorous interactions between computers, and provisioned networks in classrooms dedicated to the particular events. In addition to significant network changes, the Regis staff and faculty must welcome large numbers of students and faculty from other institutions, and a highly diverse range of cybersecurity professionals supporting the event.

Cyber defense training is a more complex capability. When The State of Colorado and National Guard visited a RMCCDC competition and short training exercises performed by Regis for the professional organization ISSA (Information Systems Security Association), they requested that Regis host a cyber defense training event on the Regis campus using the Cyber Range.

Cyber outreach programs generally serve children in public schools starting at about age 13. Regis used several pre-existing extracurricular programs to forward this work either on a Regis campus, or on-site at the schools. The programs used are the nationally recognized CyberPatriot and locally organized Cyber Girls. The goal is for boys and girls in underserved and established middle school and high schools to harden these systems in particular ways that score points based. Students receive a list of vulnerabilities and must mitigate the vulnerabilities locally on the VM to score points.

### 4.1 Ethical Policy and Agreement

In general, where cybersecurity guidelines extend beyond standard institutional policies, the institution relies on the Association of Computing Machinery [8] and various ethical standards publications within the sector professional organizations such as EC Council.

Upon enrollment, students must agree to the student handbook. The section Responsible Use of University Technology Resources generally covers technology behavior on the Regis network and on the Internet in general. These rules cover the prohibition of unauthorized access, malware distribution, impersonation, exploitation of system vulnerabilities, and misuses of data. The Regis University Catalog covers plagiarism, cheating, and other types of academic integrity issues. Beyond this initial policy, course content covers ethics training, and is described here under the section on adjudication.

The Outreach programs for children with public institutions and for college students at the RMCCDC events, student groups must have a faculty sponsor for guest teams from each institution represented. This is important to adjudicate behavioral issues as students participate at their home institutions, or as a group at Regis. Students inherit their institutions behavioral policies, but Regis considers the maturity of the institutions they are working with. The RMCCDC boundaries of acceptable behavior to maintain the game rules [9] were set for all regions by the National Collegiate Cyber Defense Competition (NCCDC), focusing on defensive practices known as "Blue Team" work rather than attack practices known in the competition as "Red Team" work.

Generally, for joint events like the RMCCDC and training challenges, adjudication can happen within the competition, including things like time limits for performance, prohibition of social engineering other teams, and restrictions from accessing off-site data stores. Of more significant interest is the directives associated with the long-term ethical behaviors the competition is attempting to instill in participant behavior as persistent personal and professional traits. These significantly also address the protection of the game infrastructure, and the institutional infrastructure on which the game resides. In the RMCCDC specifically, each Blue Team does not counterattack, but follows the rules of engagement that civil institutions must follow in the professional and local government worlds [10]. The Red Team is an active part of the game space provided by the game hosts to provide adaptive attacks as part of the competition.

Professional and cyber defense training depends on the ethical guidelines of the partner institutions and professional organization for reducing risk, as they establish the relevant boundaries of behavior for the activities pertinent to those organizations. This suggests that a professional development workshop for the Information Systems Audit and Control Association would have different boundaries of behavior than a joint cyber defense training exercise with the Colorado National Guard.

## 4.2 Technical Cybersecurity Controls

The Regis Cyber Range operates under a separate Internet connection. It uses its own firewalls and internal security monitoring, and has its own methods of compartmentalization, assigning clusters of system to various classes using virtualization software. The only link between the Cyber Range and the Regis production network is the federation of accounts that allows for access to be controlled in-part on the affiliation status with Regis University.

The Regis Laboratory Network environment is on the same infrastructure as competition activities. To divide these functions, networks are segmented into separate virtual networks that are adapted to the particular goal. When a cyber competition is hosted, a part of the Cyber Range can be "virtual air-gapped" to emulate a logically independent network. For Regis, this makes deployment much more agile than a physical detachment, and would generally have traffic filtering for security control. This type of containment has been sufficient given the greater separation with the Regis Production Network. The technical controls apply only to the Regis campus, and so behavior at home must rely on the policy and adjudication for reducing risk (Fig. 1).

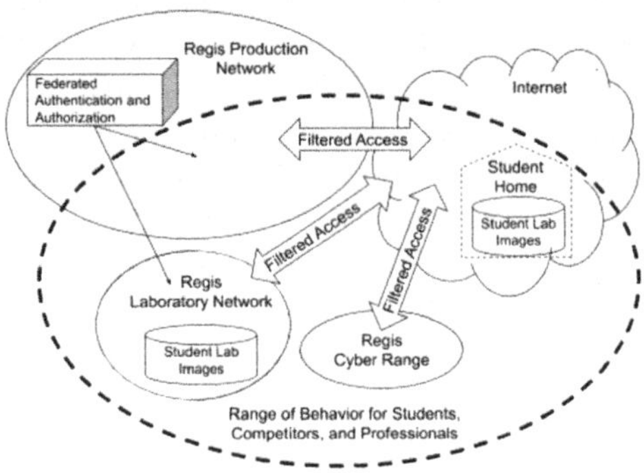


**Fig. 1.** Range of encouraged student, competitor, or professional behavior at Regis University

Outreach programs offered to public school children by Regis University, regardless of whether at the student's local school or on the Regis campus, are offered through stand-alone hardware not connected to a network. Programs like CyberPatriot have specific curriculum to load, and in other cases Regis develops and loads software. This means that the technical controls on risky student behavior and the possibility of disruptive hacks from the Internet are greatly reduced. Therefore, this function is not drawn on the diagram of technical controls, except that the range of student behavior after the event still extends to the Internet and home where Regis must rely more on ethical training to mitigate risk.

### 4.3 Ethical Training and Adjudication

For Regis students, the adjudication of policy violations for both academic integrity and inappropriate use of technology resources is handled by the Integrity Committee with an appeal to the Academic Integrity Board of the appropriate college. To give students an active understanding of issues related to Students have embedded sections in each course that provides ethical content engaged in the topics appropriate to course content. The process invokes corrective actions is the primary resolution but sanctions and potentially expulsion are possible.

The adjudication of fairness of the competition; the persistent ethics that the RMCCDC is working to instill in participants; and the aspirational skills that the competition is encouraging are all reinforced through practice. These two levels of rules published prior to the event provide students with guidelines that focus their efforts on defending systems.

For professional adjudication, Regis requires that the organizational representative for any particular group respond appropriately to resolve issues and enforce policy. Regis reserves the right to exclude disruptive, unethical, and malicious network or human behavior from its premises. This is handled by the Regis staff hosting an event, and can be escalated through the appropriate college.

### 4.4 Limits on Teaching Risky Content Areas

Regis University educates and trains a range of student and professional learners looking to engage in the cybersecurity community in both professional cybersecurity and cyber defense roles. But Regis does not allow it's systems to be repurposed for those activities, or produce disruptive effects outside the Regis controlled Cyber Range environments. The Regis production network may not be used as an experimental network for visitor or student exploits or security experiments.

In order to establish and maintain these boundaries of content, demonstration, and laboratory work Regis refers to the general ethical guides for staff and faculty. Specifically, course content is the responsibility of the Regis Program Chair, ensuring that course content is free of high risk activities. Course content that has proactive cybersecurity work such as penetration testing, and malware reverse engineering have extensive ethical components so that students understand the professional constraints and ethical expectations associated with these activities.

## 5 A Case of Cybersecurity Education and Extracurricular Programs for Children

Adams 12 Five Star Schools is a public school district north of Denver, Colorado USA serving just under 40,000 children with just under 5,000 staff. Like many districts in the region, Adams 12 is adopting cybersecurity curriculum and extracurricular activities to support both the career potential of graduates and the interest of students. Adams 12 offers several opportunities for students to gain experience, skill, and knowledge in cybersecurity.

The cybersecurity curriculum taught in Adams 12 is based on the Cybersecurity Curriculum Framework published on the National Cryptologic Museum Foundation [11] website. This framework, along with the text: Cyber Security Principles and Practices 4th Edition by Stallings and Brown [12], units from the NICERC Cyber Society curriculum [13], and resources from Clark Center [14] make up the instructional materials for the class.

Curricular hands-on opportunities beyond general safety start with an 8th grade course lasting about three months emphasizing privacy, encryption, and decryption. At the high school level, students can take a year-long course in cybersecurity that progresses along the NIST Framework [15], and uses the CIA triad of confidentiality, integrity, and availability [16] of data as a framing perspective when dealing with each topic. While both 8th grade and high school coursework have modules covering ethics, the High school course has a section emphasizing law.

Currently CyberPatriots is the only extracurricular cybersecurity activity offered at Adams 12, available from 6th grade through graduation at 12th grade. This program comes with strict behavioral and ethical guidelines for all participants that the District follows. A particular characteristic of CyberPatriot in relation to other cyber competitions available is that it is focused exclusively on cyber defense and does not involve attack training as other competitions offer offensive security competition, red teaming, or capture the flag competitions [17].

### 5.1 Ethical Policy and Agreement

Adams 12 employs several policy strategies to ensure that students and parents are aware of the districts behavioral expectations and to create a safe community where the risks of using the Internet are reduced in general. Specific policies and practices are enforced through both teacher oversight, and through the formal policy development process of the Institution. District policy goes through a policy review board and the students and parents sign a technology use agreement that refers to the District policy of acceptable use. Cybersecurity presents specific risks that may not be fully covered by the Adams 12 district policy, so additional controls are implemented as described below.

As cybersecurity classes start, the teachers communicate during the first two weeks of school, students receive the class syllabus. The syllabus lays out the units and skills taught in the course, and class expectations. The syllabus has a page that is required to be signed by students and parents. The page that is signed by students and parents collects current parent contact information, preferred method of contact, information about if parents want a code to be able to monitor the work students complete and submit in Schoology, and information about the ways parents can be involved in the classroom and school community. This includes being a guest speaker, volunteering, sitting on the district CS Advisory Committee, or helping with co-curricular events.

In regards to extracurricular policy, Adams 12 and the CyberPatriot organization require teams to register. Once teams are registered, students sign-up for one of the teams via online access If a parent does not complete the verification, and the student competes in the competitions, the team score will be withheld until parents have signed off on allowing their student to participate. In January of each year, Adams 12 hosts an open house. During the open house parents and potential students learn about all of the computer science programs available at Adams 12 including cybersecurity. Families are given an overview of what is taught in each class. In April of each year, Adams 12 hosts Pre-Acceptance night. During Pre-Acceptance Night parents and students come and learn about the specifics for each class. A presentation is given on the specific curriculum in the class. If a student is interested in taking the class once they have heard more about it, they fill out an application that evening. The counselors check to see that each student has met the prerequisites for the class, has appropriate grades and attendance to be successful in the class. This spring we will be introducing the parent cybersecurity course agreement during pre-acceptance. Both parents and students will sign the agreement when applying for the course. Similar to the Advance Placement

(AP) contract that parents and students sign when applying for AP computer science. At the end of August, students register for CyberPatriot and form teams and parent approval is required. In October, Adams 12 hosts parent-teacher conferences. Both parents and students attend the conferences. During the conferences, parents have the opportunity to ask any questions that they currently have. Parents are shown the curriculum and resources that students have access to including Schoology, Co-Curricular calendars, and Plural Sight. Parents have the opportunity to get a parent code for Schoology to monitor their student's assignments and work.

## 5.2 Technical Cybersecurity Controls

Adams 12 runs a production network to perform the operations of the business and schools, using various forms of network segmentation including Virtual LANs and access control lists between them that isolate where the traffic from varying systems to what is required. Figure 2 illustrates the range of network types available within Adams 12 including the Production Network, Cyber Competition Network, and Air Gap Network.

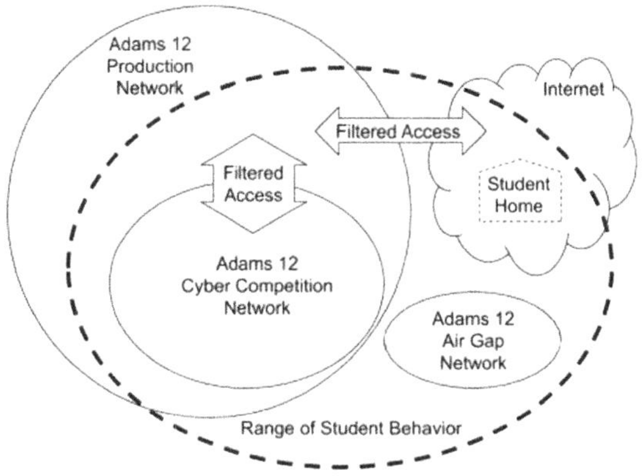


**Fig. 2.** Range of encouraged behavior at Adams 12

The Production Network provides functions a general business and education network of the institution can be carried out, and which generally has physical and/or logical links to all departments of the institution, as well as to the broader Internet. Cybersecurity students use this for their normal classroom activities and for research in their cybersecurity courses. This migration of students raises the risk that learned behavior on the air gap network may transfer to the production network. This network has standard security configurations set up in response to contemporaneous threat analytics, but was not initially designed to support cybersecurity training activities.

As cybersecurity training was introduced for students, several additional options as a Cyber Competition Network were required because students needed access to administrative controls over computers and network devices in order to gain the skills for learning and for competition. Adams 12 provisioned designated machines on a

Guest network that still allowed students to connect to the CyberPatriot scoring engines on the Internet, while eliminating peer-to-peer activities. As the network engineer reviewed required activities, this pre-existing network matched the required access closely. However, the Guest Network had to be deployed manually to student computers in Pods, switching from the Production Network for each competition. Therefore, a dedicated Cyber Competition Network is being planned to remove the manual process and allow for security controls customized to cyber competitions. Provisioning a dedicated network should also help supporting CyberPatriot programs across multiple sites as the competition becomes more popular. The competition computers are dedicated to the CyberPatriot students and Adams 12 pre-loads them with virtualization software that runs the as a virtual PC. These machines also have a different security posture with a unique local administrator password, and hardware-protecting password.

To support both the cybersecurity curriculum and the CyberPatriot program with training experiences proven out on actual computer and network hardware, the team designed an Air Gap Network that could operate as a sandbox for students to experiment with systems, network devices. This is a place where students can be encouraged to try things even if they have a chance of breaking, and work to fix them without consequences. This network does not have any wireless devices, and is located away from open network jacks. Any devices containing wireless electronics needed in the Air Gap Network have their wireless devices disabled at the BIOS layer before they are added. The Air Gap Network also includes warning labels about connection and has a significant distance or "air gap" between these devices and any connection to other Adams 12 networks.

### 5.3 Ethical Training and Adjudication

A significant part of mitigating the school district's risk is establishing a formal consent relationship with parents and students that transparently describes the skills students will learn, the activities they engage in, and the knowledge they will gain. While parents must sign a form consenting to the activities, a structured set of meetings begins prior to the course and proceed through the first quarter of the course session. This category covers both where students experience control of behavior based on policy and also walk through scenarios to learn self-control later on in life.

When discussing the syllabus with the students, teachers set class behavioral expectations. These expectations include logging off of the computer before leaving the classroom for the day. If a student fails to log out of the computer and another student in the next class period goes to the computer to work on it, the expectation is for that student to log out the previous user and log into their own account. Any student who is caught working on a computer logged into another student is written up. If it happens more than one time students can lose lab access. Then, they have to hand write everything, including any code for the programming classes. Academic honesty is also discussed when discussing the syllabus, but this is general to all coursework.

### 5.4 Limits on Teaching Risky Content Areas

The Adams 12 cybersecurity coursework currently sets limits on content, particularly hands-on activities. This is an acknowledgement that skills taught in the cybersecurity curriculum can create risks for children if they acquire skills and habits that translate readily into inappropriate, disruptive, or illegal activities. Exclusions include things like scanning networks, working with malware, and some scripting activities.

While current technical controls help reduce these risks when students are on Adams 12 networks, the school district leadership understands that the student takes cybersecurity skills with them into a broad range of technology environments at home, at the library, and at other institutions. Limiting content is also a protection measure because students daily migrate from the Challenge Network environment to the computers on Adams 12's production network that is used for their other classes.

## 6 Analysis

One thing that became apparent in case review is that the risk reduction measures were prompted by the level of engagement of student content. Students learning how to harden a system were less likely to be disruptive or to misuse the skills they had acquired, either on the network or in the larger community. A matrix of levels along with the original risk reduction categories makes the discrete work at each level clearer, and provides a context for the type of prompts that might lead to these risk reduction measures. We designed the matrix, shown in Table 2, with the expectation that it could be used to track institutional cyber resilience in relation to both the presence of cybersecurity education programs generally, and the practices within the risk reduction categories.

One obvious factor that came up with Regis was the need to completely mitigate the network risk associated with outreach programs to children. The isolation of laptop machines removed the need for internet filtering, eliminated peer-to-peer digital behavior, and reduced dramatically the threat of malware or malicious network activity. At Adams 12, significant effort goes into maintaining a safe and secure environment for children with multiple isolated networks directly addressing concerns related to children. Therefore, the boundaries in Table 2 between levels 3 and 4 is a strong boundary for consideration. Children, levels 1–3 require significant constraints on the actual content, and strong involvement of parents. Adults, at Regis, required strong institutional relationships through agreements or sponsoring staff, while placing significant emphasis on the adherence to professional ethical guidelines of aspiration or affiliation. Each cell within Table 2 provides a defined point of reference designed so that a rating of risk coverage can be applied as a way of highlighting areas across the institution and cybersecurity program where curricular overreach creates risk beyond standard cybersecurity threat assessment.

**Table 2.** Matrix of cybersecurity deployment

| L | Level Title | Groups | Curricular Limits | Technical Controls | Ethical Engagement | Institutional Behavioral Policy |
|---|---|---|---|---|---|---|
| 1 | Theory and basic skills | Minor and adult college/ Prof. Dev. | Password security, cryptography, least permission,.privacy, ethics, and law (No scan or scripting tools) | Network segmentation, edge firewalling, competition computer hardening | Meetings with parents and students prior to the course | Institutional policy, parental permission for extracurricular, |
| 2 | Systems defense | Minor and Adult College/ Prof. Dev. | Endpoint Protection and patching, System Hardening, Permissions, Unauthorized Access Response. (No scanning or scripting tools) | Network Segmentation, Edge, Host & East-West Firewalling, competition computer hardening | Mid-class parent meetings, technical explanation of student skills and capabilities | Institutional policy, parental permission for extracurricular, |
| 3 | Network defense, system Investigation and alerts | Minor and Adult College/ Prof. Dev. | Firewall rules, forensics with autopsy. (No scanning tools) | Network forensics, device monitoring, log analysis and reporting. | Parent participation encouraged as a part of awareness building. | Institutional policy, parental permission for extracurricular, |
| 4 | Service attack/ defense | Adult College/ Prof. Dev. | No construction of Malware or active Internet-based attacks | Isolation of Laboratory Environments, Layer 7 Firewalling. | Institutional Computer Usage Agreement, Course-embedded Ethical and Policy Content | Student identity confirmation. visiting students must have institutional liability insurance and a responsible guest faculty member. |
| 5 | Process attack/ defense | Adult College/ Prof. Dev. | No targeting proprietary or operational systems: Financial software, etc. or weaponizing | Whitelist-only web application firewalling | Engage through professional societies, employers, partner institutions, and certifications | Invitation or approval only for current practice. |

## 7 Conclusion

Because of the increasing societal need for cybersecurity education and training programs, regularizing and formalizing the risk mitigation methods that are needed to keep these programs running smoothly is becoming more significant. While the matrix for risk reduction presented here is developed on two cases that span across, public education of children, university level education, and professional training, it is likely that two customizations of this matrix will need to occur if others intend to use it. First, technology content changes over time, as does the expectations of learners at various levels, so the content will need to be adapted. Second, the threatscape that all institutions face regardless of their curricular content is advancing, so more lower level risk controls will become redundant with the institutions baseline of cybersecurity controls and risk reduction.

Another important implication of doing this work well, is that a matrix like this can help institutions address shortages of educators at all levels. The risks addressed here are not just institutional and societal risks. To make potential educators, parents, and students comfortable participating and contributing, we must find proactive and comprehensive ways to reduce their risk. Otherwise this becomes a high barrier for those considering entry into the field. Table 2 represents at least a framework for this consideration that is leveled to various learning environments.

## References

1. Marcum, C., Higgins, G., Ricketts, M., Wolfe, S.: Hacking in high school: cybercrime perpetration by Juveniles. Deviant Behav. **35**(7), 581–591 (2014)
2. Marquardson, J., Gomillion, D.: Cyber security curriculum development: protecting students and institutions while providing hands-on experience. Inf. Syst. Educ. J. **16**(5), 12–21 (2018)
3. Boylan, A., Tepe, A., Davis, D.: Texas governance and authorities for cyber attack response: a summary. https://cybersecurity.tamu.edu/wp-content/uploads/2019/11/Cyber-Response-State-Authorities_13-NOV-19.pdf. Accessed 3 July 2020
4. Fujs, D., Mihelič, A., and Vrhovec, S.: The power of interpretation: qualitative methods in cybersecurity research, tile of a proceedings paper. In: 14th International Conference on Availability, Reliability and Security (ARES 2019), Article 92, pp. 1–10. Association for Computing Machinery, New York (2019)
5. Creswell, J., Creswell, J.: Research Design: Qualitative, Quantitative, and Mixed Methods Approaches, p. 7. Sage Publications, Thousand Oaks (2017)
6. Carl, D.: Perkins Career and Technical Education Act of 2006, Public Law 88-210; 18 December 1963, As Amended Through P.L 116-6 Enacted 15 February 2019, United States of America (2019)
7. Knowles, M., Holton III, E., Swanson, R.: The Adult Learner. Routledge, London (2012)
8. https://www.acm.org/code-of-ethics. Accessed 10 Feb 2020
9. National Collegiate Cyber Defense Competition Rules. https://www.nationalccdc.org/index.php/competition/competitors/rules. Accessed 10 Feb 2020
10. Rocky mountain collegiate cyber defense competition. https://plantzmasters.net/rmccdc/. Accessed 10 Feb 2020
11. Cryptologic foundation framework. https://cryptologicfoundation.org/visit/goal/cyber security-curriculum-framework-portal-login.html. Accessed 10 Feb 2020
12. Stallings, W., Brown, L., Bauer, M., Bhattacharjee, A.: Computer security: principles and practice, pp. 0–978. Pearson Education, Upper Saddle River (2012)
13. NICERC cybersociety curriculum. https://nicerc.org/curricula/cyber-society/. Accessed 10 Feb 2020
14. Clark center home. https://www.clark.center/home. Accessed 10 Feb 2020
15. NIST cybersecurity framework. https://www.nist.gov/cyberframework. Accessed 3 July 2020
16. Nieles, M., Dempsey, K., Pillitteri, V.: NIST Special publication 800-12 revision 1 an introduction to information security. https://nvlpubs.nist.gov/nistpubs/SpecialPublications/NIST.SP.800-12r1.pdf. Accessed 3 July 2020
17. Lockheed Martin Cyberquest™ competition, https://www.lockheedmartin.com/content/dam/lockheed-martin/eo/documents/CyberQuest/2019/LM-CYBERQUEST-Challenge-Overview_PIRA.pdf. Accessed 10 Feb 2020

# Education for the Multifaith Community of Cybersecurity

Steven Furnell[1,3(✉)] and Matt Bishop[2]

[1] School of Computer Science, University of Nottingham, Nottingham, UK
steven.furnell@nottingham.ac.uk
[2] Department of Computer Science, University of California at Davis, Davis, CA, USA
mabishop@ucdavis.edu
[3] Security Research Institute, Edith Cowan University, Perth, WA, Australia

**Abstract.** The demand for cybersecurity professionals is growing. Many cybersecurity academic and training programmes exist to prepare students and professionals for these jobs. The programmes cover many areas of cybersecurity with considerable overlap, but with different emphases. Some are highly technical and cover little non-technical; others do the opposite. Cybersecurity jobs typically require some technical knowledge, an ability to place security problems in a larger context, and an ability to communicate this information effectively and convincingly. The problem with treating technical and non-technical subjects as silos rather than recognizing the two are tightly related and need to be taught together. This paper shows how seven common cybersecurity frameworks and ten masters' courses from the UK and US cover both technical and non-technical content. It examines the balance of technical courses, non-technical courses, and courses that mix both technical and non-technical material. It argues that these topics cannot be siloed, and their balance is critical to meeting the goals of the frameworks and programmes.

**Keywords:** Certifications · Curricula mapping · Cybersecurity frameworks · Masters degrees · Qualifications

## 1 Introduction

Over the last two decades, the need for improved cybersecurity has become more visible and more critical. Newspapers report compromises of major vendors and organizations daily; nation-states engage in cyberwarfare by attacking other countries' infrastructure; and attacks increase in sophistication. The damage from these attacks has repercussions throughout societies. As an example, the Equifax compromise exposed tens of millions of credit records, putting their subjects at risk for identity theft and other nefarious purposes [1].

There is no doubt that the profession is suffering from a shortage of qualified and skilled workers. As an example, according to a survey of 267 cybersecurity professionals conducted by Enterprise Strategy Group (ESG) and the Information Systems Security


Published by Springer Nature Switzerland AG 2020
L. Drevin et al. (Eds.): WISE 2020, IFIP AICT 579, pp. 32–45, 2020.
https://doi.org/10.1007/978-3-030-59291-2_3

Association (ISSA), three quarters felt that the skills shortage had impacted them in recent years, with a third indicating that it had done so significantly [2]. Similarly, the latest cybersecurity workforce study from $(ISC)^2$ reports a global skills gap of 4.07 million, and further suggests that 65% of organisations have a skills shortage, with 51% considering themselves to be at moderate or extreme risk as a result [3].

Reflecting the resultant demand for skilled workers, there has been a growth in both academic programmes and industry certifications targeting the topic area, which should in theory begin to help in offsetting the shortage. However, while there are many education and training options on offer, there is a question of whether the full breadth of the cybersecurity discipline is receiving the attention that it requires.

Cybersecurity spans many technical and non-technical skills, ranging from technical and low-level aspects of computing to human, organizational, and business skills. The latter, often called "soft skills," seem to be considered less important in many communities, even though in practice, they are as important as the former ("hard skills"), and indeed are skills that employers seek when hiring – especially given the need to understand the effects of security problems on the company, not just the technical implications.

The paper examines the balance of technical and non-technical topic coverage that exists within the various cybersecurity topic frameworks and standards that may be guiding academic and industry perspectives, and how this coverage aligns to areas of employer demand in terms of job openings. It then considers how the topic is represented within academic qualifications in cybersecurity, with an assessment of the coverage within a series of Masters degrees from the United Kingdom and the United States. The findings enable a comparison to be made between the coverage in the reference frameworks and market demand, and the focus provided by the academic programmes.

## 2 Cybersecurity Skills – Spectrum or Silos?

Players within the cybersecurity community often have conflicting perspectives of what cybersecurity actually is, with the consequence that the technical and business camps often cannot relate to each other and are even dismissive. Management often views the technology staff through the lens of the established stereotype of being a group of geeks and nerds who lack the ability to understand and properly communicate the aspects of their work relevant to the business or organization. Technical practitioners often consider the business and human side of cybersecurity to be some sort of sanctuary for those who can no longer keep up with the technology. Such attitudes foster a "them and us" culture within the discipline of cybersecurity. The key argument of this paper is that, to move things forward effectively, it is important to accept that cybersecurity is a multifaith community, and educating accordingly is critical to improving the state of the art and its effectiveness. Some topics are central, some are peripheral, but they are all cybersecurity. In practice, the key needs vary according to the party involved:

- for providers - knowing how education maps to roles; and
- for employers - knowing what is needed to get the job done.

The authors have already examined the second point in an accompanying paper that considers the relationship between skills, certifications and roles, recognising that this is what employers will ultimately need to understand when looking to recruit talent that addresses their needs [4]. The focus of the current paper is more towards the first point, considering the extent to which academic programmes are effective in addressing the breadth of the domain.

Training and education clearly need to be aligned to target roles. For example, someone trained to conduct risk assessment cannot be expected to use that training as a basis to do penetration testing. It is interesting that most of the industry and professional certifications have a technical flavour, not least because many of them are geared towards securing a particular product or platform. This provides learners with expertise in a particular area, but not with the breadth required of most cybersecurity specialists.

Table 1 lists the relative importance of different forms of cybersecurity qualifications and experience, according to the $(ISC)^2$ Cybersecurity Workforce Study 2018 [5] (based upon responses from 1,452 cybersecurity professionals from across North America, Latin America, Asia-Pacific and Europe). Looking at the ranking, it is rather notable that degree qualifications are at the bottom of the list. The survey does not comment upon the reason for this, but one might hypothesize that a potential contributor could be that employers have not found current offerings to be delivering graduates with the knowledge and skills that they need. Academic institutions and educators should not necessarily expect anything they do to be able to *change* this, but they at least need to *recognise* it and ensure that their degrees remain relevant.

**Table 1.** Importance of different types of cyber security qualifications and experience.

| Characteristic | Respondents rating as important |
|---|---|
| Relevant cybersecurity work experience | 49% |
| Knowledge of advanced cybersecurity concepts | 47% |
| Cybersecurity certifications | 43% |
| Extensive cybersecurity work experience | 40% |
| Knowledge of basic cybersecurity concepts | 40% |
| Strong non-technical/soft skills | 39% |
| Cybersecurity qualifications other than certifications or a degree | 37% |
| Knowledge of relevant regulatory practices | 37% |
| Cybersecurity or related graduate degree | 21% |
| Cybersecurity or related undergraduate degree | 20% |

It is also notable that non-technical skills are rated ahead of most of the qualification-related options, highlighting the fact that those working in cybersecurity are expected to be able to communicate and integrate within the business context. This finding is echoed in a report from Infosec, suggesting the top ten skills that security professionals needed to have in 2018 [6]. Looking at the list below, it clear that soft skills and non-technical aspects have a significant presence alongside the ones that are clearly technical:

1. Security analysis
2. Penetration testing
3. Secure application development
4. Incident response
5. Cloud security
6. Data science and analytics
7. Customer service
8. Communication
9. Collaboration
10. Curiosity and passion for learning

This is not to suggest that it is an either-or situation. The most desirable scenario is to have an effective *combination* of skills, as illustrated the following quotes from two further reports:

> "*Currently, the most-prized hire in a cybersecurity team is a technically proficient individual who also understands business operations and how cybersecurity fits into the greater needs of the enterprise*" [7]

> "*the really good people in the security industry are far more than just technically skilled. Especially in the higher ranks, you will see people who have a good mix of technical and soft skills, which enables them to implement control frameworks that really work*" [8]

This need to look beyond technical ability broadly aligns with earlier work from Dawson and Thomson, who suggest six key traits that the members of the future cyber security workforce are likely to need: systemic thinking, teamwork, continued learning, strong communication ability, a sense of civic duty, and a blend of technical and social skill [9]. This does not devalue the importance of the technical skills. It emphasizes the importance of not seeking them in isolation, because knowing which cybersecurity issues are critical to the functioning of the enterprise, and being able to present cybersecurity issues so that non-computer people can understand them and act appropriately, require the aforementioned blend of technical, social, organizational, and business skills.

In practice the technical and non-technical aspects are not distinct and separated. They overlap, interact and affect each other (e.g. technologies are deployed within a legal and regulatory context; choices are informed by policy and risk assessment; effectiveness is influenced by user education and awareness). So, we need emerging cyber professionals to be taught to think of them holistically and not to regard them as competing views (i.e. recognising that effective cybersecurity benefits from a spectrum of skills rather than placing them within silos).

## 3 Examining Coverage Within Cyber Security Frameworks

Although there is clear agreement that a range of underlying topics fit within the overall cyber security discipline, there is currently no single source that definitively specifies what the topics are or how they are structured. There are, however, a number of key sources that describe the information/cyber security discipline (and which in several cases are used to directly inform education and training activities). With this in mind, it is relevant to look at the topic coverage within these, and the extent to which they cover the technical and non-technical perspectives. Table 2 identifies seven such sources, and summarises the categories under which they have grouped their security topics. It should be noted that of these some are formal standards, whereas some bill themselves as frameworks, guidelines and bodies of knowledge. However, for the purposes of this discussion, we will use the term *framework* as the generic label by which to reference them, while further examining the ways in which each elect to classify and divide the overall topic space.

**Table 2.** A summary of the selected cybersecurity frameworks.

| Source | Framework | Description/Coverage |
|---|---|---|
| ACM/IEEE/AIS/IFIP | Cybersecurity Curricula 2017 (CSEC2017) [10] | Produced by the ACM/IEEE/AIS/IFIP joint task force in 2017, the guidelines provide a structure for the cybersecurity discipline, defining its boundaries and outlining key dimensions of a curricular structure<br>It identifies 8 Knowledge Areas: Data Security; Software Security; Component Security; Connection Security; System Security; Human Security; Organizational Security; Societal Security |
| CIISec | Skills Framework v2.4 [11] | The Skills Framework describes the range of competencies expected of Information Security and Information Assurance Professionals in the effective performance of their roles.<br>It is based on 11 Security Disciplines: Information Security Governance and Management; Threat Assessment and Information Risk Management; Implementing Secure Systems; Assurance, Audit, Compliance and Testing; Operational Security Management; Incident Management, Investigation and Digital Forensics; Data Protection, Privacy and Identity Management; Business Resilience; Information Security Research; Management, Leadership, Business and Communications; Contributions to the Information Security Profession and Professional Development |
| CyBOK project | Cyber Security Body of Knowledge (CyBOK) [12] | An initiative funded by the UK's National Cyber Security Programme and seeking to codify the foundational and generally recognised knowledge on cyber security.<br>It proposes 19 Knowledge Areas: Risk Management & Governance; Cyber Physical Systems; Law & Regulation; Physical Layer and Telecommunications Security; Human Factors; Secure Software Lifecycle; Privacy & Online Rights; Operating Systems & Virtualisation |

(*continued*)

**Table 2.** (*continued*)

| Source | Framework | Description/Coverage |
|---|---|---|
| | | Security; Adversarial Behaviours; Malware; Network Security; Security Operations & Incident Management; Cryptography; Software Security; Authentication, Authorisation & Accountability (AAA); Web & Mobile Security; Hardware Security; Distributed Systems Security; Forensics |
| $(ISC)^2$ | Common Body of Knowledge (CBK) [13] | The CBK is used as the underlying knowledge base for $(ISC)^2$'s series of professional certifications including CISSP, SSCP and CCSP<br>It identifies 8 domains: Security and Risk Management; Asset Security; Security Architecture and Engineering; Communications and Network Security; Identity and Access Management; Security Assessment and Testing; Security Operations; Software Development Security |
| ISO/IEC | 27002:2013 - Code of Practice for Information Security Controls [14] | An International Standard designed as a reference for organizations to use in selecting common security controls, as well as offering guidance on their use<br>It is structured around 14 main clauses: Information Security Policies; Organization of Information Security; Human Resource Security; Asset Management; Access Control; Cryptography; Physical and Environmental Security; Operations Security; Communications Security; Systems Acquisition, Development and Maintenance; Supplier Relationships; Information security Incident Management; Information Security Aspects of Business Continuity Management; Compliance |
| NIST | National Initiative for Cybersecurity Education (NICE) Cybersecurity Workforce Framework [15] | The NICE Framework aims to provide a common, consistent lexicon that categorizes and describes cybersecurity work, and a reference for describing and sharing information about the knowledge, skills, and abilities involved<br>It is based upon 7 Categories: Analyze; Collect and Operate; Investigate; Operate and Maintain; Oversee and Govern; Protect and Defend; Securely Provision |

(*continued*)

**Table 2.** (*continued*)

| Source | Framework | Description/Coverage |
|---|---|---|
| NSA | Centers of Academic Excellence (CAE) Knowledge Units [16] | The Centers of Academic Excellence program identifies four classes of Knowledge Units: *Fundamental* (Cybersecurity Foundations; Cybersecurity Principles; IT Systems Components), *Technical Core* (Basic Cryptography; Basic Networking; Basic Scripting and Programming; Network Defense; Operating Systems Concepts), *Non-Technical Core* (Cyber Threats; Cybersecurity Planning and Management; Policy, Legal, Ethics, and Compliance; Security Program Management; Security Risk Analysis), and *Optional* (spanning 56 further units covering both technical and non-technical aspects of security, as well as more general computing and communications topics). The Knowledge Units are then used within designated specialisations for Cyber Defence Education (CAE-CDE), Cyber Defence Research (CAE-R) and Cyber Operations (CAE-CO). All designations require the Fundamental units to be covered, and various percentages and combinations of the others |

The frameworks present various views of what cyber looks like. While they are not necessarily *competing* views, they are not entirely *consistent* either (particularly when looking into their various categories in more detail). However, here we consider how the broad areas map onto the technical and non-technical perspectives of cybersecurity. Figure 1 demonstrates the proportion of coverage allocated to technical and non-technical aspects of cybersecurity, based upon a classification of the top-level topic categories listed in Table 2. In some cases, the topics covered a mix of technical and non-technical aspects (such as the *Adversarial Behaviours* Knowledge Area within CyBOK, and the *Operate and Maintain* category within the NICE Framework). The CIISec Skills Framework is unique in having a discipline that seemed to be a non-cybersecurity topic (namely *Management, Leadership, Business and Communications*, which nonetheless remains relevant *within* cybersecurity as it relates to the much-needed soft skills). The entry depicting the Knowledge Units from the NSA's Center of Academic Excellence is only considering the split of coverage amongst Fundamental and Core units, as it is felt that representing the optional units could give a misleading impression (given that they will be taken in significantly different combinations and many have a non-security focus).

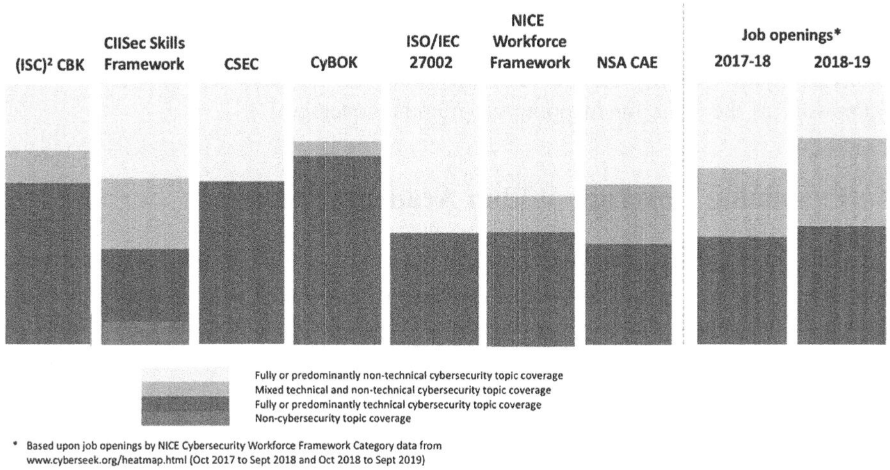


**Fig. 1.** Topic coverage within alternative cybersecurity frameworks.

The representation in the figure does not take account how large or extensive each category is, and these can decompose in rather different ways. For example, in ISO/IEC 27002, the non-technical clause of *Organization of Information Security* has seven underlying controls, whereas the largely technically focused *Access Control* clause is home to fourteen associated controls. Similarly, within the CIISec Skills Framework, the discipline of Information Security Governance and Management hosts seven underlying skills groups, whereas Implementing Secure Systems has just three. Nonetheless, it was considered most appropriate to keep the focus at the high-level categories on the basis that each of the frameworks selected these to represent their main structure (and so presumably considered the resulting categories to be of broadly equal merit and importance within cybersecurity as a whole, regardless of the number of underlying points within them).

The goals of the cybersecurity frameworks lead to differences in emphasis. The CSEC2017 and arguably CyBOK frameworks are intended for academic education, and the others are for professional certification or training. The academic frameworks tend not to mix technical and non-technical subjects, as these are generally seen as separate courses. Hence, in Fig. 1, these have little to no green. ISO/IEC 27002, a code of practice, also makes the same delineation. The professional certification and training frameworks, on the other hand, mix technical and non-technical aspects of cybersecurity, because practitioners must take into account the non-technical needs when designing and implementing technical controls.

The frameworks offer a point of reference for other activities to map against, including academic courses, professional certifications, and training programmes. Indeed, in some cases this is specifically what they exist to provide, with the CSEC guidelines offering a framework specifically for undergraduate academic curricula and the $(ISC)^2$ CBK being used as the reference point for $ISC)^2$'s own certifications. Meanwhile, other frameworks have a more general purpose, but can still be applied in this context. For example, Hallett et al. [17] have mapped other security frameworks to

CyBOK and indicated its potential as a reference point for curricular mapping. Similarly, the national certification programme for academic degrees operated by the UK's National Cyber Security Centre has been using an adapted version of the CIISec framework as the basis for mapping programme coverage [18].

# 4 Examining Coverage Within Academic Degrees

Having looked at the overall composition of the various guiding frameworks that reflect and inform the way we understand cybersecurity, it is interesting to apply the same high-level mapping exercise to the content of academic degrees. With the in mind, we have taken a sample of Masters programmes offered by a range of UK and US universities, and then examined the breakdown of taught module/unit topics offered within each of them. We considered Masters programmes rather than Bachelors degrees because the former are expected to have a more cyber-specific coverage, whereas undergraduate programmes and other earlier-stage qualifications are expected to include a fair volume of more general computing/IT content, which would complicate the task of seeing how security is addressed. In addition, in the Masters, all topics are being covered at the same academic level, whereas attempting to fairly assess undergraduate degrees would also involve some consideration of the years of study at which different security topics were being introduced.

We examined two broad categories of topic coverage within cybersecurity. *Technical cybersecurity* covers material such as system, device, and network security, plus a range of underlying technical mechanisms that support computing and networking. For example, penetration testing, digital forensic analysis, cryptography, authentication, and access control fall into this category. Meanwhile, *non-technical cybersecurity* focuses on the managerial, human, legal, and physical protection. Issues such as risk assessment, business continuity planning, development of security policies, delivery of security awareness training, and cyberlaw fall into this category.

Looking firstly at the UK market, there are more than 100 cybersecurity-related Masters programmes, and the investigation specifically focused upon those titled 'Cyber Security' (as opposed to any more specific - and typically technical - variants such as forensics, network security or ethical hacking). We are looking at a set of programmes that all claim to offer coverage across the discipline as a whole. The sample used here was drawn from a range of universities around the UK (spanning different levels of teaching versus research intensity), with a mix of newer and more established programmes, and nothing inherent within the sample would be expected to skew the results.

The coverage of the degrees was assessed based upon publicly available information from websites (which varied from titles only, to summary paragraphs, to more detailed lists of underlying topic coverage). In terms of content, some programmes include a broad range of options that allow candidates to choose their own route and coverage balance through the selection of electives. Equally, there are some cases in which the syllabus is fully mandated, or the extent of optionality is limited. All also offer substantial project modules, but these are excluded from the assessment as the specifics of their focus will vary depending upon candidates' preferences or topics made available by academic supervisors.

The overall findings are summarised in Fig. 2. It is clear that the situation is generally far less balanced than amongst the frameworks discussed earlier. With one exception, the non-technical aspect of cyber appears to receive little treatment. In programme 5, half of the content is based around more generic computing and network material rather than anything security specific; the rest predominantly cover cybersecurity topics. While it is accepted that wider computing knowledge in areas such as programming, operating systems, and networking can legitimately be relevant in the context of supporting cybersecurity (as well as requiring security aspects to be considered in such areas), this level of coverage seems excessive in a degree claiming to be specifically about cyber. The relevance of the content to employer needs is questionable. Indeed, comparing the spread of job openings illustrated in Fig. 1 to this raises the question of whether the resulting graduates will have topic knowledge and skills that are market-aligned.

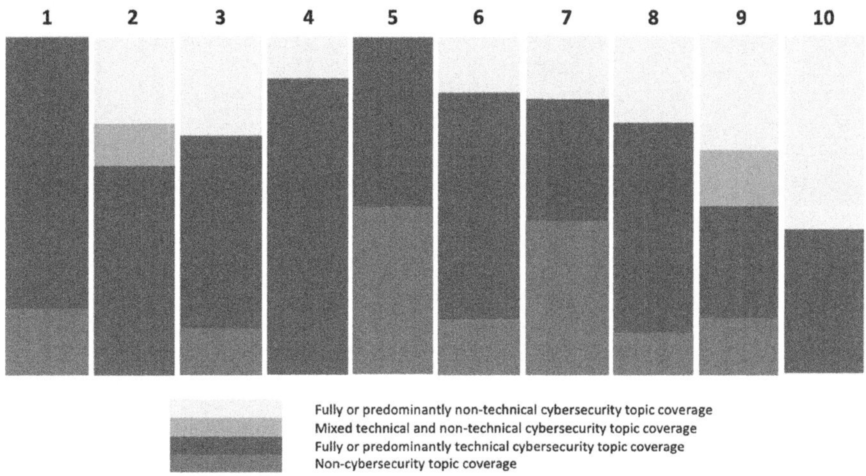


**Fig. 2.** Topic coverage of ten 'MSc Cyber Security' degree programmes in the UK

There is also the question of how and where the courses deliver the soft skills that employers say they need and rate highly. At first glance, there appears to be little direct attention to these aspects. As these are postgraduate courses, these skills will have been promoted and developed during earlier study. Additionally, there is a good chance that in many cases they will be embedded within other modules, with elements such as group work, presentation and writing skills being a specific part of the assessed activities.

Looking at the wider UK cybersecurity degree market and the specialisms represented, the volume of digital forensics degree programmes seems to outstrip the apparent demand for the 'Investigate' strand of the workforce framework. Meanwhile, other topic specialisations that arguably address market need are less represented within degree programme titles, possibly because universities do not consider them to be sufficiently attractive to students coming *into* the process (e.g. 'risk and governance' is not as applicant friendly as 'ethical hacking').

We also looked at a sample consisting of ten Masters programmes in US universities. As with the UK, there is a plethora of such programmes. We again chose ones with the words "Cyber Security" as opposed to anything more general or more specific. This allowed us to compare the breakdown of the programmes with the breakdown of the UK programmes.

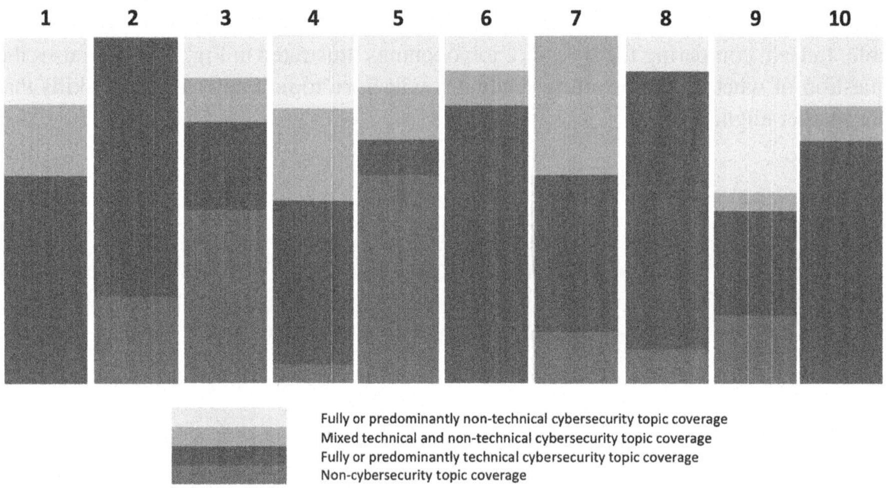


**Fig. 3.** Topic coverage of ten 'MSc Cyber Security' degree programmes in the US

The programmes have both required courses and electives. Only one school prescribes all courses; the rest allow students to select from among the electives, sometimes with the approval of their advisor. The ratios in Fig. 3 include all required courses and electives except those that could not be properly categorized. For example, a capstone project could be very technical or focus on the use of the technology; hence, it could not be assigned to one category.

Four of the US universities had multiple tracks. The tracks in universities 2 and 6 were all technical. University 7 had an interdisciplinary track and a technical track; we used the interdisciplinary one. University 9 had 3 tracks, each of which prescribed some courses and constrained how the electives could be selected. It also had an untracked degree. Because of the myriad of possible combinations, we used all courses to compute the statistics.

Of the ten universities, eight were R1 (doctoral programme – very high research activity), one was R2 (doctoral programme – high research activity), and one was M1 (Masters programme – larger programme) under the Carnegie Classifications. Eight were DHS/NSA Centers of Academic Excellence, seven having CAE-CD (education) classification, five with CAE-R (research) and two with CAE-CO (cyberoperations) classifications; six institutions had more than one such classification [19]. Six were public institutions; the rest were private not-for-profit institutions. Considering the entire university, one had fewer than 10,000 students; four had between 10,000 and 245,999 students, and the remainder had at least 25,000 students [20]. Information on the number of students in each Masters programme was not available.

The results show an overarching focus on technology. Of the ten programmes, only one has more than 20% of the courses being primarily non-technical. That programme is focused on risk management, which explains the predominance of non-technical cybersecurity-related courses. Three of the programmes have a fifth of the courses being primarily non-technical. One is from a school of information science, which is traditionally broader than programmes in computer science. The other is an interdisciplinary track degree, which would be expected to be broader than a strictly technical degree.

The others are primarily technical, and the courses fall into two groups: those directly related to cybersecurity (such as courses on cryptography and network security) and those that are not (such as courses on compilers and operating systems). Except for the three schools mentioned above, these courses account for over 70% of the curriculum. Further, the number of technical courses is greater than the number of mixed technical, non-technical courses in all but 2 of the schools, sometimes by a large percentage. One of those universities focuses on public policy, while the second figure comes from a school where interdisciplinary work is emphasized.

The mixture of technical and non-technical cybersecurity elements in a Masters course is necessary to show that cybersecurity is not solely a technical endeavour. This work used a sampling of 20 university programmes (10 from the UK and 10 from the US) to examine whether this was commonly done. A more comprehensive study would shed further light on how widespread this confluence of technical and non-technical material in cybersecurity programmes is. Such a study would lead to a deeper understanding of how the two should be integrated to meet the particular goals of the academic programme. A major point of this study was to show how widely varied the focus of a programme called "Cyber Security" can be, and a more comprehensive study would undoubtedly provide more details on the extent of the variation.

## 5 Conclusions

Multiple frameworks provide structure for the field of cybersecurity. These frameworks each take a slightly different view of what constitutes the field of cybersecurity. As the frameworks were developed for different purposes, and in different cultures, none can be definitive. Nevertheless, the overlap among them is striking.

Frameworks have two uses. The first is to provide a basis for asserting that a certification or an academic programme meets the desired goals. The content of the courses is mapped into the framework's topics, and from that the educators can determine gaps in coverage, or places where more (or less) depth of coverage is required. The second is to provide a basis for comparison. If two programmes are mapped into the same framework, the differences in them will show up as inconsistencies in the coverage of the framework's topics.

Which framework to choose is driven by the needs of the students, the practitioners, and the employers. They are all fit for various purposes – but the evaluator, students, teachers, and institutions need to be clear on what their purpose is. The same cannot be said for the MSc degree programmes that were examined. In these cases, some include far less balanced coverage of cybersecurity than others. Given that they are called programmes in "cybersecurity", often by exactly the same names, both candidates and employers must understand how this coverage positions graduates for entry into the job market.

Recognising the need for balanced coverage is not enough. It is also necessary to recognise how the programmes and frameworks balance the technical and non-technical topics needed by cybersecurity practitioners, managers, and policy setters.

**Acknowledgements.** Matt Bishop gratefully acknowledges the support of grants DGE-1303211 and DGE-1934279 from the National Science Foundation to the University of California at Davis. Any opinions, findings, and conclusions or recommendations expressed in this material are those of the author(s) and do not necessarily reflect the views of the National Science Foundation.

## References

1. Berghel, H.: Equifax and the latest round of identity theft roulette. IEEE Comput. **50**(12), 72–76 (2017). https://doi.org/10.1109/MC.2017.4451227
2. Oltsik, J.: The life and times of cybersecurity professionals 2018. Research report. Enterprise strategy group and information systems security associate, April 2019 (2019). https://www.esg-global.com/hubfs/pdf/ESG-ISSA-Research-Report-Life-of-Cybersecurity-Professionals-Apr-2019.pdf
3. (ISC)$^2$. Strategies for building and growing strong cybersecurity teams: (ISC)$^2$ cybersecurity workforce study (2019). https://www.isc2.org/-/media/ISC2/Research/2019-Cybersecurity-Workforce-Study/ISC2-Cybersecurity-Workforce-Study-2019.ashx
4. Furnell, S., Bishop, M.: Addressing cybersecurity skills: the spectrum not the silo. Comput. Fraud Secur. **2020**, 6–11 (2020)
5. (ISC)$^2$. Cybersecurity professionals focus on developing new skills as workforce gap widens: (ISC)$^2$ cybersecurity workforce study (2018). https://www.isc2.org/-/media/ISC2/Research/2018-ISC2-Cybersecurity-Workforce-Study.ashx
6. Infosec. Top 10 skills security professionals need to have in 2018, 17 August 2018 (2018). https://resources.infosecinstitute.com/top-10-skills-security-professionals-need-to-have-in-2018/#gref
7. ISACA (2019). State of cybersecurity 2019 - part 1: current trends in workforce development. https://cybersecurity.isaca.org/state-of-cybersecurity
8. Symantec. High alert: tackling cyber security overload in 2019. Symantec corporation (2019). https://resource.elq.symantec.com/LP=7421

9. Dawson, J., Thomson, R.: The future cybersecurity workforce: going beyond technical skills for successful cyber performance. Front. Psychol. **9**, 744 (2018). https://www.frontiersin.org/articles/10.3389/fpsyg.2018.00744/full
10. CSEC2017 joint task force. Cybersecurity curricula 2017–curriculum guidelines for post-secondary degree programs in cybersecurity. Version 1.0 Report 31 December 2017. Association for Computing Machinery (ACM), IEEE Computer Society (IEEE-CS), Association for Information Systems Special Interest Group on Information Security and Privacy (AIS SIGSEC) and International Federation for Information Processing Technical Committee on Information Security Education (IFIP WG 11.8) (2017). https://cybered.hosting.acm.org/wp-content/uploads/2018/02/newcover_csec2017.pdf
11. CIISec. CIISec skills framework, version 2.4, chartered institute of information security, November 2019 (2019). https://www.ciisec.org/CIISEC/Resources/Capability_Methodology/Skills_Framework/CIISEC/Resources/Skills_Framework.aspx
12. Rashid, A., Chivers, H., Danezis, G., Lupu, E., Martin, A.: The cyber security body of knowledge. Version 1.0, 31 October 2019 (2019). https://www.cybok.org/media/downloads/cybok_version_1.0.pdf
13. $(ISC)^2$. The $(ISC)^2$ CBK (2019). https://www.isc2.org/Certifications/CBK. Accessed 1 Apr 2020
14. ISO/IEC. Information technology—Security techniques—Code of practice for information security controls. International Standard ISO/IEC 27002. Second edition 2013-10-01. International Organization for Standardization and International Electrotechnical Commission (2013)
15. Newhouse, B., Keith, S., Scriber, B., Witte, G.: National initiative for cybersecurity education (NICE) cybersecurity workforce framework. NIST Special Publication 800–181, August 2017 (2017). https://nvlpubs.nist.gov/nistpubs/SpecialPublications/NIST.SP.800-181.pdf
16. NSA. CAE-CD 2020 knowledge units. CAE requirements and resources (2019). http://www.iad.gov/NIETP/documents/Requirements/CAE-CD_2020_Knowledge_Units.pdf. Accessed 1 Apr 2020
17. Hallett, J., Larson, R., Rashid, A.: Mirror, mirror, on the wall: what are we teaching them all? Characterising the focus of cybersecurity curricular frameworks. In: 2018 USENIX Workshop on Advances in Security Education (2018)
18. Furnell, S., Michael, K., Piper, F., Chris, E., Catherine, H., Ensor, C.: A national certification programme for academic degrees in cyber security. In: Drevin, L., Theocharidou, M. (eds.) WISE 2018. IAICT, vol. 531, pp. 133–145. Springer, Cham (2018). https://doi.org/10.1007/978-3-319-99734-6_11
19. The CAE in cybersecurity community (2020). CAE Institution Map. https://www.caecommunity.org/content/cae-institution-map. Accessed 1 Apr 2020
20. Indiana University Center for Postsecondary Research. (2018). The Carnegie classification of institutions of higher education. https://carnegieclassifications.iu.edu/index.php. Accessed 1 Apr 2020

# Quality Criteria for Cyber Security MOOCs

Simone Fischer-Hübner[1(✉)], Matthias Beckerle[1], Alberto Lluch Lafuente[2], Antonio Ruiz Martínez[3], Karo Saharinen[4], Antonio Skarmeta[3], and Pierantonia Sterlini[5]

[1] Karlstad University, Karlstad, Sweden
simofihu@kau.se
[2] Technical University of Denmark, Kongens Lyngby, Denmark
[3] University of Murcia, Murcia, Spain
[4] Jyväskylä University of Applied Science, Jyväskylä, Finland
[5] Trento University, Trento, Italy

**Abstract.** Cyber security MOOCs (Massive Open Online Courses) can enable lifelong learning and increase the cyber security competence of experts and citizens. This paper contributes with a review of existing cyber security MOOCs and MOOC quality assurance frameworks. It then presents quality criteria, which we elicited for evaluating whether cyber security MOOCs are worthy to be awarded with a quality seal. Finally, an exemplary evaluation of six selected European MOOCs is presented to exercise the quality seal awarding process. Additionally, the evaluation revealed that criteria for assuring privacy, ethics, meeting professional expectations and openness were on average not clearly met.

**Keywords:** Cyber security · Security education · MOOCs · Quality assurance and evaluation

## 1 Introduction

The CyberSec4Europe project will, as one of the EU H2020 pilot projects for a future European Cyber Security Competence Network, test and demonstrate potential governance structures for such a network of future competence centres. One area, for which the project will define and evaluate governance structures, is the area of quality assurance for cyber security education provided by MOOCs (Massive Open Online Courses), which have emerged over the last years as an alternative to formal education and as an enabler for life-long learning to a broad group of students. Cyber security MOOCs can thus increase the cyber security competence of experts but also a larger group of the population in Europe. For defining a quality assurance process, a list of quality criteria is needed for evaluating MOOCs if they are worthy to be awarded with a quality seal by a


L. Drevin et al. (Eds.): WISE 2020, IFIP AICT 579, pp. 46–60, 2020.
https://doi.org/10.1007/978-3-030-59291-2_4

European Cyber Security Competence Network. For eliciting such quality criteria, we have first conducted an initial review of existing cyber security MOOC offerings and of existing rules and practices of operating them at EU level for assuring quality. While MOOC quality assurance frameworks were already proposed by different organisations, we have been particularly interested in eliciting those quality assurance criteria that should be met specifically by cyber security MOOCs, including cyber range MOOCs, in addition to generic MOOC quality assurance criteria. The objectives of this paper is to present and motivate quality criteria for cyber security MOOCs, and to present and discuss the exemplary evaluations of selected cyber security MOOCs according to those criteria and conclusions drawn from it.

The remainder of this paper is structured as follows: Sect. 2 provides a short review of existing offerings of cyber security MOOCs in Europe and the existing rules and practices of operating them for providing quality, and concludes with requirements for quality criteria and open issues. Section 3 is briefly summarising the related work of existing Quality Assurance frameworks for MOOCs. In Sect. 4, we are presenting quality criteria for cyber security MOOCs, which are extending the existing MOOC quality criteria and are addressing the identified open issues. These criteria are then used for an exemplary evaluation of selected cyber security MOOCs for testing a process for awarding a quality seal to cyber security MOOCs based on these criteria, as presented in Sect. 5. Finally, Sect. 6 is presenting overall conclusions and next steps to be taken.

## 2 Review to Existing European Cyber Security MOOCs

This section summarises the review of the landscape of European cyber security MOOCs and the rules for operating them that we conducted for Cyber-Sec4Europe. Our survey of the current landscape showed that cyber security specific topic channels or platforms do not exist yet - existent cyber security MOOCs are rather offered on the dominant learning platforms, such as Coursera, EdX, FutureLearn, Udacity, Edemy, or Canvas. Cyber security MOOCs can be grouped into academic level MOOCs, continuous learning MOOCs and MOOCs utilising cyber ranges, or can be combinations of those categories, and will be reviewed in the following sections.

Among the different MOOC offering, the EIT Digital (a division of the EIT, European Institute of Innovation and Technology) stands out with its focus on the area of Innovation and Entrepreneurship (I&E) education in ICT and the implementation of blended I&E courses. We will review them in the Academic level section albeit they may also fit the Continuous Education section.

### 2.1 Academic Level MOOCs

Academic level courses or programmes are those offered primarily to students enrolled at a University and award credit points or academic degrees to those enrolled students. Online academic courses can be divided into classical MOOCs that are open to all kinds of participants in addition to enrolled students, and other online courses or programmes, which can only be accessed by students that are formally enrolled at the offering academic institution.

While classical MOOCs for cyber security topics are mostly offered by academic institutions, most of them are MOOCs for continuous learning, whereas classical academic MOOCs are still rare and only a handful of them could be identified via a search on Class Central and via the Web [1].

Academic courses are typically already governed by existing regulations and university's own rules and quality plans for guaranteeing high quality education. For instance, national higher education acts and ordinances usually regulate student admission criteria, qualification requirements for course instructors and for the publication of course evaluations. For issuing ECTS credits, the university must have an accreditation approved by the Education Accreditation Commission (EQAC) and must provide transparency on course workload and learning outcome, as required by the EU Commission.

The EIT Digital approved courses are slightly different than classical academic MOOCs from the perspective of the governance and approval process.[1] The qualification of the proposing institutions is guaranteed by the involvement of the EIT Digital Network of European universities. The approval of the MOOCs follows a submission-based model similar to the traditional calls for research funding, that typically involves a consortium. More specifically, the development of the courses is based on a cross-university collaboration in accordance with the current EIT Digital I&E education guidelines. The partners submit a proposal to the EIT Digital for co-financing the implementation of a specific MOOC and, if approved by the EIT Digital, the MOOC is realised and ported in the learning platform for the actual execution.

### 2.2 MOOCs as Continuous Education Courses

Continuing education courses are meant to provide all citizens with specialised education through all phases of their lives and are characterised by a huge variety of formats and characteristics. The dominant classes of providers of Cyber Security MOOCs are higher education institutions and private companies, but some are also offered by non-profit organisations or individuals. Most MOOC platforms have headquarters in the US, hence not necessarily adhering to EU regulations such as the EU General Data Protection Regulation 2016/679 (GDPR).

Access to the courses is often unrestricted, but there are cases in which enrolment is limited by several criteria that may include nationality constraints, for example due to sanctions to specific countries, typically dictated by the platform's legal headquarters: the US in most cases. Academic qualifications are rarely a mandatory criteria to access a course. Most courses, indeed, are offered with no specific criteria on the students' qualifications and previous knowledge,

[1] An example of technical specialisation is available at: https://www.coursera.org/specializations/embedded-systems-security whereas a I&E specialization is available at: https://www.coursera.org/specializations/value-creation-innovation.

although informal recommendations are usually given. Platforms tend to provide information about content, learning objectives, and professional expectations in an informal way. Certificates are sometimes issued automatically upon completion of the course but without a formal verification.

The typical qualification for courses provided by higher education institutions is that of a teacher at the corresponding institutions (lecturer/professor). In the rest of the cases, teachers are often experienced professionals with a variety of profiles, but qualification criteria for those instructors are usually not provided by the platforms.

### 2.3 MOOCs Utilising Cyber Ranges

The definition of a cyber range currently varies greatly between organisations giving cyber security education. The size of the cyber range currently varies from one virtual machine to thousands. Thus declaring a MOOC to a "Cyber Range MOOC" is troublesome and needs clear criteria.

MOOCs in particular have the problem of being tied to the platform providing registration and distribution of material for the MOOC. Larger platforms might not support technical laboratories (other than basic quizzes or multiple-choice answers) leaving out the technical aspect of cyber security. This leaves universities with the problem of hosting the cyber range by themselves. Generating accounts and instructions on how to use the cyber range next to the MOOC platform requires automatisation and integration of the environments. This also provides challenges to the student, with multiple accounts or environments, who thus may require online support, which in turn increases costs and may hinder the scalability of the cyber range course.

These reasons might be the troublesome parts of the cyber range MOOCs, which without answers leaves the industry without competent, technically oriented workforce. For this reason cyber range MOOCs are currently basically non-existent yet, while rather traditional cyber range courses are offered by several European Universities, such as Tallinn University of Technology (in collaboration with NATO), NTNU and JAMK University of Applied Sciences. Apart from that, also the openness (which is one of the inherent MOOC characteristics) of course attendance and of course material is often, due to the security sensitivity of the course content, an issue for courses on cyber ranges, which therefore typically have restrictions in place.

### 2.4 Conclusions and Gaps

From our review, we want to highlight especially the following conclusions in terms of quality assurance criteria needed for the different types of cyber security MOOCs: In general, criteria for assuring fairness and transparency in regard to course admission, access to course content and evaluations will need attention. This is especially important for cyber security MOOCs teaching sensitive information about hacking and vulnerabilities. So far, cyber range MOOCs are non-existent, but if developed in future, they will require ethical rules on the openness of course content, student admission and course material.

Furthermore, MOOC platforms and channels are typically hosted by US providers, which means that personal data including student attendance and performance tracking may be transferred to the USA, which raises privacy and issues of compliance with the GDPR (EU General Data Protection Regulation), especially in regard to the transfers of personal data to third countries regulated in Chapter V of the GDPR.

## 3 MOOC Quality Assurance and Validation Frameworks

In CyberSec4Europe, we are particularly interested in eliciting quality assurance criteria for cyber security MOOCs including future cyber ranges MOOCs. The definition of such criteria is fundamental for course recognition, certification, and accreditation, and for awarding quality seals to MOOCs. As pointed out by Gaebel (2014) [2] for MOOCs making a change in higher education, they have to award credits, and thus quality assurance criteria for credentialisation play an important role too.

The OpenCred report by JRC [3] addressed the recognition practices of open learning achievements by European non-formal open learners. This study identifies elements of MOOC recognition by another Higher Education Institution (HEI) or employer, including the identity verification of learners, suitable supervised assessment, informative credential that acknowledge learning, and the award of credit points.

For the definition of the quality assurance criteria for cyber security MOOCs, we have considered the review of the main existing MOOC quality assurance and validation frameworks: the OpenupEd label [4], the Quality Reference Framework (QRF) for the Quality of Massive Open Online Courses (MOOCs) [5], and the Instructional and Assessment Design Framework (IADF)[2]. Such specific frameworks for MOOCs were developed, since, as indicated by Hood and Littlejohn (2016) [6], the quality measures and indicators used so far for other type of courses are not always suitable for MOOCs, and quality is not objective because it is a purpose-specific measure. These measures could be even dependent on pedagogy [7], which means that they could differ between MOOCs and courses taught in another form.

The OpenupEd Quality Label [4] is a framework designed to improve the quality of OpenupEd's MOOCs. OpenupEd is an alliance of institutional MOOC providers, which is coordinated by the European Association of Distance Teaching Universities (EADTU). Their MOOCs have eight distinctive features: openness to learners, digital openness, learner-centred approach, independent learning, media-supported interaction, recognition options, quality focus, and spectrum of diversity.

[2] https://www.eitdigital.eu/eit-digital-academy/.

The OpenupEd Quality Label has been derived from the E-xcellence label [8], which provides a methodology to assess the quality of e-learning in higher education and it is based on several benchmark statements. These statements are arranged into six dimensions: Strategic Management, Curriculum Design, Course Design, Course Delivery, Staff Support, and Student Support. As e-learning in HEIs is evolving and changing, the E-xcellence label has undergone several updates from the feedback of its reviewers to reflect this evolution. Through a mapping between the benchmarks and the OpenupEd distinctive features, it is possible for a MOOC to provide evidence confirming that it supports OpenupEd features. These evidences can be gathered by different stakeholders such as management, academics, course designers, tutors, and students.

The Quality Reference Framework (QRF) for the Quality of MOOCs [5] is a development of the European Alliance for the Quality of Massive Open Online Courses (MOOCs), called MOOQ. For the definition of this framework, MOOQ has been based on ISO/IEC 40180. The research they have made by means of Global MOOC Quality Surveys, semi-structured interviews, and the feedback from several MOOQ workshops. In the QRF, they have defined three dimensions: Phases, Perspectives, and Roles. The phases, in turn, are divided into processes. Furthermore, for the design and development of MOOCs, the framework provides the QRF Key Quality Criteria and the QRF Quality Checklist. The former are action items for those actions that could be performed in different processes. The latter consists of leading questions for the defined dimensions to remind the key issues to be considered in the MOOC design and development.

The Instructional and Assessment Design Framework (IADF) has been developed by EIT Digital with the other Knowledge and Innovation Communities (KIC) to assess the quality assessment of courses. This framework consists of four components: Instructional Design, Assessment, Functional Requirements, and Learning Analytics. These components have to be considered by teachers for the design of their courses and by evaluators to evaluate the product developed. However, this is an *evaluation framework that is not tailored to security.*

To the best of our knowledge, no cyber security specific quality assurance or validation framework is existing yet.

## 4 Proposed Quality Criteria for Cyber Security MOOCs

Our quality assurance criteria for Cyber Security MOOCs presented in this section were (1) derived the conclusions from our review of existing European MOOCs in Sect. 2 in terms of gaps to be addressed and are (2) also based on criteria taken from existing quality assurance frameworks that were presented in Sect. 3. Moreover, some of the criteria are (3) based on existing best practices and our experiences, as well as (4) derived from regulations and ethical standards.

Some of the criteria require the involvement of relevant stakeholders for cyber security MOOCs, which may include cyber security experts from industry or government, data protection officers, privacy activists, representatives from (ethical) hacker organisations and/or from national cyber security agencies.

The categories of quality criteria that we present in the following subsections are corresponding to categories used in the other quality assurance frameworks referred to in the previous section. In addition, we added categories for ethical rules, privacy and for cyber range specific quality assurance criteria, which as our review and gap analysis in Sect. 2 showed, need special attention when it comes to cyber security MOOCs. Cyber security-specific criteria including criteria for future cyber range MOOCs in each category are especially highlighted, except for three categories that have no cyber-security-specific criteria. The detailed list of all criteria for each category and the sources from which they were derived are available in the CyberSec4Europe project deliverable [1].

### 4.1 Criteria for the Qualification of the Proposer

In order to create and offer a MOOC of high quality, the proposing institution (proposer) should have the proper qualification and experiences to be able to develop, run and evaluate the MOOC in a professional manner. The quality of the proposer is also essential for the recognition of the MOOC by the community and for the recognition of credentials.

**Cyber Security Specific Criteria:** The proposer should especially be recognised by relevant stakeholders in cyber security, either through academic recognition or through their long experiences in the cyber security domain. Proposers of cyber range MOOCs should have expertise in applied technology & private-public partnership. The proposer's cyber range should be technical, work-life oriented which can mimic realistic phenomena (attack campaigns, threat actors, techniques & tools) from the cyber security field.

### 4.2 Admission Criteria and Qualification of Participants

It is important that participants (students) know what is expected from them in terms of prerequisites and that the teachers know what to expect from the participants. However, prerequisites that are not essential for the MOOC should not be used for excluding participants, as in principle the aim should be to be as inclusive as possible for enhancing cyber security competence in Europe. Participants must also be able to find out whether they are qualified for a MOOC and/or why they are not accepted for enrolment. Therefore, the acceptance process should be legit and transparent.

**Cyber Security Specific Criteria:** For cyber range MOOCs, the participant should have the skills necessary to operate a technical cyber range platform or the learning objective of the course should be that the participant learns how to operate such platform.

### 4.3 Criteria for the Qualification of Instructors

The qualification of the instructors (teachers) is fundamental to ensure a high quality MOOC. Instructors should usually have an academic degree and should have undergone pedagogical training - for academic MOOCs, national higher education acts often require that the academic degree of the examiner should be higher then the degree that is awarded by the course. For continuous learning MOOCS, relevant working life or industrial experiences should be required.

**Cyber Security Specific Criteria:** Since the cyber range requires technical operation, the instructor of a cyber range MOOC should have such technical skills for conducting and supervising such operations or the course should have dedicated personnel for this task (e.g. cyber range specialists).

### 4.4 Criteria for Examination, Credentialisation and Recognition

For awarding credits or certificates, course examination has to verify that the participant has achieved the goals of the education and assure that the awarded credits or the certificate correctly reflects the quality with that the goals were achieved. The examination must be fair and the goals must be transparent, so that the participants know what is expected from them in the exam and that the risk of fraud is minimised. For promoting life long learning, course certificates should be issued enabling recognition of the educational achievements in the professional or life-long/blended learning context. For ensuring recognition in the academic context, academic European MOOCs should be recognised as a valid credit-awarding course within the European credit transfer system.

**Cyber Security Specific Criteria:** The cyber range activities, laboratory work, and assignments that need to be completed for obtaining a course credential should be clearly stated.

### 4.5 Course Evaluation Criteria

MOOC evaluations allow student to give feedback and ratings for continuously improving the course quality, and by this, reduce the number of course dropouts. Published course evaluations provide information allowing to judge a MOOC and its usefulness from a participant's perspective. Course evaluations are commonly regulated in the academic sector. In particular, the Massive Online Open Education Quality (MOOQ) QRF Framework [5] provides key quality criteria for the evaluation planning, realisation, review and resulting improvements, which we propose as quality criteria together with criteria from rules and established practices from the academic sector.

**Cyber Security Specific Criteria:** An evaluation review and follow-up process should be in place that should involve relevant stakeholders, such as the MOOC design team, instructors, director of studies, but also relevant cyber security stakeholders, as the ones named above.

### 4.6 Criteria for Meeting Professional Expectations

For meeting professional expectations, suitable stakeholders, especially from working life and the employment side, should be involved in different MOOC phases.

**Cyber Security Specific Criteria:** When providing a cyber range course to a company or an organisation, it should be "realistic enough", i.e. simulate operational and supporting services and systems available for the participants. The extent of realism should be discussed and agreed upon during designing the course. When participants from an organisation attend a course given for that organisation which utilises a cyber range, the participants should, if there is agreement with the instructor, follow their own organisations' processes and guidelines when detecting abnormal or malicious activity and when starting or even performing incident management. This approach should bring to awareness the need to update the organisation's guidelines and process documentation.

### 4.7 Course Structure and Course Content Criteria

Criteria for the course structure guaranteeing the quality of the course content were partly taken from the OpenupEd suggested distinctive features [9], and some others were motivated by the Checklist for MOOC Accreditation in [10]. These criteria are requiring to clearly specify learning outcomes that can be achieved by the course content. We also require that continuous learning MOOCs offered by companies should not with an inappropriate bias promote commercial products or systems of that company, unless the entire focus of the MOOC is on the teaching or training of the usage of these products or systems.

### 4.8 Course Platform and Channels Criteria

Quality criteria for platforms and channels are derived from legal requirements. In particular, GDPR compliant platforms and channels must be selected. Moreover, the functionality of the platform should comply with the EU Directive 2016/2102 on the accessibility of the websites and mobile applications of public sector bodies for ensuring inclusiveness.

### 4.9 Openness Criteria

Openness is a key element of a MOOC and important both in terms of the MOOC content and material (by using an open licensing, e.g. CC-BY-SA, allowing to freely reuse, mix and redistribute material), and in terms of being open to the learner's needs, enabling them to study at any time, place and pace of choice.

**Cyber Security Specific Criteria:** There should be clear, transparent and justifiable policies for defining any restrictions to digital openness (e.g. for the use of malicious or attack code for teaching purposes) and/or openness of course elements (e.g. those that are hacking-related or for other reason security-sensitive) to learners for ethical or security reasons.

### 4.10 Ethics and Privacy Criteria

Education in cyber security by its nature must also cover attack methodologies and how vulnerabilities arise and/or could be misused. This knowledge is needed for teaching how to secure systems against threats and weaknesses in computer-based systems, e.g. administrative systems, industrial control systems and computer networks. A deeper understanding of threats and risks is also needed when performing risk assessment, risk analysis and risk management. However, this knowledge could also be exploited for malicious purposes. Because of this dual nature of this knowledge, it is important to define, teach and enforce ethical principles for cyber security courses in regard to ethical hacking, handling security-sensitive information and personal data.

Moreover, many teaching platforms today store personal information about the participants for different purposes. In some cases, this information is used to profile participants for either platform improvement or for market purposes. This profiling can reveal sensitive personal data like political opinions, religious believes or ethical origin e.g. when tracking and storing course preferences and browsing patterns. On platforms like YouTube or other types of "free" channels, the information is used for targeted advertisement and in some cases sold on for market purposes. With this in mind, it is important to give the participants choices for where to access the learning material and not force the student to disclose more personal data than it is necessary for fulfilment of the course and the examination. For example, if video course material is made available through YouTube, there should be an alternative more privacy friendly channel made available for accessing the material. It is also important that the "owner" of the course (i.e. the data controller) has an appropriate data processor agreement with the sites that distribute the course material stating how personal data may be processed in compliance with Art. 28 GDPR. There must be GDPR compliant privacy policy statement, both from the platform provider and the course owner that process personal data. The platform and course instances storing personal data about the participants must be secured by appropriate security controls and should be designed by the Data Protection by Design and Default principle (Art. 25 GDPR).

**Cyber Security Specific Criteria:** While ethics and privacy criteria should be enforced for all types of MOOCs, they are especially relevant to Cyber Security MOOCs teaching security and privacy, for demonstrating that privacy and ethics taught in the course are also enforced in practice, i.e. the course should live up to the standards taught.

### 4.11 Cyber Ranges Criteria

For cyber ranges to be utilised for future cyber range MOOCs certain quality criteria, in particular in regard to the technical and operational capabilities and capacities should be fulfilled. For instance, the institution's cyber range should provide systems and services for planning, running and doing post-exercise analysis and also provide systems and services for the defending team to prevent, detect, mitigate and recover from cyber incidents.

# 5 Exemplary Evaluation of MOOCs

The project partners conducted an exemplary evaluation of selected cyber security MOOCs by applying a subset of the defined quality criteria, with a focus on those criteria that are cyber security specific. Therefore, Table 1 does not include all criteria categories from Sect. 4. In addition, since no Cyber Range MOOCs were available, those criteria could not be tested.

The objective of the exemplary evaluation was twofold: First, we wanted to test a process for awarding quality seals to cyber security MOOCs based on our quality criteria in order to propose governance rules for awarding MOOC quality seals by a future European Cyber Security Competence Center and to test the applicability of our criteria. Second, we wanted to test how far information for evaluating the quality of exemplary cyber security MOOCs is openly available online, so that the MOOCs can be easily assessed by interested students and to what extent the criteria are fulfilled.

## 5.1 Selection of Exemplary MOOCs

For the evaluation exercise, we selected the following six MOOCs from different European countries in the form of academic and/or continuous learning MOOCs offered by academic institutions and/or industry for having a broad range of different types of MOOCs:

- Continuous learning MOOC: "Information Security: Context and Introduction" by Royal Holloway, UK [11]
- Continuous learning MOOC: "Managing Security in Google Cloud Platform" by Google [12]
- Academic MOOC: "Netzwerksicherheit" by Technische Hochschule Lübeck, Germany [13]
- Academic MOOC: "Privacy by Design" by Karlstad University, Sweden [14, 15]
- Academic MOOC: "Development of Secure Embedded Systems Specialization", EIT Digital Cyber Security course [16]
- Academic and continous learning MOOC: "Cyber Security Base with F-Secure, Academic", by the University of Helsinki and F-Secure, Finland [17]

## 5.2 Evaluation Procedure

Our evaluation procedure had three phases and basically implemented a peer-review process, which was especially needed for evaluating those criteria that were rather subjective and open for interpretations. In the first phase, each

MOOC was independently evaluated by five or six project partners. For each quality criterion, each partner decided to which degree the criterion was fulfilled and assessed it as "yes", "partly", or "no". If information was not retrievable from the openly published course information and material, the assessment was marked as "unclear". In addition, the source of information used for the assessment and a short explanation of the decision process were noted. In the second phase, these five to six evaluation lists were collected and combined into a single document. Afterwards, one partner, assigned for taking the lead, consolidated any unanimous ratings into a combined evaluation list. In the third phase, in case of deviating ratings for criteria, a consensus discussion among involved partners took place. Afterwards, the evaluation was finalised and graphical representations were generated.

### 5.3 Results and Discussion

**Ratings and Openness of Information:** Our evaluation exercise showed that not all information for evaluating the quality of MOOCs is openly available. This is illustrated in Table 1, which shows the average percentages of unclear ratings due to a lack of available information for different criteria categories.

Information about the proposing institute were rather visibly published. Also, information needed to evaluate the course examination, credentialisation, and recognition criteria as well as the course structure and content criteria were mostly available online. Considering that students that are interested to enrol, need that information to decide if a MOOC is suitable for them, this comes at no surprise. Nevertheless, it is astonishing that for several of these criteria information could not be found on the related websites.

Ethical considerations for teaching cyber security, including ethical rules for students for handling security-sensitive information, were only clearly addressed for a quarter of the analysed courses. One may argue that some of the selected MOOCs are not including ethical hacking exercises, and thus do not require such ethical instructions for students. Nonetheless, ethical standards are in general of relevance for cyber security experts and should thus be preferably addressed by any cyber security MOOC.

On average only a third of the privacy criteria were clearly fulfilled. In particular, most of the evaluated MOOCs did not have clear policy statements specifying how student-performance related data collected by the course platforms are used by the course owners. Hence, those MOOCs provide no good example of how to implement privacy requirements in practice. Finally it is also notable that criteria about meeting professional expectation were on average only clearly fulfilled in less than 15%. In particular, many of the courses missed to involve cyber security stakeholders in the course in the course design, implementation, realisation, and/or periodic review. This is a further shortcoming, as practical working-life cyber security experiences and perspectives may thus not be well reflected.

**Table 1.** Average distribution of criteria assessment ratings per criteria category for the evaluated MOOCs in percent.

| Category of criteria | Yes | Partly | No | Unclear |
|---|---|---|---|---|
| Qualification of the proposing institution | 80.5 | 2.4 | 12.2 | 4.9 |
| Course structure and content criteria | 55.2 | 12.8 | 3.2 | 28.8 |
| Qualification of instructors | 52.8 | 8.3 | 2.8 | 36.1 |
| Course examination, credentialisation, and recognition | 40.6 | 4.2 | 32.3 | 22.9 |
| Privacy requirements | 37.1 | 8.6 | 14.3 | 40.0 |
| Openness | 33.3 | 0.0 | 0.0 | 66.7 |
| Ethical considerations for teaching cyber security | 25.0 | 4.2 | 20.8 | 50.0 |
| Meeting professional expectation | 14.3 | 0.0 | 21.4 | 64.3 |
| Average | 45.2 | 7.0 | 14.7 | 33.1 |

**Quality Seal Awarding Process.** The three phase evaluation process consisting of independent evaluation by several experts, consolidation, and moderated consensus discussions and decisions, worked very well and is thus recommended as part of a governance structure for awarding the quality seal to MOOCs by a European Cyber Security Competence Network. We recommend to only award a quality seal for MOOCs that clearly fulfil all quality criteria that are not formulated as optional. For any criteria that are not met, partly met or that are unclear, the proposer should be requested to address these open issues first and then resubmit the application for a quality seal. An evaluation process based on openly published information only, does not seem to work, even though this is not inline with the inherent openness characteristic of MOOCs. Nonetheless, we conclude that the MOOC proposers will have to add documentation demonstrating how quality criteria have been met by them when they submit their application for a quality seal. Ultimately, active participation in a MOOC might be needed to reliably retrieve all information needed for the evaluation.

## 6 Conclusions

In this paper, quality criteria for cyber security MOOCs were elicited and tested with an evaluation exercise for selected European cyber security MOOCs. The results provide a basis for defining a quality assurance process for MOOCs to be awarded with a quality seal by a European Cyber Security Competence Network. As a next step, governance models for a quality seal awarding process will be further developed and refined by the CyberSec4Europe project. Our exemplary evaluations revealed issues in regard to the openness of course meta information that restrain evaluators and interested students to assess the quality of MOOCs. Moreover, criteria for assuring privacy, ethical rules for course participants, as well as for ensuring that professional expectations of cyber security stakeholders are met, were to a large extent not fulfilled by the selected MOOCs. We therefore hope that our quality criteria will also enable cyber security MOOC designers, developers, and owners to generate better courses that will fulfil our criteria. Our criteria are especially important for enabling the development of high quality cyber range MOOCs in future, which will be further investigated by CyberSec4Europe.

**Acknowledgements.** This work was funded by the European Commission's H2020 Programme under the Grant Agreement Number 830929. We thank all contributors to the CyberSec4Europe Deliverable 6.1, especially Hans Hedbom, Fabio Massacci, Yani Päijänen, Petri Muka, Marko Vatanen, Lejla Islami and Mahdi Akil, for their valuable input.

## References

1. Fischer-Hübner, S., et al.: CyberSec4Europe deliverable 6.1 - case pilot for WP2 governance (2019). https://cybersec4europe.eu/publications/deliverables/
2. Gaebel, M.: MOOCs Massive Open Online Courses. European University Association, Brussels (2014)
3. Witthaus, G.R.: Validation of non-formal MOOC-based learning: an analysis of assessment and recognition practices in Europe (OpenCred). Joint Research Council, European Union (2016)
4. Rosewell, J., Jansen, D.: The OpenupEd quality label: benchmarks for MOOCs. Int. J. Innov. Qual. Learn. **2**(3), 88–100 (2014)
5. Stracke, C.M., et al.: Quality reference framework (QRF) for the quality of MOOCs (2018). http://www.mooc-quality.eu/QRF
6. Hood, N., Littlejohn, A.: MOOC quality: the need for new measures. J. Learn. Dev. - JL4D **3**(3), 28–42 (2016)
7. Aloizou, V., Villagrá Sobrino, S.L., Martínez Monés, A., Asensio Pérez, J.I., García Sastre, S.: Quality assurance methods assessing instructional design in MOOCs that implement active learning pedagogies: an evaluative case study. In: Proceedings of Work in Progress Papers of the Research, Experience and Business Tracks at EMOOCs 2019, pp. 14–19. CEUR Workshop Proceedings (2019)
8. Williams, K., Kear, K., Rosewell, J.: Quality Assessment for E-learning: A Benchmarking Approach, 2nd edn. European Association of Distance Teaching Universities (EADTU) (2012)
9. Jansen, D., Rosewell, J., Kear, K.: Quality frameworks for MOOCs. In: Jemni, M., Kinshuk Khribi, M. (eds.) Open Education: from OERs to MOOCs. Lecture Notes in Educational Technology, pp. 261–281. Springer, Heidelberg (2017). https://doi.org/10.1007/978-3-662-52925-6_14
10. Commonwealth of Learning. Guidelines for Quality Assurance and Accreditation of MOOCs (2016)
11. Holloway, R.: Information security: context and introduction. https://www.coursera.org/learn/information-security-data. Accessed 21 Jan 2020
12. Google. Managing security in google cloud platform. https://www.coursera.org/learn/managing-security-in-google-cloud-platform. Accessed 21 Jan 2020
13. Technische Hochschule Luebeck. Netzwerksicherheit. https://www.oncampus.de/weiterbildung/moocs/netzwerksicherheit. Accessed 21 Jan 2020
14. Karlstad University. Privacy by Design. https://www.kau.se/cs/pbd. Accessed 21 Jan 2020

15. Fischer-Hübner, S., et al.: A MOOC on privacy by design and the GDPR. In: Drevin, L., Theocharidou, M. (eds.) Information Security Education - Towards a Cybersecure Society. WISE 2018. IFIP Advances in Information and Communication Technology, vol. 531, pp. 95–107. Springer, Cham (2018). https://doi.org/10.1007/978-3-319-99734-6_8
16. EIT digital. Development of secure embedded systems specialization. https://www.coursera.org/specializations/embedded-systems-security. Accessed 21 Jan 2020
17. University of Helsinki and F-Secure. Cyber security base with F-secure, academic. https://cybersecuritybase.mooc.fi/. Accessed 21 Jan 2020

# An Analysis and Evaluation of Open Source Capture the Flag Platforms as Cybersecurity e-Learning Tools

Stylianos Karagiannis(✉), Elpidoforos Maragkos-Belmpas, and Emmanouil Magkos

Department of Informatics, Ionian University, Plateia Tsirigoti 7, 49100 Corfu, Greece
{skaragiannis,pl3mara,emagos}@ionio.gr

**Abstract.** Capture the Flag (CTF) challenges are typically used for hosting competitions related to cybersecurity. Like any other event, CTF competitions vary in terms of context, topics and purpose and integrate various features and characteristics. This article presents the results of a comparative evaluation between 4 popular open source CTF platforms, regarding their use for learning purposes. We conducted this evaluation as part of the user-centered design process by demonstrating the platforms to the potential participants, in order to collect descriptive insights regarding the features of each platform. The results of this evaluation demonstrated that participants approved the high importance of the selected features and their significance for enhancing the learning process. This study may be useful for organizers of learning events to select the right platform, as well as for future researchers to upgrade and to extend any particular platform according to their needs.

**Keywords:** Capture the flag platforms · CTF challenges · Cybersecurity · e-Learning

## 1 Introduction

Cybersecurity is a fast-growing topic and a compound industry that is rapidly changing following the lightning fast evolution of technology. Large sums are consistently invested in security research and training of professionals in order to protect critical infrastructures against possible threats [1]. As part of their cybersecurity strategy, many companies choose to train their employees in order to sharpen their skills and increase their security awareness [2]. Traditional methodologies of teaching cybersecurity and information security topics may not allow trainees to use and test their knowledge in realistic conditions [3]. *Capture the Flag* (CTF) competitions [4] are very popular for testing skills and presenting challenges for practice on various security topics such as cryptography, steganography, web or binary exploitation and reverse engineering among others. The game takes place in the digital world, while each team must protect and attack vulnerable systems and collect the flags which are alphanumeric strings. Each challenge has a description, related files or website links, featuring potential hints


Published by Springer Nature Switzerland AG 2020
L. Drevin et al. (Eds.): WISE 2020, IFIP AICT 579, pp. 61–77, 2020.
https://doi.org/10.1007/978-3-030-59291-2_5

and the amount of reward points which each participant or team collects after a successful flag submission [4]. Groups or individual participants are trying to collect as many reward points as possible within a certain time. The winner is the individual or the team with the most collected reward points.

CTF competitions could be categorized according to their purpose. The first category involves the use of CTF tools by educational institutions as an alternative way of teaching security concepts [5, 6]. This gives the participants the opportunity to acquire practical experience as well as to better understand context related to academic topics. The second category involves the use of CTF tools by organizations and even governments for recruiting purposes [7]. Organizing CTF competitions is an ideal way for companies or organizations to find competent people and evaluate their skills. The third and final purpose for organizing a CTF is entertainment and self-directed learning [4]. CTFs have greatly evolved in the past decade, while modern CTF competitions use gamification elements [8–11] such as storytelling, rich graphics, prizes, even augmented reality that transform them into interesting and fun activities. Over the years this has led to the creation of entire online communities which could be considered as social networks that unite people that share the same passion [12].

Depending on the category a CTF belongs, some features could be more important than others. Our study aims to review the technical elements and key components of 4 open source CTF platforms focusing on their use for educational purposes [13–15]. Towards this direction, this article addresses the following research questions:

**RQ1:** Which are the features that CTF platforms have for presenting information regarding the included CTF challenges?
**RQ2:** How and which are the features that could enhance the learning curve?
**RQ3:** Are there any missing features which could be important for supporting the learning process?
**RQ4:** Which are the potential features of the CTF platforms which could enhance the gamification attribute?

RQ1 and RQ2 intend to evaluate the current options which the current CTF platforms support, in terms of the options which affect the challenge presentation and flag submission, while RQ3 and RQ4 focus on possible missing key components and possible extensions which could enhance the learning process. Towards this direction, we conducted an empirical study, using direct observation on 4 open source CTF platforms, from the perspective of the facilitator and organizer. Furthermore, qualitative research was conducted and more specifically an experimental study using one-on-one interviews in order to extract evidence on the impact of each individual key component from the participants' perspective.

### 1.1 Related Work

Noor et al. [16] conducted an evaluation of the most popular open source and online CTF platforms. By focusing on usability, their research does not delve into a holistic analysis of each platform leaving many important aspects unclear. Raman et al. [17] also evaluated various CTF contests along with their key differences, mostly from a technical point of view. Other important researches are that of Chung [18, 19], presenting the key elements of CTFd in comparison to other CTF platforms such as OpenCTF, picoCTF, TinyCTF, Mellivora, and the iCTF framework. Key differences for each platform are mentioned; however, the details are more generic and do not include specific evaluation criteria. Similarly, Kucek and Leitner [21] present a survey and a comparison of 8 open source CTF platforms. More specifically, they present technical details and features of the selected CTF platforms. Most of the above studies are focused on the organizers' perspective and mostly on the technical aspects, while our research is focused on the capability of using the CTF platforms for educational purposes.

### 1.2 Our Contribution

Our research focuses on an in-depth analysis for evaluating CTF platforms and extracting their key components as e-Learning tools in higher education, in order to provide a more complete perspective of the special characteristics, limitations and capabilities of each platform. Specifically, we evaluated 4 open source CTF platforms, using both a systematic comparative study and an experimental study based on one-on-one interviews on undergraduate computer science students. The students expressed interest after an open call for participation by providing their opinion and comments. Towards this direction we conducted open-ended questions in order to gather information from the participants' perspective about the features and key components of the selected CTF platforms which reflect to specific attributes.

The results of this research could be important for organizers or facilitators to select the most suitable CTF platform for learning or training purposes and to highlight potential features which could be important according to their needs.

## 2 Analysis and Evaluation of CTF Platforms

### 2.1 Methodology

CTF platforms vary in multiple aspects such as design, complexity, capabilities, graphics, and used technologies. The selected CTF platforms are open source and can be directly deployed without any cost for individual purposes. The 4 open source platforms we selected were FBCTF[1], CTFd[2], Mellivora[3] and Root the Box[4]. To this extend, it is important to mention CTF platforms that include both CTF challenges and management tools for maintaining events and for individual training, such as Hack the Box[5], CTF365[6] and Shelter Labs[7] among others. Some of the above platforms could be

[1] https://github.com/facebook/fbctf.

[2] https://github.com/CTFd/CTFd.

[3] https://github.com/Nakiami/mellivora.

[4] https://github.com/moloch–/RootTheBox/.

[5] https://www.hackthebox.eu.

[6] https://ctf365.com.

[7] https://shellterlabs.com.

used for hosting a CTF event; however, they require a premium account, including extra costs. Finally, CTF365 is a fully commercial product with a 30-day free trial. Most of the challenges presented in such platforms are usually restricted to cybersecurity topics, without providing any other educational context and are appropriate mostly for experienced users. In contrary, open source CTF platforms can be used for deploying educational context and presenting custom challenges including specific topics which could be extended further from ethical hacking and penetration testing.

The criteria for the selected CTF platforms regarding the key components were selected by combining criteria from *Systems and software Quality Requirements and Evaluation (SQuaRE)* and *ISO/IEC 25010:2011* [20] as well as criteria related to the educational perspective, using a rubric for the evaluation of e-learning tools in higher education [21, 22]. The selected criteria reflect various attributes which are affected from the platforms' features. Evaluation rubrics related to the higher education have also been presented elsewhere [23]. Towards this direction, our research is not focused on the strictly technical attributes of the platforms and therefore we customized the evaluation attributes to rubric categories which represent not only the instructors' perspective, but the participants' perspective as well [23]. Most of the mentioned disadvantages of the CTF platforms include, among others, objective factors such as incomplete documentation, insufficient reporting and lack of migration tools. However, some of the factors directly affect the learning experience while some other factors are not that important on specific perspectives. For example, the use of gamification features in virtual learning environments has been shown to have positive effects [19] and the platforms include specific features which enhance this attribute.

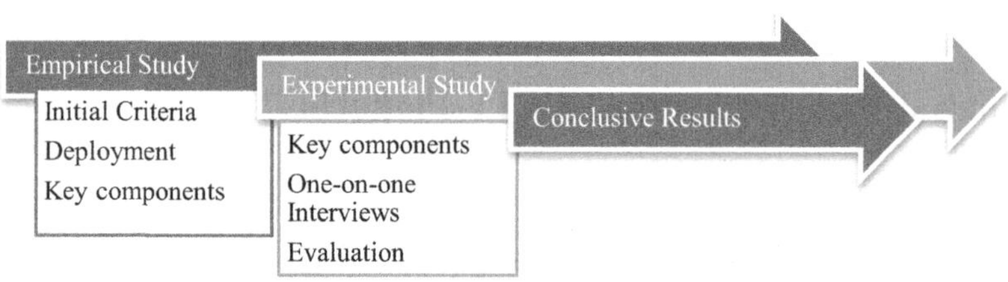


**Fig. 1.** Research methodology

For conducting this research, we deployed the selected CTF platforms and extracted the features each platform provides (Fig. 1). During the deployment we successfully added five main challenges which include 5 to 12 sub challenges each one. After extracting the criteria for evaluation, we conducted an experimental study using one-on-one interviews with undergraduate students of the 4$^{th}$ semester or higher of the Department of Informatics, Corfu, Greece. More specifically, an open request for participation was distributed to students of academic courses in information security for providing their perspective on each CTF platform; a total number of nine (9) participants were responded, and were asked to provide us feedback for each CTF platform. The interviews were conducted both physically and remotely using sound and screen recording, maintaining at about 1-h duration for each one. Informed consent was explicitly requested and documented from candidates prior to the interview and recording process commencing, while all recording and data collection has been done without retaining any personal information.

**FBCTF.** The Facebook CTF platform (FBCTF) was developed by Facebook security engineers, in order to provide an easy way for organizing CTF competitions. The platform stands out for its ease of installation, the capability to host King of The Hill type competitions, its rich graphics in the form of a world map that work as gamification elements and finally, the capability of multilingualism.

**CTFd.** CTFd was developed for the needs of Cyber Security Awareness Worldwide (CSAW[8]). The ease of installation, use and customization options combined with its rich features, make it a particularly attractive choice for the organizers. This platform focuses on extensibility, along with descriptive information related to the reporting tools and statistics.

**Mellivora.** Mellivora is a CTF platform developed in the PHP programming language and might not be as popular as the other platforms, however its simplicity makes it a particularly attractive choice for CTF contest organizers.

**Root the Box.** Root the Box focuses mostly on presenting the challenges as a "box", meaning that each challenge includes minor steps for being able to complete the main challenge. The reward system is more complex than the others and reward points are virtual credits which the participants could use in order to acquire extra features.

## 2.2 Criteria-Based Evaluation

The key components for each of the selected CTF hosting platforms were identified and matched with the criteria for evaluating the platforms [22]. The results derive from the deployment and our experience as facilitators. Since some of the features and attributes could not be distinct as either strengths or weaknesses, these have both been included as comments for each platform. The criteria and the comparison might include subjectiveness and for that reason we conducted the evaluation experiment from one-on-one interviews in order to clarify our initial assumptions (Sect. 2.3).

**Evaluation Criterion 01 – Functionality.** This criterion is related to the extent to which the tool's operations and processes facilitate or make easier to use the platform as a learning environment. Such attributes include visualization, ease of use, sufficient documentation and hypermediability. The strengths and weaknesses of each platform are presented on Table 1. For instance, the attribute of visualization includes all the related elements which present visualized information such as scoreboards, scenarios, a map and challenge categories among others. Ease of use (EoU) is evaluated for both administrators and participants. Regarding EoU, Root the Box includes a lot of complex elements which in some cases might be difficult to use and to get familiar with. Table 1 highlights a distinct advantage of FBCTF, mainly because of its rich graphics and engaging environment. FBCTF maintains sufficient documentation while CTFd

[8] https://csaw.engineering.nyu.edu.

was the easiest to deploy by following the documentation. For Mellivora we had to look further into setting up the localhost and some steps were not described extensively. Root the Box was easy to deploy as well using the documentation. CTFd provides extensive documentation for developing extra plugins and themes providing extensive information related to the platforms' capabilities.

**Table 1.** Evaluation of functionality

| Functionality | FBCTF | CTFd | Mellivora | Root the Box |
|---|---|---|---|---|
| EoU - admin | ++++ | +++++ | ++++ | +++++ |
| | A bit complex | Clean and minimal | Clean and minimal | Rich and functional |
| EoU-participants | +++ | +++++ | ++++ | +++++ |
| | Rich graphics | Clean and functional | Minimal | Rich and functional |
| Documentation | ++++ | +++++ | +++ | +++ |
| | Gitpage (Extensive documentation) | Read the docs | Gitpage (More information could be included) | Gitpage (Moderate content) |
| Hypermediality | +++ | ++++ | +++ | ++ |
| | Size limit (2 MB by default) | No size limit | Size limit (2 MB by default) | Embedded media, not supporting uploading of files |
| Multi-rank | No | No | Yes | No |
| Visualization | +++++ | +++ | ++ | ++++ |
| | Map and scoreboard | Scoreboard, challenge categories, themes | Challenge categories | Challenge categories, themes |

The attributes which reflect to the visualization, usually have direct impact in terms of usability. Hypermediability includes the ability to upload hypermedia such as images, videos and other documents inside the platform. All platforms except Root the Box included the support for uploading files.

**Evaluation Criterion 02 – Extensibility.** This criterion includes attributes such as Ease of Use which is affected from features such as support for extra plugins and themes among others (Table 2). Plugins and themes already exist for CTFd and Root the Box includes some end-user themes as well.

**Table 2.** Evaluation of extensibility

| Extensibility | FBCTF | CTFd | Mellivora | Root the Box |
|---|---|---|---|---|
| Extensions | ++ | ++++ | +++ | +++++ |
| | No themes and plugins | Plugins and central themes. Python | No plugins and themes. PHP | Front-end themes |
| Customization | +++ | ++++ | +++ | +++++ |
| | Relatively complex | Clean and minimal | Poor graphics, minimal | Rich and functional |
| Multilingual | ++++ | +++ | ++ | +++++ |

CTFd includes specific advantages related to customization options and for providing an easy way for customizing the theme through a CSS editor. Custom plugins exist for CTFd such as a world map and a plugin for maintaining multiple-choice questions. Most of the CTF platforms are customizable and open source, however CTFd maintains an easier way for maintaining any changes and customizations and already has published themes and plugins[9], while Root the Box maintains specific themes and seems extendable by maintaining a lot of extra features; for example, it maintains the option for having bonus challenges which the participants could unlock using virtual credits giving them the opportunity to unlock bonus content and extra features.

**Evaluation Criterion 03 – Teaching Presence.** This criterion is very important for our approach, which is the usage of CTF platforms in the classroom and includes the features which could be used in order to enhance the learning environment and process. More particularly this criteria category includes options which could enhance the learning processes and facilitators better presenting their challenges. For example, CTFd includes the option for creating and maintaining extra webpages inside the platform, featuring HTML and rich context (Table 3). Maintaining specific prerequisites for unlocking challenges could be important for students to engage more to the learning process and for facilitators to gradually present educational context.

**Table 3.** Evaluation of teaching presence

| Teaching presence | FBCTF | CTFd | Mellivora | Root the Box |
|---|---|---|---|---|
| Facilitation | +++ | +++++ | +++ | ++++ |
| | Interactive announcements' box | Popup messages. Announcements page | No popup messages. Announcements on homepage | Popup message and announcements on homepage |

(*continued*)

[9] https://github.com/CTFd/plugins.

**Table 3.** (*continued*)

| Teaching presence | FBCTF | CTFd | Mellivora | Root the Box |
|---|---|---|---|---|
| Personalization | +++ | ++++ | +++ | ++++ |
| | Minor user personalization | Extra pages and main themes | BBCode and extra pages | No main theme, focused on the client's view |
| Statistics | +++ | +++++ | ++ | ++++ |
| | Logs, scoreboard | Logs, pie charts, scoreboard | Scoreboard | Logs, pie charts, scoreboard |
| Readability | ++ | +++++ | +++ | ++++ |
| | Not clear for large text | Clean and readable | Clean, readable but poor visual elements | Rich but complex for beginners |
| Filters | ++++ | +++ | ++ | ++++ |
| | Team names and usernames | Team names, awards, fails, missing flags | Usernames, team names and emails | Usernames, team names, emails |
| Rewards | +++ | ++++ | ++ | +++++ |
| | Team scoreboard | Team scoreboard, badges/awards | Team scoreboard, without timeline | Team scoreboard, MVP scoreboard for each participant, bonus features |
| Hidden or Locked Challenges | ++ | +++++ | ++++ | +++++ |
| | No sub-challenges, no prerequisites | Sub-challenges, prerequisites, hidden challenges | Sub-challenges, prerequisites | Sub-challenges, prerequisites |

Regarding facilitation and more specifically the options for interactive communication with the participants, FBCTF provides an announcement window which might be possible to miss, while CTFd provides notifications by using alerts such as sound indications, popup windows and a subpage for announcements. Mellivora provides the notifications on the homepage without any alerts. Root the Box provides 4-s pop-up notifications for each announcement and kept on the homepage. Other attributes which affect the teaching presence and the learning process include statistics, readability, filters, the option for hide or lock specific challenges and the rewarding system which is related to the gamification elements.

**Evaluation Criterion 04 – Flag and Challenge Management/Submission.** This criterion concerns the way the selected platforms are maintaining and handling the flags (Table 4). CTFd for example not only maintains the ability to open a challenge when meeting a set of prerequisites, but a published plugin extends this option further.

**Table 4.** Evaluation of challenge management

| Challenge management | FBCTF | CTFd | Mellivora | Root the Box |
|---|---|---|---|---|
| Flag management | +++ | ++++ | ++ | +++++ |
| | Penalty, regex, case insensitive, hints | Penalty, regex, case insensitive, hints, multiple flags | Penalty, hints | Penalty, regex, case insensitive, hints, flag validation |
| Flag awards | ++++ | ++++ | +++ | +++++ |
| | Scoreboard per team, rich visuals | Scoreboard per team, personal awards - badges, category impact | Scoreboard per team, minimal visuals | Scoreboard per team, credits, MVP per player, bonus media or features |
| Categories | Yes, a bit unclear | Yes, clear categorization | Yes | Yes, category as boxes |

Regarding Root the Box, the option to evaluate the flag submission as an administrator is important. MVP (Most Valuable Player) on the scoreboard was also considered as a benefit for increasing competitiveness for Root the Box.

**Evaluation Criterion 05 – Social Presence.** This specific criterion relates to features such as integration of the scoreboard with online communities, features for identifying and authenticate the participants (Table 5). Moreover, it is related to the popularity of each platform and the ability to be socially identified.

**Table 5.** Evaluation of social presence

| Social presence | FBCTF | CTFd | Mellivora | Root the Box |
|---|---|---|---|---|
| Social interaction | +++ | +++ | +++ | ++++ |
| | | | | Team pastebin |
| Integration | ++ | +++++ | ++++ | +++ |
| | LDAP authentication, registration with Google or Facebook | MajorLeagueCyber (MLC) and JSON export MLC | JSON export for CTFtime | JSON export for CTFtime |
| Identifiability | ++++ | ++++ | ++++ | +++++ |
| | | | | Tools for prohibiting DoS |

**Evaluation Criterion 06 – Sustainability.** Sustainability includes features such as licensing and the system requirements for maintaining the platform as well as their total social presence (Table 6).

**Table 6.** Evaluation of Sustainability

| Sustainability | FBCTF | CTFd | Mellivora | Root the Box |
|---|---|---|---|---|
| Presence | ++++ | +++++ | +++ | ++ |
| | No logo but well known for the immersive user interface, popular because of the name | Own domain name, logo, used very frequently | No domain name, logo, used frequently on events | Own domain name, logo |
| Scaling | ++++ | ++++ | ++++ | +++ |
| | Distribution of services | Scaling and caching | Scales well on Amazon elastic | |
| Low resources | ++ | ++++ | +++++ | +++ |
| | High resources - scaling | Low resources | Low resources | Low to medium resources |
| Licensing | (CC BY-NC 4.0) | Apache 2.0 | GNU Gen. Public 3.0 | Apache 2.0 |

FBCTF requires quite a lot of system resources, while CTFd, Root the Box and Mellivora are lighter environments. Especially, Mellivora is appropriate for low resource systems or for conducting large scale competitions that would increase the demand for resources. FBCTF, CTFd and Mellivora are frequently used on events (especially CTFd and Mellivora), while Root the Box is not very popular, maintaining low presence.

**Evaluation Criterion 07 – Portability.** This specific criteria category relates to features which consider compatibility with various screen resolutions, responsiveness and options for offline access (Table 7). CTFd is ultra-compatible and out-of-the-box responsive, maintaining all the functionality.

**Table 7.** Evaluation of Portability

| Portability | FBCTF | CTFd | Mellivora | Root the Box |
|---|---|---|---|---|
| Responsiveness | ++ | +++++ | ++++ | +++ |
| | Partially compatible | Full responsive | Partially compatible | Partially compatible |
| Browser compatibility | +++ | ++++ | +++ | ++++ |
| | Minor issues except Firefox | Well supported | Well supported | Well supported |
| Installability | +++ | +++++ | ++ | ++++ |
| | Small issues with docker, slow installation | Easy and fast deployment | Small issues with localhost from network | Easy and fast deployment |
| Offline access | ++++ | +++++ | +++ | +++++ |
| | Restore and easy deployment, sections restore | Restore and easy deployment | Issues with Localhost, No restore tools except MySQL import | Restore and easy deployment |
| Backup tools | +++++ | ++++ | ++ | ++++ |
| | Full export and export of specific sections | Full export | No out-of-the-box tools | Full export |

## 2.3 Results from One-on-One Interviews

The selected CTF platforms were presented to the participants which, during the presentation, were asked questions regarding their opinion on each of them.

**Table 8.** Attributes and features presented to the participants

| Attribute | Explanation |
|---|---|
| Visuals - immersion | Visuals and graphics that offers immersion to the participants |
| Sense of control | The ability for the participant to understand which challenge is next and to monitor the total progress |
| Readability | The ability of the platform to present clear, understandable and complete information regarding the challenges to the participants |
| Reward system | The options which the platforms providing for rewarding the participants |
| Structure | Taxonomies, filters and every feature which ensures a good structure of the various CTF challenges. It is important if the number of challenges is large |
| Socializing | Features which establish good connection from the facilitator and of the team members |

*(continued)*

**Table 8.** (*continued*)

| Attribute | Explanation |
|---|---|
| Scoreboards | The amount of information that the scoreboards provide. Visuals might affect this attribute |
| Storytelling elements | This attribute relates to how the platform itself could enhance the presentation of storytelling elements of the CTF challenges |
| Hypermedia support | The ability to maintain context such as images, video, documents and other files |
| Flag submission | The options which the platforms maintain for creating a flag. For example, regular expression might be present or multiple flags per challenge |
| Extensibility | The ability for the platform to be extensible and if there are already developed extensions such as themes or extra plugins |
| Educational acceptance | The ability of using the CTF platform as an educational tool |
| Event | Defines which of the CTF platforms and how it is better to use it for creating short-term or long-term events |
| Total acceptance | The total acceptance and feedback for the platforms |

The attributes which were affected from the features and were set for the evaluation are presented on Table 8. All selected attributes were mentioned as important from the participants (mean values higher than 3.6/5 and most of them higher than 4/5). In the first place, all the participants expressed highly acceptance for FBCTF, since the visuals and immersion of this platform are promising. However, some of the other platforms (CTFd and Root the Box) were distinguished later as more appropriate for educational purposes (Fig. 2). For each attribute the participants were asked to provide scores regarding the importance (Fig. 2) and to set score for each platform.

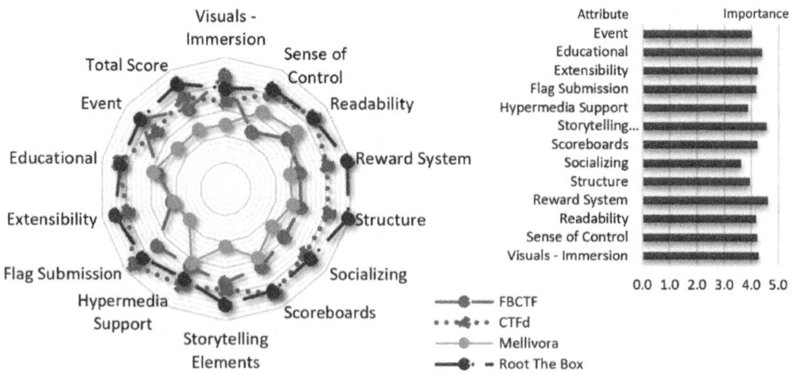


**Fig. 2.** Attributes and scores from participants

The results, presented in Fig. 2 and Fig. 3, refine and enhance our assumptions regarding each platform. The attributes in each of the figures include minor differences, however we can distinguish the similarities. Through this approach we were able to distinguish the psychological and personal characteristics, related to their opinion and to define which elements are important for each participant.

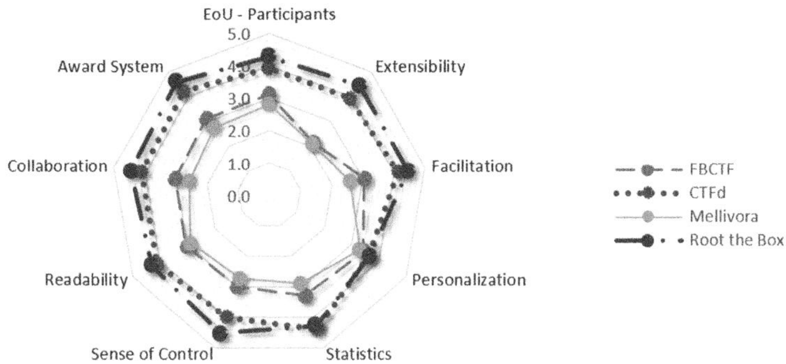


**Fig. 3.** Scores from our own perspective

CTFd was already designed having in mind the educational perspective. The ability to create dependencies on each challenge is important for the facilitators to present challenges in linear sequence or by condition. Root the Box maintains a very extensive reporting system, which is very important for the facilitators or educators. Moreover, the reward system of Root the Box enhances the gamification elements and promises highly engagement levels to competitive players. However, most of the participants identified that Root the Box is a bit complex and difficult for beginners to understand and use. The choice of Mellivora would seem to be the most appropriate if we are interested in simple design and especially in high performance with minimal hardware resources. More specifically, Mellivora is designed with a combination of methods and tools in order to be able to host very large competitions with minimum hardware required and to remain extremely stable and fast. FBCTF is recommended as a platform in competitions in which organizers are interested in introducing strong gamification elements in order to increase the students' engagement and active participation. Since CTFd offers better scoreboard and result graphs and especially team-based statistics it is a more attractive platform for the facilitators.

Based on the above, it is possible to confirm that both Root the Box and CTFd are the most suitable for educational purposes, while FBCTF is suitable for conducting CTF competitions as an event. Finally, Mellivora is suitable when the system resources are limited. The key components which the participants recognized as very important were the following:

**Visuals and Immersion.** Participants mentioned the importance of visuals and rich graphics on their first impression after seeing the platforms. User experience is also affected by such attributes and most participants mentioned that FBCTF was the most appealing, however a bit complex. Root the Box was mentioned also for having high complexity in terms of the visuals, while CTFd was described as an easy way to engage beginners, mentioning that customization options such as customized themes will be very important. Mellivora was underrated and criticized for not presenting rich graphic elements.

**Sense of Control.** This attribute was mentioned as important for being able to know the progress and understanding what to do next. To this extent, it is important to mention that usually participants are discouraged if they cannot make any significant progress. Finally, the ease of use and the user experience seem to be highly affected from this attribute.

**Hypermedia.** Participants mentioned the importance of maintaining hypermedia in order to enhance the storytelling elements and to engage more to an enhanced gamified version of the challenges.

**Capabilities to support Events.** For conducting the events, participants mentioned the importance of presenting the live scoreboard on a large screen during the event. They highlighted the importance for conducting events in order to engage newcomers. For maintaining events, FBCTF was approved as the most appropriate platform because of the highly immersive environment it provides.

**Scoreboards.** Participants recognized the importance of scoreboards, since scoreboards could increase the completeness and could provide useful information regarding the progress of each team. Furthermore, the participants mentioned the importance of maintaining a scoreboard as a self-evaluation process and for the facilitators to monitor each team or participant. Competitive players mentioned that information from the scoreboards will be used to determine the difficulty of a specific challenge. Therefore, the scoreboard from the participants' perspective was identified very important and an especially motivational element for competitive players.

**Reward System.** Rewards were identified as a benefit for increasing the motivation and competence from the participants. The option for the participants to unlock hidden challenges using their rewarding points was mentioned as an interesting feature. Towards this direction, many participants mentioned the possibility to add extra context or hidden challenges as bonus challenges in order to increase their engagement.

**Personalization.** Most of the participants mentioned that the personalization attributes are important for enhancing the storytelling elements. Therefore, the appropriate usage of themes, colors and context could improve the process of embedding storytelling elements related to the challenges.

**Flag Submission Options.** Participants mentioned that the flag submission should be easy. However, a specific participant mentioned that it is important for someone to stick on the details and to provide the correct flag appropriately. The support for multiple flags and embedding regular expression could be helpful as well as the validation tool for the flags which the Root the Box provides.

**Storytelling Elements.** Storytelling elements were unexpectedly mentioned as an important feature from the reviewers. Participants mentioned this as a very engaging attribute and a motivation to finish the challenges. However, some of the participants mentioned that this attribute is mostly related to games and it could be distracting for some people who are not interested on that perspective.

**Structure.** CTF challenges mostly suffer from the lack of not presenting structured challenges, meaning that each challenge is separate from the other, without distinct categorization or taxonomy. Most participants mentioned their preference for presenting a structured way of the challenges in order to enhance the learning process. Moreover, for educational purposes is best to separate a main challenge to smaller sub challenges for the participants to proceed gradually. Finally, the ability to maintain well-structured challenges is important if we have a large number of challenges.

**Educational Appropriateness.** Participants found that the usage of CTF platforms and challenges would be very interesting for educational purposes, especially for beginners and people who are not very familiar with IT topics. CTFd was mostly approved for making it easy for beginners to engage quickly and for presenting the challenges in a clear and readable way.

## 3 Conclusions and Future Work

This main purpose of this study was to compare four popular open source CTF platforms as possible learning platforms. For investigating all aspects of the CTF platforms, a comparative study was conducted highlighting the distinct features of each platform, and we were able to draw conclusions about the advantages and disadvantages of each platform. Given that each platform maintains different features and characteristics, it turns to be quite difficult for the organizers to choose the most appropriate platform, depending on the purpose and the audience. To this end, a number of one-on-one interviews refined our assumptions providing important information regarding the usage of CTF platforms for learning purposes. Extra features which could improve the platforms were discussed as well. In our case we tried to identify the most suitable platform for setting up a hands-on lab at the Ionian University, Corfu, Greece and to highlight CTF challenges as a complementary learning method. For learning purposes, CTFd scored the highest on the criteria of teaching presence.

Future work includes the creation of custom CTF challenges focusing on the learning perspective and on presenting extensive educational context. Towards this direction, specific features could be updated or extended in order to provide enhanced gamification elements, quizzes and evaluation processes. An important aspect would be to embed storytelling elements in order to discover and to evaluate the potential of using the CTF platforms and customized CTF challenges for learning purposes, not only in cybersecurity but also to related topics such as user privacy and privacy-aware data governance, towards capitalizing on the results of related projects such as DEFeND [24].

**Acknowledgements.** This project has received funding from the GSRT for the European Union's Horizon 2020 research and innovation programme DEFeND under grant agreement No 787068.

## References

1. Hendrix, M., Al-Sherbaz, A., Victoria, B.: Game based cyber security training: are serious games suitable for cyber security training? Int. J. Serious Games **3**(1), 53–61 (2016). https://doi.org/10.17083/ijsg.v3i1.107
2. Matias, P., Barbosa, P., Cardoso, T.N., Campos, D.M., Aranha, D.F.: NIZKCTF: a noninteractive zero-knowledge capture-the-flag platform. IEEE Secur. Priv. **16**(6), 42–51 (2018). https://doi.org/10.1109/MSEC.2018.2875324
3. Bowen, B.M., Devarajan, R., Stolfo, S.: Measuring the human factor of cyber security. In: 2011 IEEE International Conference on Technologies for Homeland Security (HST), pp. 230–235. IEEE, Boston (2011). https://doi.org/10.1109/THS.2011.6107876
4. Davis, A., Leek, T., Zhivich, M., Gwinnup, K., Leonard, W.: The fun and future of CTF. In: Proceedings of the 23rd USENIX Summit on Gaming, Games, and Gamification in Security Education 2014 (3GSE 14), San Diego. USENIX (2014)
5. McDaniel, L., Talvi, E., Hay, B.: Capture the flag as cyber security introduction. In: 2016 49th Hawaii International Conference on System Sciences 2016 (HICSS), Koloa, USA, pp. 5479–5486. IEEE (2016). https://doi.org/10.1109/HICSS.2016.677
6. Mansurov, A.: A CTF-based approach in information security education: an extracurricular activity in teaching students at Altai State University. Russia. Mod. Appl. Sci. **10**(11), 159–166 (2016). https://doi.org/10.5539/mas.v10n11p159
7. Cherinka, R., Prezzama, J.: Innovative approaches to building comprehensive talent pipelines: helping to grow a strong and diverse professional workforce. Syst. Cybern. Inform. **13**(6), 82–86 (2015)
8. Boopathi, K., Sreejith, S., Bithin, A.: Learning cyber security through gamification. Indian J. Sci. Technol. **8**(7), 642–649 (2015)
9. Burket, J., Chapman, P., Becker, T., Ganas, C., Brumley, D.: Automatic problem generation for capture-the-flag competitions. In: Proceedings of the 24th USENIX Summit on Gaming, Games, and Gamification in Security Education 2015 (3GSE 15), Washington. USENIX (2015)
10. Chapman, P., Burket, J., Brumley, D.: PicoCTF: a game-based computer security competition for high school students. In: Proceedings of the 23rd USENIX Summit on Gaming, Games, and Gamification in Security Education 2014 (3GSE 14), San Diego. USENIX (2014)
11. Schreuders, Z.C., Butterfield, E.: Gamification for teaching and learning computer security in higher education. In: Proceedings of USENIX Workshop on Advances in Security Education 2016 (ASE 16), Austin, USA (2016)
12. Conti, G., Babbitt, T., Nelson, J.: Hacking competitions and their untapped potential for security education. IEEE Secur. Priv. **9**(3), 56–59 (2011). https://doi.org/10.1109/MSP.2011.51
13. Eagle, C., Clark, J.L.: Capture-the-flag: learning computer security under fire. In: Proceedings of the 6th Workshop on Education in Computer Security 2004 (WECS), pp. 17–21. Naval Postgraduate School, Monterey, CA (2004)
14. Antonioli, D., Ghaeini, H.R., Adepu, S., Ochoa, M., Tippenhauer.: Gamifying education and research on ICS security: design, implementation and results of S3. In: Proceedings of the 3rd Workshop on Cyber-Physical Systems Security and PrivaCy 2017, Dallas, Texas, USA, pp. 93–102. ACM (2017)

15. Leune, K., Petrilli Jr., S.J.: Using capture-the-flag to enhance the effectiveness of cybersecurity education. In: Proceedings of the 18th Annual Conference on Information Technology Education 2017, Rochester, New York, USA, pp. 47–52. ACM (2017). https://doi.org/10.1145/3125659.3125686
16. Noor Azam, M.H., Beuran, R.: Usability evaluation of open source and online capture the flag platforms. Japan Advanced Institute of Science and Technology (JAIST), Technical report, IS-RR-2018-001 (2018)
17. Raman, R., Sunny, S., Pavithran, V., Achuthan, K.: Framework for evaluating Capture The Flag (CTF) security competitions. In: The Proceedings of the International Conference for Convergence for Technology 2014 (I2CT 2014), Pune, India, pp. 136–140. IEEE (2014). https://doi.org/10.1109/I2CT.2014.7092098
18. Chung, K., Cohen, J.: Learning obstacles in the capture the flag model. In: Proceedings of the 23rd USENIX Summit on Gaming, Games, and Gamification in Security Education (3GSE 2014), San Diego, CA. USENIX (2014)
19. Chung, K.: Live lesson: lowering the barriers to capture the flag administration and participation. In: Proceedings of USENIX Workshop on Advances in Security Education (ASE 2017), Vancouver, BC, Canada (2017)
20. Ahmad, R., Hussain, A., Baharom, F.: Software sustainability characteristic for software development towards long living software. WSEAS Trans. Bus. Econ. **15**, 55–72 (2018)
21. Kucek, S., Leitner, M.: An empirical survey of functions and configurations of open source capture the Flag (CTF) environments. J. Netw. Comput. Appl., 102470 (2019). https://doi.org/10.1016/j.jnca.2019.102470
22. Martínez-Torres, M.R., Toral Marín, S.L., Garcia, F.B., Vazquez, S.G., Oliva, M.A., Torres, T.: A technological acceptance of e-learning tools used in practical and laboratory teaching, according to the European higher education area. Behav. Inf. Technol. **27**(6), 495–505 (2008). https://doi.org/10.1080/01449290600958965
23. Khan, J.A., Rehman, I.U., Khan, Y.H., Khan, I.J., Rashid, S.: Comparison of requirement prioritization techniques to find best prioritization technique. Int. J. Mod. Educ. Comput. Sci. **7**(11), 53–59 (2015). https://doi.org/10.5815/ijmecs.2015.11.06
24. Piras, L., et al.: DEFeND architecture: a privacy by design platform for GDPR compliance. In: Gritzalis, S., Weippl, E.R., Katsikas, S.K., Anderst-Kotsis, G., Tjoa, A.M., Khalil, I. (eds.) TrustBus 2019. LNCS, vol. 11711, pp. 78–93. Springer, Cham (2019). https://doi.org/10.1007/978-3-030-27813-7_6

# Cybersecurity Knowledge Within the Organisation

# Designing Competency Models for Cybersecurity Professionals for the Banking Sector

Andrey Vybornov[1], Natalia Miloslavskaya[2](✉), and Alexander Tolstoy[2]

[1] Bank of Russia, 12 Neglinnaya Street, Moscow, Russia
vaol@mail.cbr.ru

[2] The National Research Nuclear University MEPhI (Moscow Engineering Physics Institute), 31 Kashirskoye shosse, Moscow, Russia
{NGMiloslavskaya,AITolstoj}@mephi.ru

**Abstract.** The research results for the main stages of designing competency models (CMs) for cybersecurity (CS) professionals are presented. A strategy for designing such models was formulated. The CS-related terminology and conceptual framework were clarified. Areas, objects, and types of professional activity (PA) as a whole for CS professionals and the banking sector, in particular, were determined. It is proposed to use the role and process models to determine the tasks that employees of banking organizations should solve. The practical issues of developing CMs, which allowed to determine the order of their development and the typical structure, as well as to formulate recommendations on the content of a specific CM, are considered.

**Keywords:** Design · Cybersecurity · Space · Environment · Competency · Model · Professional · Bank · Processes · Management · Knowledge · Skills · Role

## 1 Introduction

At present, we witness a growing need for professional staff in the rapidly developing field of Cybersecurity (CS). The modern approach to determining qualification requirements for such personnel is based on the formulation of professional competencies (PCs) as the ability to solve assigned tasks and perform certain work within the framework of professional activity (PA) [1, 2]. Moreover, it was recognized that it is correct to form a set of PCs in the form of competency models [3–5].

Currently, there are a large number of definitions of the "competency" term [1–6]. For completeness of the research topic discussion, we will focus on the following definition: competency is a certain personality characteristic, which is necessary to perform certain work and which allows its holder to obtain the necessary work results [6]. Competency traditionally refers to a combination of observable and measurable indicators: knowledge (K), Skills (S), and Abilities (A) (together denoted by KSA).


L. Drevin et al. (Eds.): WISE 2020, IFIP AICT 579, pp. 81–95, 2020.
https://doi.org/10.1007/978-3-030-59291-2_6

A model is a logical description of components and functions, which display the essential properties of a simulated object. Competency models (CMs) are structured sets of necessary, identifiable, and measurable competencies [6]. Existing approaches to the development of competency-based models take into account the PA scope (fields and types), as well as the focus of the application of such models.

For CS, the most interesting is the CM presented in the report of Apollo Education Group, Inc and the University of Phoenix [5, 7] and based on tools developed by the Department of Labor (US). The CM is presented in the form of organizational structure [8, 9], divided into nine levels forming three clusters.

Cluster 1: Fundamental competencies unite three levels (groups) of competencies. Levels 1 to 3 at the bottom represent a group of basic competencies, which are required from almost any person as a workforce. Together they reflect skills, which are common to all PA fields and types. At level 1, there are competencies of personal effectiveness/qualities, such as integrity, reliability, and adaptability, which are formed at an early age in the family, at school or through connections with religious or other community-based values. Level 2 consists of academic competencies, which are usually formed through formal education (primary, secondary, higher). Level 3 includes competencies in the workplace, such as teamwork, planning, and organization, which are necessary to perform certain job functions.

Cluster 2: Industry competencies unite two levels of competencies. Levels 4 and 5 include general PCs related to a specific PA field without reference to a certain profession or roles. Level 4 contains the general PCs relate to the formation of concepts related to the entire PA field. Level 5 includes general PCs that are associated with the formation of concepts relating to specific sectors of the PA field.

Cluster 3: PCs unite three levels of competencies. PCs are located at levels 6 through 8. They relate to special PCs and reflect a specific PA type with a focus on a particular profession and the performance of specific professional roles. To do this, it is necessary to form special PCs related to special knowledge for a specific PA type (level 6), special skills and abilities to perform certain roles (level 7), requirements for performing specific roles (level 8) and management processes when performing them.

The organizational structure of the CM presented above is universal. Its effectiveness can only be tested when developing specific CMs.

Thus, the main goal of the paper is to design CMs for CS PA and the types of professional activities that are associated with professions being in demand in banking institutions when implementing specific roles to ensure CS. This goal can be achieved by solving the following tasks: developing a CM design strategy, clarifying the CS term, defining on this basis the PA fields, objects, types, and tasks for banking organizations, determining the CM types applicable in this case, defining the requirements for the CM structure and content, and considering practical issues of developing a CM for professionals in CS for banking organizations. Key findings conclude the paper.

## 2 Competency Model Design Strategy

When developing CMs, it is necessary to solve the strategic tasks presented on Fig. 1.

*Task 1: Setting the goal of developing a specific CM.* It is primarily determined by the practical significance of the developed model's usage in a specific field of activity. Currently, the following areas of CM use can be distinguished.

1. The area of an educational activity (academic education). The purpose of developing CMs is to create a regulatory framework for improving the quality and effectiveness of training professionals in various PA fields with a variety of PA types, objects, and tasks, for which graduates of educational institutions should be trained. In the CM, the universal (personal, general educational), general and special PCs, which should be formed after graduation, should be defined. At the same time, general and special PCs should be consistent with the requirements of the labor market (organizations-employers). The process of training professionals has certain "inertia". Therefore, CMs developers should predict the needs of the labor market for several years to come. For example, this period in the bachelors' training is 3–4 years, and in the masters' training is 2–3 years. It should also be noted the nature of the professional training at the academic education level, which does not allow the formation of a wide range of practical skills that affect the content of CMs.

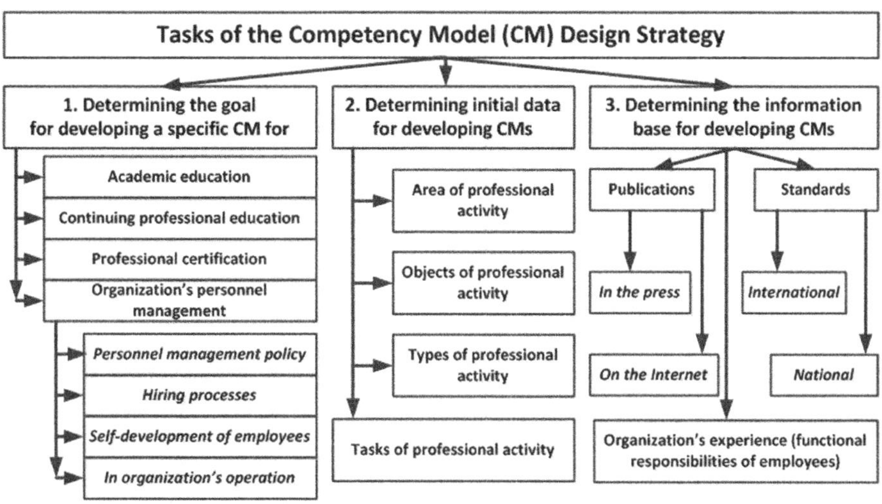


**Fig. 1.** The structure of the tasks of the competency model design strategy

2. The area of continuing professional education. The purpose of developing CMs is to create a regulatory framework for improving the quality and effectiveness of the implementation of professional refresher courses and retraining programs in a specific field and for specific PA objects, types, and tasks. Continuing education is aimed at developing a certain special PC (to acquire additional practical skills and

the corresponding knowledge). Retraining is aimed at the formation of a new special PC (to acquire new skills and the corresponding knowledge). CMs should include general professional (for retraining programs) and special professional (for professional refresher courses and retraining programs) competencies, which should be formed among students who have been trained in these programs. Moreover, CMs should be coordinated with specific organizations that are either employers or centers for independent certification of specialists in a specific PA field.

3. The area of activity of a particular organization for work with its personnel. The CMs developing purpose is to create a regulatory framework for improving the quality and effectiveness of personnel management. In this case, the CM can be developed and applied for the following organization's personnel management processes:

   - Development and implementation of an organization's personnel management policy. At the same time, this policy can be developed as a separate document or part of a document related to the policy of managing a specific process (for example, a CS ensuring policy). The use of CMs simplifies greatly the work to strengthen the organizational culture, helps to create clear guidelines that indicate what is expected from its employees, and gives it the added benefit of improving professional development programs. In this case, when developing CMs for a specific PA field (determined by the specifics of a particular organization), it is advisable to determine the PA object, type, and tasks in the framework of the description of the roles that an employee should fulfill and which should be related to the relevant competencies. The role-based approach should be fixed in the personnel management policy, which should imply the order of their development and connection with CMs, as well as the principles of the role formation and distribution (assignment). An important feature of the organization's personnel management is the establishment of a procedure for the development and use of competency and role models in the case of the organization growth that is associated with changes in its business, as well as the PA field, objects, types or tasks;
   - Personnel management during their hiring (hiring processes). CMs provide clear criteria for selecting candidates based on requirements for knowledge and skills levels, as well as existing work experience. These requirements should be included in the CMs that distinguishes them from the CMs developed, for example, in educational institutions;
   - Personnel management during the organization's operation. Together with role models, CMs can be used during periodic certification of employees to determine whether their competencies correspond to the roles performed, as well as to identify the opportunities for specific employees in their career growth. It is also important to draw up and implement plans for raising awareness, modernizing the existing PCs of employees, or creating new PCs for them. The latter is important in the context of the development of the organization noted above;

- Improving the professional level of the organization's employees on an individual basis. Based on the provisions of CMs, the employees can independently form a required level of knowledge and skills. This may be due to the desire to maintain constantly the roles assigned to them in the best way or with plans to apply for the roles related to a higher position.

4. The areas of professional certification. The goal is to increase the effectiveness of independent certification centers that implement certification programs for professionals in a particular field and related specific PA objects, types, and tasks. The implementation of certification programs is aimed at determining the level of knowledge and skills of specific specialists. This work can be carried out within the framework of an order of specific organizations of employers, companies-developers of specific devices and systems, or with the individual application of specific professionals who want to receive a certificate confirming a certain level of their PCs. The effectiveness of certification centers is determined by many factors; a particular factor is a focus on modern CMs developed in educational institutions and organizations-employers.

The features of the first problem solution discussed above allow us to conclude that there are a large number of CM types that differ not only in the goals of their development but also in the source data necessary for the development of a specific CM.

*Task 2: Defining initial data.* It includes the description of a specific field, as well as specific PA objects, types, and tasks. In some cases (e.g., personnel management), it is possible to describe the source data in the form of role models. Further, the solution of this problem for the selected field will be considered.

*Task 3: Defining the information base necessary to determine the source data and formulate the relevant competencies.* This information base can include publications, including on the Internet, reflecting the experience of developing CMs (among them are publications containing general recommendations on the development of CMs [4, 8–12], recommendations on CMs in the information security (IS) field [1–3, 6], information on PCs in the field of CS [5, 7, 13–16]), standards, including those containing recommendations on competencies in the IS field at the international [17] or national [18, 19] levels, and the experience of organizations in their personnel management (documented functional responsibilities and job descriptions of employees).

Special attention should be paid to the experience of Russia in developing a competency-based approach for formulating requirements for the professional qualifications. Professional standards for various PA fields were developed and implemented. Among them, there is a group of six IS professional standards. They formulate general and special labor functions that specific professionals can implement and requirements for the levels of knowledge and skills, corresponding to these labor functions and related to the levels of basic education and experience acquired in a practical field [18]. These professional standards are used by organizations to create and implement their personnel management systems. A group of seven Federal Educational Standards (FESs), related to the training of bachelor, masters, and specialists (engineers), is linked directly to these IS professional standards. They formulate general and general PCs and normalized the development of special PCs.

## 3 Cybersecurity and PA Fields

The ISO/IEC 27032:2012 with the guidelines for CS defines the CS as a "preservation of confidentiality, integrity and availability of information in the Cyberspace. Besides, other properties, such as authenticity, accountability, non-repudiation, and reliability can also be involved" [20]. It is a security in the Cyberspace. In turn, the Cyberspace refers to a "complex environment resulting from the interaction of people, software and services on the Internet by means of technology devices and networks connected to it, which does not exist in any physical form". This standard is in the conceptual field, which constitutes the methodological basis of the provisions of the standards of the ISO/IEC 27000 series related to IS. This area is associated with concepts such as asset, threat, vulnerability, and risk [21], which is related directly to the field of CS.

An analysis of these definitions shows the following. The CS definition complies fully with the IS definition. The difference lies in clarifying the CS scope (the Cyberspace). From the CS definition, it follows that the concept of an interaction environment is associated with it. It should be noted that the "space" and "environment" terms are not synonymous. Therefore, clarification of the definitions of these terms is required. ISO/IEC 27032 connects directly the environment of interaction to the Internet, which does not contradict the IS field.

The features highlighted above show that there is no clear distinction between CS and IS concepts at present. It can be assumed that the CS term refers to a narrower conceptual field than the IS term. In our opinion, all the problems of providing security services can be solved within the framework of security management. Despite this conclusion, the fact that the CS term has found very wide use today can be stated [22, 23]. In this case, it seems very important to make the following clarifications. Firstly, the CS term alone (as well as the IS term) does not have a clear definition. If we connect CS with the CS space and environment, then it is necessary to consider the conceptual area in the context of specific objects (so called CS objects). Secondly, when formulating the definition of the CS object term, it is necessary to take into account the modern approach to providing IS, the methodology of which is presented in the ISO/IEC 27000 standard series. In this case, the following definitions are proposed.

*The CS space* is a collection of CS objects that takes into account their relative position and has its structure (Fig. 2). As a rule, the CS space is a virtual space in which the position of a CS object is specified by a logical address. In some cases, it may be appropriate to determine the position of the CS object in real space. In the general case, CS objects can be represented in the structure of CS space, having their addresses, which are needed to determine the relative position of the CS objects. In Fig. 2, CS objects are combined into groups (parties) representing individual organizations.

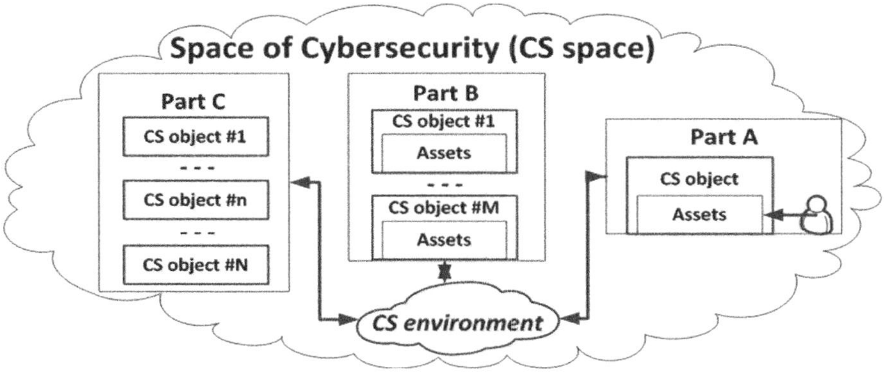


**Fig. 2.** The structure of the CS space and environment

*The CS environment* is a virtual environment implemented based on the Internet technology, ensuring the interaction of CS objects and having its structure. This structure corresponds to the situation that is associated with the provision of CS during the interaction of CS objects. In this case, it is important to identify stakeholders [20], which are organizations or persons with their CS objects that interact with each other using the Internet technology. A typical case is the presence of the following parties of the interaction presented on Fig. 2. Party A (provider) is an organization (person) that provides its services based on the operation of a specific CS object. Party B (consumers) is organizations (persons) that consume these services (there may be several), using their CS objects. In the general case, the number of such organizations (persons) or CS objects will be from 1 to M. Party C (external intruders) is organizations (persons) that by organizing the interaction of their CS objects with the CS objects of the provider or consumer will realize threats aimed at the assets of the CS objects of Parties A and B. In general, the number of such organizations (persons) or CB objects related to Party C will be from 1 to N. The interest of the parties to interact will be different: Parties A and B have a common interest in preserving their assets, and the purpose of Party C is to harm Party A and/or Party B.

It should be noted that there is a possibility when a threat may come from the organization's employee - the provider, who has authorized access to the assets of the CS object and uses its capabilities to harm the organization. This corresponds to the source of threats inside the organization - the provider or the internal intruder.

*The CS object* is a real object implemented using IT and the Internet technology.

*The CS framework* is a combination of the CS space and environment.

*An object's CS* refers to a property inherent in the object to maintain the state of object's asset protection when there are threats in the CS framework, which corresponds to the value of damage (or risk) associated with the possible implementation of these threats, not exceeding a predetermined level. At the same time, the state of asset protection is determined by their properties: confidentiality, integrity, availability, authenticity, non-repudiation, etc.

*Ensuring the object's CS* refers to an activity of forming the necessary properties of an object in the CS framework.

Thus, it is possible to formulate a definition of *the PA field* (in the broad sense) as a field of science, engineering, and technology, covering a set of problems associated with ensuring CS of objects. This definition is of a general conceptual nature and has no practical significance.

The terminology analysis of the object's CS concept and the structural features of the CS space and environment allows us to draw the following conclusion about the absence of a single PA field related to CS. This means that professionals are needed in various fields for solving problems in CS, taking into account the specifics of a particular field and the CS framework.

For further applicability, including the development of CMs, it is appropriate to identify at least three PA fields (they reflect the narrow sense of this concept):

- Areas of science, engineering, and technology covering problems associated with:
  - IT implemented taking into account the requirements for ensuring CS. This area includes IT professionals with competencies in CS;
  - The processes of ensuring CS in key systems of information infrastructure of organizations. Professionals in CS with competencies in IT belong to this area;
- Separate areas of engineering and technology, in which it is necessary to implement separate processes for ensuring CS when using IT while solving basic professional problems. This area includes professionals in a specific field of activity with additional competencies in IT and CS.

## 4 CS Objects and PA Types in Banking Sector

To describe the CS objects, it is necessary to determine the basic technological processes (TPs) implemented in banks. There are two groups of them: main and auxiliary. The first group includes banking TPs that carry out operations to change and/or determine the state of the organization's banking assets used in the operation or necessary for the implementation of banking services [24]. Operations on the assets of a banking organization can be performed manually or be automated (for example, using IT). Depending on the type of activity, there are banking payment and information TPs. *Banking payment TPs* (BPTPs) are a part of banking TPs that implement banking operations on information related to the transfer of funds from one account to another and/or control of these operations. In this case, the information contained in the documents refers to the payment information, based of which operations related to the transfer of funds from one account to another, are performed [24]. *Banking information TPs* (BITPs) are banking TPs that carry out operations to change and/or determine the state of information necessary for the functioning of a banking organization and which is not payment information. Non-payment information may include, for example, data from statistical reporting and on-farm activities, analytical, financial, and background information [24].

Automation of banking TPs is carried out, as a rule, with the help of automated banking systems (ABS), which are complexes consisting of personnel and automation tools that implement information and telecommunication technologies for performing the established functions of TPs. There are two groups of ABS: automated banking payment (ABS1) and bank non-payment (ABS2) TPs. The difference lies not only in the processing of different types of information (payment and non-payment), but also in the fact that they have different structures. The ABS1 may have in its structure executing devices (ATMs, payment acceptance devices) and remote access devices for clients when receiving banking services (smartphones, laptops, personal computers). The ABS2, as a rule, does not have logical (in some cases physical) connections with the ABS1, it does not have executing devices in its structure and can use remote access technologies only for employees of a banking organization.

In the banking structure, there may be several ABS1 and ABS2. The second group includes TPs that implement auxiliary functions. Taking into account the specifics of the area under consideration, these TPs include CS ensuring processes integrated into specific systems. The CE Ensuring System (CSES) consists of two systems: Information Protection System (IPS) and CS Management System (CSMS) (Fig. 3).

The IPS combines the following processes [25]: P1. Securing information during access control: 1.1. Management of accounts and rights of entities of logical access; 1.2. Identification, authentication, authorization (access control) in the implementation of logical access; 1.3. Protection of information during physical access; 1.4. Identification, classification and accounting of resources and access objects. P2. Securing computer networks: 2.1. Segmentation and firewalling of computer networks; 2.2. Identification of network intrusions and attacks; 2.3. Protection of information transmitted over computer networks; 2.4. Wireless Security. P3. Monitoring the integrity and security of the information infrastructure. P4. Protection against malicious code. P5. Prevention of information leaks. P6. IS incident management: 6.1. Monitoring and analysis of IS events; 6.2. Detection of IS incidents and response to them. P7. Protecting the virtualization environment. P8. Prevention of information during remote logical access using mobile (portable) devices.

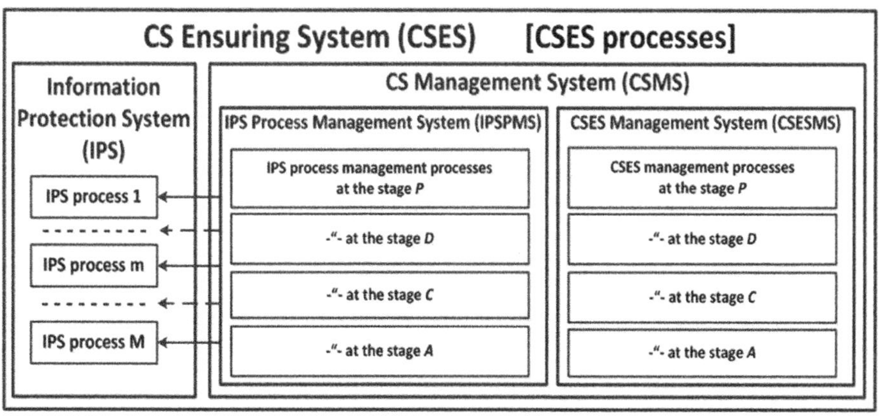


**Fig. 3.** The structure of the CSES

The CS Management System (CSMS) consists of two systems (Fig. 3): the IPS Process Management System (IPSPMS) at the design (P), implementation (D), control (C) and improvement (A) stages of the specific IPS process and the management system for the entire CSES (CSESMS) at the stages P, D, C and A according to the cyclic Plan (Plan) - Implementation (Do) - Check (Check) - Action (Act) model [21].

The management processes of the CSES include: *At the stage P*: identification of assets to be protected, description of CS threats, assessment of CS risks and selection of information protection processes and measures, development of a CS ensuring policy and development of internal organization documents related to ensuring CS; *At the stage D*: implementation of a CSES; *At the stage C*: carrying out various types of management of the CSES (processing the data of monitoring the IPS processes, conducting an internal and external audit of the CSES, conducting a self-assessment), *At the stage A*: development and implementation of measures to improve the CSES processes, including the IPS processes and the CSES management processes.

When creating a CSES, it is important to identify assets to be protected. For a banking organization, such assets will be objects that have value and are located in its location. Moreover, it is important to describe (identify) those assets that are used or consumed in the implementation of banking TPs. In this case, they are considered in the form of resources related to a particular banking TP. A banking organization has the following assets (resources) related to the scope of ensuring CS [25]: Information assets, which include payment and non-payment (financial, analytical, official, managing, personal data, etc.) information divided into two groups (public information and with a limited access) with different IS requirements; Assets related to the information asset processing environment (ABS automation systems (tangible objects): objects of storage, transmission, processing, destruction, etc.); Financial (monetary) funds of the bank; Employees (personnel) of the bank; Banking TPs (payment and information); Banking products and services provided to customers; Intangible assets (reputation, image of the bank).

The above analysis of the processes in banking structures allows us to determine:

- CS objects: ABSs that implement various banking TPs;
- The PA objects of bank employees: CS objects (ABSs), CSES processes and measures that implement these processes, assets (resources);
- PA types: operational (implementation of the IPS processes), organizational and managerial (implementation of the CSESMS management processes), design (participation in the ABS and CSES design).

It should be noted that the distinguished PA objects have features characteristic of CS: the space of their existence can be physical and virtual, and the interaction environment is predominantly virtual.

## 5 Cybersecurity PA Tasks in Banking Sector

To determine PA tasks in banking organizations, an employee role-based approach can be used [24, 26]. This approach is based on the concept of the role as a predetermined set of rules that establish an acceptable interaction between a subject and an object [24]. Subjects include persons from among the employees of a banking organization and its customers or processes initiated by them on the implementation of actions on objects. Objects can be hardware, software, information resource, service, process, system, on which actions are performed. In this case, the role model fully complies with the consideration of the CS environment as an environment for the interaction of CS objects that can be associated with PA objects and, as a result, determine the PA tasks.

The structure of the role model of an employee of a banking organization in the field of CS can be determined by analogy with a similar structure for the field of IS [26]. For this, it is necessary to consider the specifics of an employee of a banking organization (subject) performing his duties reflected in job descriptions, which are directly related to the definition of his functions (or PA tasks), rules and restrictions when interacting with various CS objects (PA objects). From this one can form an expanded role concept as a set of functions of an employee of a banking organization, the fulfillment of which requires payback (by function - a type of work performed or planned to be performed by the employee) a set of authority. This definition allows us to propose a model for the role description, the structure of which is shown in Fig. 4. Each role can correspond to one or more functions related to ensuring CS. To perform a certain function, the CS authority is required, each of which establishes a set of rules and restrictions aimed at the CS PA objects (CS objects, assets, CSES processes).

Analysis of the role model structure allows us to conclude that there is a wide variety of roles related to the CS functions (PA tasks). Hence, it useful to classify the roles. The separation of roles into groups (categories) is possible taking into account the characteristics of assets, CS objects, and CSES structure (Fig. 5).

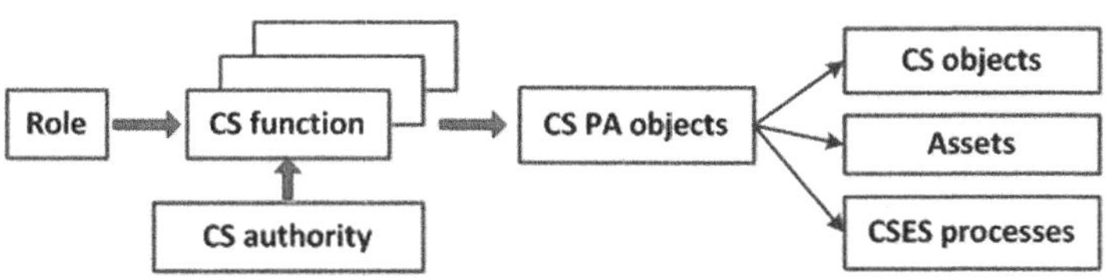


**Fig. 4.** The structure of the role model

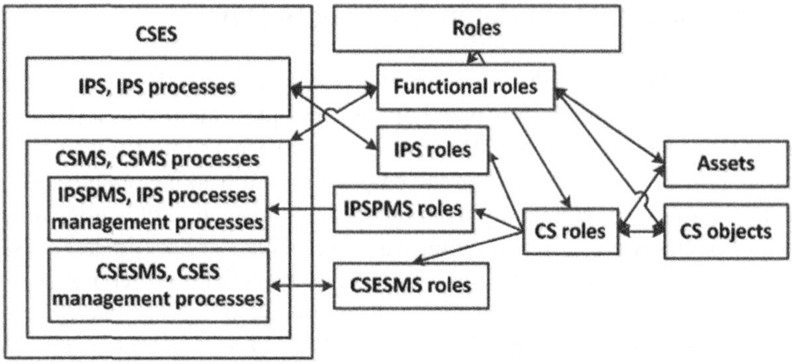


**Fig. 5.** The role categories

In a banking organization, two groups of employees can be distinguished whose basic job responsibilities are either unrelated or related to CS ensuring. For example, an accountant who processes banking information using automated workstations implements such IPS processes as ensuring the protection of information during access control and protection against malicious code (additional responsibilities). We will classify such roles as functional roles.

The CS unit employees perform functions related to CS ensuring (basic responsibilities). These functions include the implementation and maintenance of the IPS processes and the management processes of CSMS (IPSPMS and CSESMS). The corresponding roles will be categorized as CS roles (which, in turn, will be divided into the roles of IPS, IPSMS and CSESMS. Both role categories also include functions related to ensuring CS of assets and CS objects.

The banking organization should describe and document the roles related to CS ensuring. The processes of formation and distribution of roles refer to the processes of role management, which is a separate PA task in CS (the processes of managing CS roles belong to CSESMS). The description of the roles is the basis for the formulation of the PA tasks, which must be done when developing CMs. An example of defining roles in the field of IS can be found in [26].

## 6 Competency Model Development Practice

The analysis showed that the CM can be developed only for a specific PA field and application. In this case, the CM should be associated with a subject of a certain educational level (for example, a bachelor, master, specialist, engineer, etc.). Thus, the following procedure with seven stages for developing a specific CM for CS professionals for the banking sector is proposed: 1) Solving the strategic tasks of CM developing (Fig. 1); 2) Determining its structure; 3) Filling the CM with specific content; 4) CM coordinating and approval; 5) CM implementation (usage); 6) Monitoring and analysis of the CM usage efficiency; 7) Developing correction measures for the CM.

To maintain the necessary level of CMs usage efficiency, stages 3-7 should be performed cyclically in time during the CM life cycle. In the case of the CM development for use in educational institutions or certification centers, it is advisable to coordinate it with organizations-employers or organizations that have the right to approve at the state or international level (if any). In the Russian Federation, a system of training IS professionals has been created, which provides for the coordination of educational programs, syllabus and curricula (including CMs) at the state level. The capabilities of the system can be used to coordinate educational materials in the CS field.

The importance of the third stage of CM development should be noted. Here a typical CM structure (CM sections) can be proposed: S1. CM Goals and Purpose. S2. PA Characteristics: 2.1. PA Field. 2.2. PA Objects. 2.3. PA Types. 2.4. PA (by PA type). S3. Competencies: 3.1. General competencies. 3.2. General PCs. 3.3. PCs (by PA type). S4. Indicators of achievement of competencies: 4.1. Indicators of achievements of general PCs. 4.2. Indicators of achievement of PCs. S5. Information sources.

The specifics of the CM scope (CS professionals for the banking sector) is determined in the second section of CM. In the third section, the division of competencies into three groups (general, general professional, and professional) corresponds to the recommendations on the CM structure [8, 9], which suggest the presence of three clusters of competencies. The binding of general PCs to specific PA types partially corresponds to the division of a particular cluster into levels. The section of general competencies is present only in the CM of graduates of academic institutions (bachelors or masters) and sometimes in the CM used in personnel management. When formulating a specific competence, one should adhere to the following form: "has certain abilities" (for general competencies) or "ability to solve a specific problem" (for general professional and professional competencies). The formation of professionals' specific competency is associated with the presence of concrete KSA as indicators of specific competence. These indicators for each general professional or professional competence should be described in the fourth section. The "knowledge" and "skill" indicators are more often used for academic education. Professional's additional education and practical activities contribute to the formation of not only knowledge and skills, but also abilities.

CM developers should have certain CS competencies in the educational and practical fields that cannot be typically combined in one person. Therefore, it is necessary to recognize the fact that only a team of performers and representatives of educational centers and leading organizations in CS can develop a CM.

Currently, the National Research Nuclear University MEPhI (Moscow Engineering Physics Institute) has accumulated many years of experience in training professionals in the field under consideration when implementing Bachelor's and Master's degree programs. The relevant CMs can be found by the following link: http://eis.mephi.ru/AccGateway/index.aspx?report_param_gosn=3&report_param_ismagister=true.

## 7 Conclusion

The analysis of modern approaches to designing CMs, the specifics of ensuring CS area, as well as banking TPs and related CS ensuring processes allowed to obtain all the results presented in the paper. The validity of the results obtained is confirmed by the positive experience in the CM development in the framework of training professionals in the field in the implementation of specific educational programs at the NRNU MEPhI.

It should also be noted the features of the results obtained. Firstly, they have a novelty in terms of the integrity of the CM development process and its applicability to the banking sector. Secondly, the results obtained are systematic from the viewpoint of using various types of CMs for development, depending on the purpose of their application. Thirdly, the results obtained are universal. They may be applicable in the development of CM for professionals in other PA fields.

Besides, the development of a specific CM should be accompanied by the development of controls that are designed to determine the level of formation of a specific competency (the implementation of processes for assessing (measuring) competency indicators). This is important in the training of professionals, and in the certification and certification. Design issues for controls may be the subject of further research.

**Acknowledgement.** This work was supported by the MEPhI Academic Excellence Project (agreement with the Ministry of Education and Science of the Russian Federation of August 27, 2013, project no. 02.a03.21.0005).

## References

1. Miloslavskaya, N., Tolstoy, A.: Professional competencies level assessment for training of masters in information security. In: Bishop, M., Miloslavskaya, N., Theocharidou, M. (eds.) WISE 2015. IAICT, vol. 453, pp. 135–145. Springer, Cham (2015). https://doi.org/10.1007/978-3-319-18500-2_12
2. Miloslavskaya, N., Tolstoy, A.: ISO/IEC competence requirements for information security professionals. In: Bishop, M., Futcher, L., Miloslavskaya, N., Theocharidou, M. (eds.) WISE 2017. IAICT, vol. 503, pp. 135–146. Springer, Cham (2017). https://doi.org/10.1007/978-3-319-58553-6_12
3. Alsmadi, I., Burdwell, R., Aleroud, A., Wahbeh, A., Al-Qudah, M., Al-Omari, A.: Practical Information Security: A Competency-Based Education Course, p. 317. Springer, Cham (2018). https://doi.org/10.1007/978-3-319-72119-4
4. Mansfield, R.S.: Practical Questions in Building Competency Models. Workitect, Inc. (2005). https://pdfs.semanticscholar.org/91d6/2eceb2b4288bde92b46f4c58c9dc5bcf9827.pdf. Accessed 12 Jan 2020
5. Competency Models for Enterprise Security and Cybersecurity. Research-Based Frameworks for Talent Solutions. University of Phoenix. Apollo Education Group (2015). http://www.apollo.edu/content/dam/apolloedu/microsite/security_industry/AEG-UOPX%20Security%20Competency%20Models%20report.pdf. Accessed 12 Jan 2020
6. Gridin, A.: Competence model of a specialist in computer security. https://habr.com/en/post/182176/. Accessed 12 Jan 2020. (in Russian)

7. Cybersecurity Workforce Competencies: Preparing Tomorrow's Risk-Ready Professionals. Apollo Education Group, University of Phoenix, $(ISC)^2$ and $(ISC)^2$ Foundation, 2014, 2015. http://www.apollo.edu/content/dam/apolloedu/microsite/security_industry/AEG-PS-264521-CJS-STEM-CYBERSECURITY.pdf. Accessed 12 Jan 2020
8. Introduction to the Tools. Report U.S. Department of Labor «Competency Model Clearinghouse public toolkit» . http://www.careeronestop.org/competencymodel/careerpathway/cpwoverview.aspx. Accessed 12 Jan 2020
9. Competency Model General Instructions. Report U.S. Department of Labor «Competency Model Clearinghouse public toolkit» . http://www.careeronestop.org/competencymodel/careerpathway/CPWGenInstructions.aspx>. Accessed 12 Jan 2020
10. Reynolds, J.: Competency model? Explained – and how to build them. https://www.tinypulse.com/blog/competency. Accessed 12 Jan 2020
11. Forst, S.: How to build a competency model. http://hq.teamfit.co/how-to-build-a-competency-model. Accessed 12 Jan 2020
12. How to Develop a Competency Framework. https://www.lucidchart.com/blog/how-to-develop-a-competency-framework. Accessed 12 Jan 2020
13. Berry, J.: Competency Model for Cybersecurity. Memorandum for Chief Human Capital Officers. https://www.chcoc.gov/print/2667. Accessed 12 Jan 2020
14. State Government Information Security Workforce Development Model. A Best Practice Model and Framework. Final Version 1.0, June 2010
15. The U.S. National Cybersecurity Workforce Framework. https://www.dhs.gov/national-cybersecurity-workforce-framework. Accessed 12 Jan 2020
16. The Cyber Security Capability Framework & Mapping of ISM Roles. Final Report. Australian Government Information Management Office. June 2010
17. ISO/IEC 27021:2017 Information technology — Security techniques — Competence requirements for information security management systems professionals
18. Professional standards of the Russian Federation for information security professionals. http://azi.ru/professionalnye-standarty. Accessed 12 Jan 2020. (in Russian)
19. Federal Educational Standards of the Russian Federation in the Information Security Direction. http://azi.ru/obrazovatelnye-standarty. Accessed 12 Jan 2020. (in Russian)
20. ISO/IEC 27032:2012 Information technology – Security techniques – Guidelines for cybersecurity
21. ISO/IEC 27000:2014 Information technology — Security techniques — Information security management systems — Overview and vocabulary
22. Definition of Cybersecurity – Gaps and overlaps in standardisation.- Report of European Union Agency for Network and Information Security (ENISA), v1.0, December 2015. http://www.enisa.europa.eu/. Accessed 12 Jan 2020
23. Miloslavskaya, N.G., Tolstaya, S.A.: Cyber threats for organizations of financial market infrastructures. Besopasnost informachionnih technologiy **1**, 115–126 (2016). (in Russian)
24. Bank of Russia Standard STO BR IBBS-1.0-2014 «Maintenance of Information Security of the Russian Banking System Organizations. General Provisions» . (in Russian)
25. GOST 57580.1-2017. Security of financial (banking) operations. Protection of information of financial organizations. The basic composition of organizational and technical measures. (in Russian)
26. Vybornov, A.O., Kurilo, A.P., Kharlamov, V.P.: The role model of employees of a banking institution in the field of information security. Besopasnost informachionnih technologiy **3**, 90–102 (2012). (in Russian)

# Exploring the Value of a Cyber Threat Intelligence Function in an Organization

Anzel Berndt[1] and Jacques Ophoff[1,2(✉)]

[1] University of Cape Town, Cape Town, South Africa
VWYANZ001@myuct.ac.za
[2] Abertay University, Dundee, UK
j.ophoff@abertay.ac.uk

**Abstract.** Organizations can struggle to cope with the rapidly advancing threat landscape. A cyber threat intelligence (CTI) function broadly aims to understand how threats operate to better protect the organization from future attacks. This seems like a natural step to take in hardening security. However, CTI is understood and experienced differently across organizations. To explore the value of this function this study used a qualitative method, guided by the Socio-Technical Framework, to understand how the CTI function is interpreted by organizations in South Africa. Thematic analysis was used to provide an in-depth view of how each organization implemented its CTI function and what benefits and challenges they've experienced. Findings show that CTI tasks tend to be more manual and resource-intensive, but these challenges can be resolved through automation. It was noted that only larger organizations seem to have the budget and resources available to implement the CTI function, whereas smaller organizations put more reliance on tools. It was observed that skills for the CTI function can be learned on the job, but that formal education provides a good foundation. The findings illustrate the value the CTI function can provide an organization but also the challenges, thereby enabling other organizations to improve preparation before such a function is adopted.

**Keywords:** Cyber threat intelligence · Socio-Technical framework

## 1 Introduction

Cyber threat intelligence (CTI) is a collection of data regarding threat actors, exploited vulnerabilities, malware, and any other possible cybersecurity threat. It is a crucial function in knowing the threat actor by understanding how they operate [1]. A global study by the SANS Institute observed that security teams often find themselves lagging doing analyses on artefacts, trying to predict what could happen in the future. In order to bridge this gap, the CTI function has grown in "popularity, usefulness and applicability" [2]. When using threat intelligence data organizations can improve decision-making in response to the looming danger the threat actor presents to the corporation. The CTI function also looks at how to counter these attacks to proactively develop detective and reactive mitigations [3].

According to a SANS survey the global number of organizations adopting this function is increasing, with 41% of respondents having adopted a CTI function [4].


Published by Springer Nature Switzerland AG 2020
L. Drevin et al. (Eds.): WISE 2020, IFIP AICT 579, pp. 96–109, 2020.
https://doi.org/10.1007/978-3-030-59291-2_7

However, there is still a large gap in adoption which is particularly true for developing countries, such as South Africa, making them an easier target for cyber-attacks [5]. Is this poor take-up due to the lack of skills required to fully understand their attacker's methods [2], or could it be due to the lack of understanding the value of this function? In developing countries organizations are primarily focused on improving their profits and decreasing their expenses, and thus cybersecurity is considered a side factor and is usually less of a priority [5]. The consequences of not adopting the CTI function are twofold. Firstly, it renders the organization incapable of analyzing the vast number of cyber-attacks happening globally each day. Secondly, it presents a risk because this function examines the attacks' features in order to implement defensive mitigations, and the organizations miss out on the benefits of this [1].

This study explores the gap in understanding the CTI function inside an organization by examining the value this function brings along with the challenges experienced when implementing this function. It aims to answer the following primary research question: What value does a cyber threat intelligence function provide an organization? The study explores this topic through interviews with several CTI professionals in South Africa, thus adding insight in a developing country context. This study will explore the perceived gap in the understanding of the CTI function inside organizations by presenting the benefits this function brings along with the challenges experienced when implementing this role. The findings should be valuable in giving organizations greater understanding and a better chance of thoroughly preparing for such an implementation by planning for the possible challenges. It also provides a list of skills required for the CTI function which can assist in designing security curricula and training programs within organizations.

The remainder of this paper proceeds as follows. Section 2 provides a review of relevant CTI literature. In Sect. 3, the research design is discussed in detail. This is followed by the data analysis and discussion of the project findings in Sect. 4. Finally, this paper concludes by discussing the limitations of this study, along with opportunities for future research.

## 2 Background

Prior research describes CTI as a collection of data from several sources which consists of indicators of comprise which is in turn used to understand threat actors, malware and vulnerabilities to provide actionable intelligence used to protect an organization [1–3, 6]. Veerasamy [3] explained that CTI can be used during a cyber-threat attack to answer important questions such as: who is attacking us; why is there an attack; what are they attacking; how are they attacking; and, how can the attack be stopped? SANS defines CTI as the practice to collect data from several sources which creates a better knowledge base and understanding of cyber threats in the wild and how this gathered information relates to your organization. This gathered information can comprise indicators, context, and hopefully actionable advice in order to make an enlightened decision for the required mitigation to the threat [2].

Gartner defines CTI as "evidence-based knowledge, including context, mechanisms, indicators, implications and actionable advice, about an existing or emerging menace or hazard to assets that can be used to inform decisions regarding the subject's response to that menace or hazard" [7]. This is reiterated in a study by Mavroeidis and Bromander [8] which defined CTI as providing "evidence-based" data on a known cyber threat that could potentially be a new threat or an existing threat to an organization. Having a better understanding of what CTI is, it is important to understand the importance of the CTI function and the next section will explain this in more detail.

## 2.1 The Importance of a CTI Function

The CTI function is important because it can enable other cybersecurity teams to detect and respond more efficiently as it does not rely solely on signature-based detections but on understanding the techniques of a threat actor better, so that the threat can be mitigated in a more proactive manner [3, 9, 10].

The threat landscape is continuing to advance at a rapid rate and current cybersecurity teams don't have the capabilities to keep up with this [3]. The CTI function is a natural step towards hardening the security of an organization in order to prepare for the "known and unknown threats" [2]. In order to improve the detection and response to threats IT security teams are increasingly relying on the CTI function to improve their mitigation strategies [10].

Security controls normally rely on signature-based detection, so any new type of malware or technique used by the threat actor goes undetected. This is where the importance of the CTI function lies: to understand these new techniques and implementing mitigations [3]. The CTI function influences the Security Operations Centre (SOC) and Incident Response (IR) teams by providing them with greater insight into the current type of threats and attacks, while decreasing the time it takes to detect and respond to threats, because of a better understanding of the attack [10]. Up-to-date knowledge about threats, vulnerabilities, exploits and threat actors is vital to successfully defend against a cyber-attack and the CTI function provides this important service to an organization's IT security team [9].

## 2.2 Benefits of a CTI Function

To understand why the adoption of CTI is important one needs to understand the benefits and value it presents. This section looks at the benefits some organizations experience with the CTI function. The first theme is proactive defense capabilities which is seen as a CTI function to enable the organization to proactively stop malware, ransomware, and advanced attacks by having indicators of compromise which consists of threat and vulnerability details [3, 8, 10–12]. The CTI function enables the organization to have an innovative capability in detecting and preventing cyber-attacks [8]. These abilities are derived from gathering intelligence of intricate threats and threat actors, which gives more insight and develops "detective and reactive actions" [3]. This enables the organization to recognize changes in the techniques, tactics, and procedures (TTP) of a threat actor in order to plan accordingly for the appropriate protection [2].

To proactively protect the organization, the CTI function studies threat actors before they attack to learn their goals, strategies, techniques, tactics, and procedures [3, 11, 13, 14]. CTI is not just about knowing about the threats but also about understanding the threat actors' abilities and motivation [3]. By building up CTI data you are defining the threat actors' goals and strategies, which will give greater focus on what they would attack in your organization [13]. Understanding the threat actor and their TTP's is crucial in the CTI function but sharing this information amongst peers is just as important [14].

By sharing data, the CTI function can familiarize itself with the ever-changing threat landscape quicker by using sharing platform technologies which could mean the early prevention of a cyber-attack [7, 8, 14–16]. Through this exchange of data participating organizations can positively influence "collective knowledge, experience, and capabilities" in order to achieve a better understanding of the threats [17]. Another benefit is a degree of protection for other community members by hindering the threat, whether this involves the spreading of malware or a threat actor possibly attacking another organization [17]. However, sharing requires "standard formats and protocols" and a significant understanding of the different terminologies amongst communities [8]. The benefits of a CTI function don't come without challenges, which are discussed next.

## 2.3 Challenges for the Adoption of a CTI Function Adoption

Challenges include lack of funding, the time required to implement, not developing enough proactive intelligence, and a skills shortage. Implementing a CTI function which consists of analysts and tools has been experienced to be a very costly function [4, 9]. According to Brown [4], in order to provide the CTI function with the required time to analyze and disseminate the intelligence gathered, an automation tool is of great use. However, such tools are expensive and only a limited number of organizations can afford to invest in such tools; often smaller organizations are not able to participate in the threat intelligence market [9]. Time and effort to implement are some of the leading challenges experienced with this function [2, 12, 18].

Current CTI functions mostly rely on events that already occurred, but data should be studied prior to attacks in order to provide a proactive stance [6, 11, 19]. Most CTI functions primarily focus on internal intelligence data like anti-virus logs and some threat feeds, but this is a reactive approach which depend on events that have already happened. A more proactive stance should be taken when implementing the CTI function – one where more external threat feeds are analyzed to discover threat actors and malware before an attack happens [11].

Finally, a lack of skilled staff is seen as one of the prime challenges experienced in the CTI function [10]. The lack of trained staff creates a gap in the industry because a normal cybersecurity team lacks the visibility into the threat landscape without the CTI function [3, 10, 20]. According to Veerasamy [3] the skills gap for the CTI function is the leading challenge currently seen in the industry.

## 2.4 NICE Framework: SP800-181 – CTI Skills Standard

In order to formalize essential CTI skills, the NICE (National Initiative for Cybersecurity Education) Framework categorizes the CTI function as a threat/warning analyst with its specialty area being warning/threat analysis. Its description of this role is as follows: "Develops cyber indicators to maintain awareness of the status of the highly dynamic operating environment. Collects, processes, analyses and disseminates cyber threat/warning assessments" [21]. The NICE standard specifies the tasks, knowledge, skills, and abilities that are required for the threat/warning analyst, which relates to the CTI function.

According to the NICE framework, the CTI function requires the ability to perform a total of 30 tasks, knowledge in 47 areas, with a set of 17 different skills, and a set of 16 abilities. Some skills include performing non-attributable research, but also the ability to conduct research using the deep web. The CTI function should also have the skills to create a solution to a problem where the data is incomplete, as well as identifying cyber threats that could endanger the organization by understanding the target threat systems and using multiple analytical tools and techniques. The CTI function also requires skill in reviewing and writing about threat intelligence collected from multiple sources and presenting these briefings to different knowledge levels in the organization [21].

## 3 Research Methodology

To explore the topic and answer the research question a qualitative research design was employed. A qualitative study focuses on a smaller number of people but tends to produce rich data [22] through a process of "deep attentiveness, of empathetic understanding" [23]. This allows the researcher to entice certain themes from the raw data without the restrictions of using a more controlled methodology [24]. This study is based on the participants' experiences of the CTI function in their organization.

Empirical data was collected through semi-structured interviews with a selected sample of participants. Performing interviews is a method of collecting data by analyzing the participants' words, making observations, and documenting the participants' perspectives of the phenomenon [24]. A non-probability sampling method was used to target South African employees who had been working in a cyber-security team in their current organization for at least six months. Ethical clearance was obtained before data collection commenced, and participation in the study was voluntary. A total of seven participants were interviewed. After the interviews were transcribed the transcriptions were loaded into Nvivo12 for analysis.

To provide a valid interpretation during a qualitative study it is important to provide information on the dependability, credibility, transferability, and authenticity of the data collected [25]. By following the sampling method, the validity is improved and increases the quality of the study [26]. To prove dependability during the research study the theoretical framework will be used to identify themes and relationships between the participants' feedback [25]. Credibility will be established by linking the information gathered from the participants to the research question. The applicability depends on the sample that was chosen through the sampling process where the inclusion/exclusion criteria was identified [25]. Transferability is proven by using the Socio-Technology Framework, which the interview questions are constructed from.

### 3.1 Theoretical Framework

A theoretical framework functions as a "structure and support" for a study [27]. This research uses the Socio-Technical Framework as theoretical lens. The framework was developed when implementation problems were experienced and were possibly connected to a "failure to achieve the expected benefits" [28]. These issues consisted of behavioral problems due to poor designs linked to the members and their functions within an organization. The Socio-Technical framework was designed to create an increase in effectiveness through "meeting task requirements" [28]. This framework was also designed to provide a "realistic view" of an organization and its internal functions. It can be used for rebuilding current and implementing new functions [28].

There are four themes derived from this framework and a total of 13 questions drafted from the themes. The four themes are: Structuring the CTI function inside current IT Teams; Skills their CTI function possesses; The technologies used in the CTI function; and Tasks pertaining to the CTI function. Based on these themes, and CTI literature reviewed, the interview questions were derived through a five-stage process [29].

## 4 Data Analysis and Findings

During the data analysis phase of this research study a thematic analysis process was used. A thematic analysis process includes searching for important themes derived from the specific phenomenon being researched. This includes "a form of pattern recognition" where the different themes change into the different categories that are being examined during the analysis phase [30].

The data analysis process consisted of six stages: 1. Developing the coding manual; 2. Testing the reliability of codes; 3. Summarizing data and identifying initial themes; 4. Applying template of codes and additional coding; 5. Connecting the codes and identifying themes; and 6. Documenting themes [30].

During Stage 5 the codes are connected to the identified themes in the data. During this phase, the Socio-Technical framework was used to form the structure of a 'map' that includes the themes and sub-themes and presents the relationship between themes. A primary contribution of this study is the thematic analysis map (Fig. 1) which indicates the different relationships observed between the main themes of structure, technology, tasks, and people (skills).

As seen in the thematic analysis map the benefits experienced with the CTI function in the structure had a strong relationship with the tasks that applies to this function. The team where the CTI function operates and the reason for placing the CTI function in the team also had a strong relationship with the tasks interlinking with other teams due to the nature of the function. The challenges experienced with the function were mostly related to the tasks that apply to the CTI function. The technology that is advantageous for the CTI function had the strongest relations with the technology associated with the tasks of a CTI function. Open-source versus paid threat intelligence had a strong relationship with the skills a CTI function requires, due to open-source tools requiring more skills to make it operational. The skills required by the CTI function were mostly related to the tasks required by the function. Possible causes for the low adoption of the

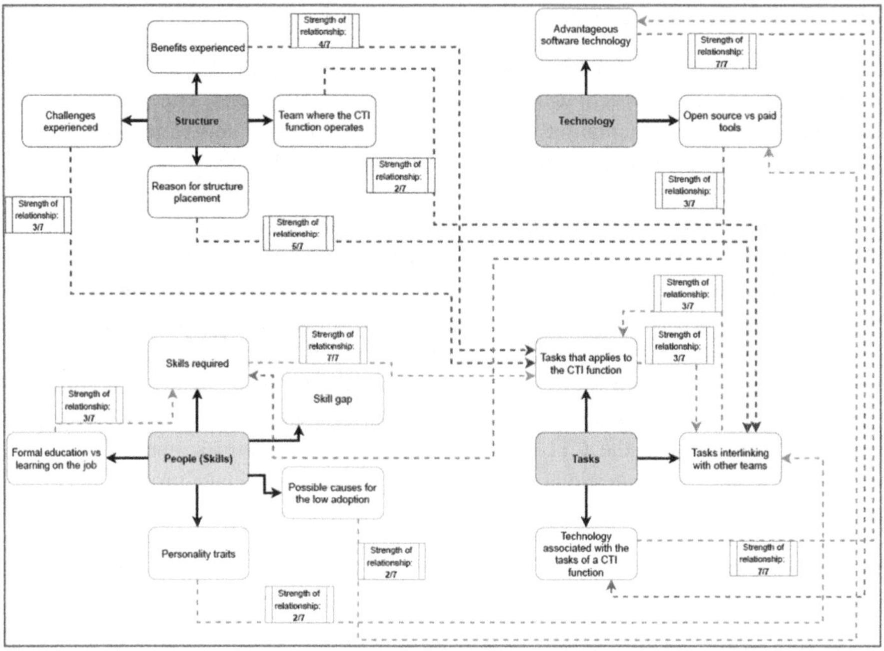


**Fig. 1.** Thematic analysis map

CTI function has some relations to the open-source versus paid tools due to the CTI function being too expensive to implement and by using open-source tools, the cost to adopt the CTI function could be reduced. The personality traits a CTI function should possess had some relations with the tasks interlinking other teams, due to the function requiring the ability to continuously work other cybersecurity teams in order to gain the maximum benefit of the function. Formal education versus learning on the job has some relationships with the skills required as a CTI function. The tasks that applies to the CTI function has a strong relationship with the tasks interlinking with other teams, due to the CTI functions' requirement to work continuously with the defense and pent testing teams.

Each code that is connected to the corresponding theme and sub-themes is documented during Stage 6 of the thematic analysis. These relationships will be explored in more detail in the following subsections. Due to space limitations certain sub-themes will not be discussed (A total of seven participants were interviewed but two of the participants worked for the same organization. To ensure the anonymity of the participants the findings will refer to them as O1–O6).

## 4.1 Structuring the CTI Function

The first main theme is the structuring of the CTI function. This theme consists of four sub-themes: where the CTI function was implemented in the organization (not discussed), the reason for implementing the function in the specific structure (not discussed), the benefits, and challenges (not discussed) experienced when the CTI function was implemented.

**Benefits Experienced When the CTI Function was Implemened.** This section will explore the benefits the organizations experienced after the CTI function was implemented in the said structure. O1 noted "greater visibility across potential threats" although this required more of a manual process when investigating specific threat indicators, tools, and tactics. Another benefit was greater confidence that the organization is not in the position of getting compromised and that the *organization is adequately defended*. O2 experienced an increase of automation on some of the work that was normally manual and very time-consuming. This drove them to build their own threat intelligence platform which sped up the process and made the team *more effective*. O3 developed monitoring for a particular threat actor targeting South African banks which included rules to alert them when a specific piece of code is identified. This solution highlighted two targeted attacks on the bank which they wouldn't have known about otherwise. O4 experienced their teams to *function more effectively*. O5 noted some benefits experienced were an increased *ability to detect attacks*. They can detect new attacks as they happen by generating their own threat intelligence and not solely relying on threat feeds. So, when they identify an attack the CTI function gathers the intelligence data and compares the IOC's (indicators of compromise) to the data from their customers to see if the same attack targeted them or not. They found that because their CTI function gathers intelligence themselves the quality of data is significantly better. O6 noted that the CTI function provides a *predictive view* in order to know what is coming down the line. Another benefit mentioned was the sharing of intelligence between organizations.

According to literature CTI is seen as assistance to cybersecurity practitioners by understanding the cyber-attack methods in order to respond in a more proactive manner [1]. This corresponds with the organizations stating that the CTI function assisted in proactively building their defenses before the attack happened. Another similarity in literature was found where the CTI function needs to study malicious threat actors before they attack the organization in order to protect the organization better [11]. This corresponds with the organizations stating that the CTI function created the process where threat actors' activity would be studied in advance and attacks down line were detected; if the CTI function wasn't present this might not have been possible. The final similarity with literature was the sharing of threat intelligence information. A higher level of CTI function data requires the need to share intelligence gathered [14]. The organizations confirmed that the CTI function enabled their organization to start sharing threat intelligence with other organizations.

Benefits that extend current literature were that the CTI function improved organizations' automation capabilities, as well as their ability to detect attacks using data from internally generated intelligence and not just threat feeds.

## 4.2 Skills Their CTI Function Possess

The second main theme is the skills within the CTI function. This theme consists of five sub-themes: what skills the CTI function should possess, is formal education required or can the skills be learned on the job, personality traits someone in a CTI function should possess, the skills gap (not discussed), and the cause of the low adoption rate of the CTI function in South Africa (not discussed).

**What Skills a CTI Function Should Possess.** This section will explore what skills the different organizations felt a CTI function should possess. O1 mentioned the CTI function should have an *attackers' mindset* in order to understand the goals of an attacker and know their tactics and techniques. The function should also have *experience building systems or infrastructure* to fully understand what typical mistakes are made. Thus, experience is a key part of understanding the potential threat for your specific organization. Another skill that is useful is *coding or development skills*, in order to decrease manual jobs and automate certain tasks (O1/O3). If automation is not present in the CTI function the resource overhead in the team would be much greater than if some automation was present. O2 stated that he came from a previous SOC analyst function before moving over to being part of the CTI function of the team. The participant noted that a SOC background gave him the ability to perform deeper research in order to make sure of the facts. An *analytical skill* is also required to perform this function. Another skill is having the curiosity for the work of a pen-tester or red teamer. O3 listed a couple of skills which a CTI function should possess. These skills include *understanding attacks* – how the organization could be attacked, how to construct a payload, and the *cyber kill chain*. The CTI function should also understand how to perform reconnaissance and how malware can get onto the network so what actions would *raise a flag*. The participant noted that if you don't understand how an attack works it is impossible to derive threat intelligence data from certain data. The CTI function should also understand how to transform data into actions that should be taken in order to defend against the attack. O4 noted some skills which include having a *broad understanding of cybersecurity* and being *open-minded*. The function should also have a *low level of bias* and needs to be *analytical*, the right personality and mindset. O5 stated that the skills that are required for a CTI function are divided into different roles. From a *response perspective* the function is required to analyze the incident in order to gather the required intelligence data from it. Looking at the *detection* side of the function, they need to understand how that data from the response team can be applied. The most important skill for this function to have the ability to perform analysis when dealing with threat intelligence. O6 noted that *analytical skills* are very important in order to work through events and understanding what happened. The function should also *know what attacks look like*. This would require the function to have some "offensive pen testing type skills".

Collectively a total of 15 different skills a CTI function should possess were identified by participants. The most important skills were analytical and offense team (pen tester) experience. According to literature some skills a CTI function should possess include analyzing intelligence, awareness of the latest attack patterns and indicators of compromise, but also knowledge on how to perform incident response and awareness on known and unknown behaviors in the organization's network [10]. This was confirmed by some of the organizations who stated a CTI function needs to be analytical, drive the outcomes with the gathered intelligence but also need a good understanding of the organizations' infrastructure.

The NIST framework states that a CTI function should perform non-attributable research and have the ability to conduct research using the deep web [21]. However, none of the participating organizations mentioned this. There were several skills mentioned by the participants not seen in literature, including: coding skills, automation skills, knowledge of how malware payloads are constructed, having the ability to reverse engineer code, and performing OSINT (open-source intelligence) investigations.

**Formal Education Versus Learning on the Job Required for Gaining the Skills.** Understanding the skills that are required for the CTI function from the participants' view and literature, this section will look at if these skills require formal education or could be learned on the job. Five out of the six organizations agreed that the skills for a CTI function can be learned on the job, but four participants noted that formal education provides an advantage. O1 mentioned that the "basics like coding, network infrastructure, and protocols" can be learned through formal education. He also stated that the OSCP (offensive security certified professional) qualification is beneficial. O5 mentioned that engineers, system administrators or network engineers that have a passion for security can develop their security skillset. There were no findings in the literature review concerning which of the two options, formal education or learning on the job is a better fit in gaining the required skills for a CTI function.

**Personality Traits Someone in a CTI Function Should Possess.** This section will explore the personality traits a CTI function should possess. O1 mentioned that someone in a CTI function should *question everything* and not accept everything at face value. O1 & O2 stated that a person in a CTI function should have the ability to interact with external companies or internal people. O2 also said that they should always *communicate clearly and quickly*. O4 stated the CTI function should be *open-minded* and have a *low level of bias*. And finally, O3 said the CTI function should *be curious to understand how things work*. There were no findings in the literature review concerning the personality traits a CTI function should possess.

## 4.3 Technology Used in the CTI Function

The third main theme is the technology used in the CTI function. This theme consists of two sub-themes: the software that is advantageous for the CTI function (not discussed) and if open-source tools could be just as effective as commercial threat intelligence tools.

**Open-Source Versus Commercial Threat Intelligence Tools.** This section will explore the views of the participants regarding open-source tools versus a commercial threat intelligence tool. Five out of the six organizations agreed that an open-source tool can be just as effective as a paid threat intelligence tool. However, one organization disagreed saying open-source tools are not as effective as paid threat intelligence tools, stating that "support for open-source tools can be challenging", and paid threat intelligence tools generates a higher quality of threat intelligence data through a *higher level of integration and automation*. O1 noted that a commercial tool is too expensive, and an open-source tool can be used to do a value evaluation to create a better motivation for a paid threat intelligence tool. However, O1, O2 & O5 stated that an open-source tools require more skills to use effectively. O6 mentioned that only a *strict intelligence sharing space* would be able to use open-source effectively.

According to literature in order to provide the CTI function with the required time to analyze and disseminate the intelligence gathered, an automation tool is of great use [4]. But such tools are expensive and only a limited number of organizations can afford to invest in such tools; smaller organizations are not able to participate in the threat intelligence market [9]. These statements share similarities to that found in the data gathered from the participants where the participants stated that *commercial tools are too expensive* but in the previous section, where the advantageous technology was discussed, it seems there is still a need for tools that provides automation. Due to the commercial tool being too expensive, more organizations are moving towards open-source tools but find it challenging due to the extra skills that are required and the lack of support.

## 4.4 Tasks Pertaining to the CTI Function

The fourth main theme are the tasks pertaining to the CTI function. This theme consists of three sub-themes: the tasks that apply to the CTI function, the tasks interlinking between the CTI function and other cybersecurity teams (not discussed), and the technology associated with the tasks of a CTI function (not discussed).

**Tasks that Apply to the CTI Function.** This section will explore the tasks pertaining to the CTI function. O1 stated that these tasks include the *gathering of information* in order to produce indicators that would discover malicious activity in the organization or attacking the organization. The gathered data is correlated which requires *visibility across your organization*. The tasks also include the implementation of an alarm or trip when something bad happens. One of the main tasks is *research* and *applying context* to the information gathered but then also implementing that intelligence in your organization in a useful way. O1 also mentioned that a very important task is to make the information actionable in order to provide value to the organization. O2 noted that the CTI function "plays a big role in your IT security strategy". O3 stated the tasks include *threat modelling* in understanding the type of threat actors who would target your organization and understanding the tools and techniques and procedures the specific threat actors use. The *behavioral aspects* when hunting the threat actors in your environment are also part of the tasks related to the CTI function. Another important task is *industry sharing* which should be automated in order to handle it more effectively. O4 noted the tasks pertaining to the CTI function include the collection and dissemination of research data, but also *reporting, investigating, advising, underground checking and social media monitoring*. O5 stated that there are different tasks within the CTI function which depends on the level of maturity. A basic level of CTI maturity only ingests feed data and then pushes it through to their technologies. A mid-range level of CTI maturity *generates their own intelligence*. Here the CTI function is required to analyze incidents and understand how the threat intelligence data can be extracted from the data. A higher-level of CTI function tasks require research to be done on the dark web and finding the threat intelligence data from more advanced sources. O6 noted the tasks pertaining to the CTI function included looking at "your threat intelligence server provider platform or portal". This is to see what's happening in the world using the available feeds. Each incident data should be collected and analyzed.

According to literature, a CTI function "collects, processes, analyses and disseminates cyber threat/warning assessments" [21]. This has strong similarities to the data from the participants. Some additional tasks include research on the dark web and social media monitoring.

## 5 Conclusion

The primary objective of this research was to understand the value experienced in organizations when the CTI function was adopted. During the literature review the importance of a CTI function was identified. It seems like a natural step to take in hardening the security of an organization in order to prepare for the known, and unknown, threats. Empirical data was collected to examine how the CTI function was implemented, what benefits and challenges were experienced with the implementation, what skills such a function requires, and the technology that would be beneficial for such a function.

Using the Socio-Technical Framework as lens it was observed that implementing a CTI function provides significant value to the organization, but requires skilled resources, process to integrate the CTI function into current cybersecurity teams, and enough budget for tools to provide the best value to the organization.

A limitation of this study is the limited number of participants which represented only large organizations. Thus, the data does not represent smaller organizations and differences in their context. The limited number of CTI professionals represents a challenge for research in this area, which might be overcome with a broad survey methodology. In addition, it would be valuable to understand how the cybersecurity industry can ensure that a CTI function is also adopted by smaller, resource-constrained organizations.

**Acknowledgements.** This work is based on the research supported wholly/in part by the National Research Foundation of South Africa (Grant Numbers 114838) [31].

## References

1. Conti, M., Dargahi, T., Dehghantanha, A.: Cyber threat intelligence: challenges and opportunities. Adv. Inf. Secur. **70**, 1–6 (2018)
2. Bromiley, M.: Threat Intelligence: What It Is, and How to Use It Effectively. SANS Security Insights (2016)
3. Veerasamy, N.: Cyber Threat Intelligence Exchange - A Growing Requirement (2017)
4. Brown, R.: SANS Institute Information Security Reading Room: The Evolution of Cyber Threat Intelligence (CTI): 2019 SANS CTI Survey (2019)
5. Mbelli, T.M., Dwolatzky, B.: Cyber security, a threat to cyber banking in South Africa: an approach to network and application security. In: Proceedings - 3rd IEEE International

Conference on Cyber Security and Cloud Computing, CSCloud 2016 and 2nd IEEE International Conference of Scalable and Smart Cloud, SSC 2016, pp. 1–6 (2016)
6. Qamar, S., Anwar, Z., Rahman, M.A., Al-Shaer, E., Chu, B.T.: Data-driven analytics for cyber-threat intelligence and information sharing. Comput. Secur. **67**, 35–58 (2017)
7. Knights, R., Morris, E., Security, V.C.W.: Move to intelligence. Netw. Secur. **2015**, 15–18 (2015)
8. Mavroeidis, V., Bromander, S.: Cyber threat intelligence model: an evaluation of taxonomies, sharing standards, and ontologies within cyber threat intelligence. In: Proceedings - 2017 European Intelligence and Security Informatics Conference, EISIC 2017, January 2017, pp. 91–98 (2017)
9. Mtsweni, J., Shozi, N.A., Matenche, K., Mutemwa, M.: Development of a semantic-enabled cybersecurity threat intelligence sharing model. In: Proceedings of the International Conference on Cyber Warfare and Security, pp. 244–252 (2016)
10. Shackleford, D.: Cyber Threat Intelligence Uses, Successes and Failures: The SANS 2017 CTI Survey. SANS Institute (2017)
11. Grisham, J., Samtani, S., Patton, M., Chen, H.: Identifying mobile malware and key threat actors in online hacker forums for proactive cyber threat intelligence. In: 2017 IEEE International Conference on Intelligence and Security Informatics: Security and Big Data, ISI 2017, pp. 13–18 (2017)
12. Shackleford, D.: SANS Institute Information Security Reading Room: CTI in Security Operations: SANS 2018 Cyber Threat Intelligence Survey (2019)
13. Bou-Harb, E., Lucia, W., Forti, N., Weerakkody, S., Ghani, N., Sinopoli, B.: Cyber meets control: a novel federated approach for resilient CPS leveraging real cyber threat intelligence. IEEE Commun. Mag. **55**, 198–204 (2017)
14. Skopik, F., Settanni, G., Fiedler, R.: A problem shared is a problem halved: a survey on the dimensions of collective cyber defense through security information sharing. Comput. Secur. **60**, 154–176 (2016)
15. Abu, M.S., Selamat, S.R., Ariffin, A., Yusof, R.: Cyber threat intelligence – issue and challenges. Ind. J. Electr. Eng. Comput. Sci. **10**, 371–379 (2018)
16. Johnson, C., Badger, L., Waltermire, D.: NIST Special Publication (SP) 800-150 Guide to Cyber Threat Information Sharing October 2016. 150 (2016)
17. Johnson, C.S., Badger, M.L., Waltermire, D.A., Snyder, J., Skorupka, C.: Guide to Cyber Threat Information Sharing. NIST Special Publication (2016)
18. Mutemwa, M., Mtsweni, J., Mkhonto, N.: Developing a cyber threat intelligence sharing platform for South African organisations. In: 2017 Conference on Information Communication Technology and Society, ICTAS 2017 – Proceedings, pp. 1–6 (2017)
19. Samtani, S., Chinn, R., Chen, H., Nunamaker, J.F.: Exploring emerging hacker assets and key hackers for proactive cyber threat intelligence. J. Manage. Inf. Syst. **34**, 1023–1053 (2017)
20. Mohaisen, A., Al-Ibrahim, O., Kamhoua, C., Kwiat, K., Njilla, L.: Rethinking information sharing for actionable threat intelligence. arXiv:1702.00548 (2017)
21. Newhouse, W., Keith, S., Scribner, B., Witte, G.: National Initiative for Cybersecurity Education (NICE) Cybersecurity Workforce Framework, p. 144 (2017)
22. Kerr, K.: Research Methods in Physical Education (2005)
23. Punch, K., Oancea, A.: Introduction to Research Methods in Education. SAGE Publishing, Thousand Oaks (2014)
24. Leitch, C.M., Hill, F.M., Harrison, R.T.: The philosophy and practice of interpretivist research in entrepreneurship. Organ. Res. Methods **13**, 67–84 (2010)
25. Seale, C.: Quality in qualitative research. Qual. Inq. **5**, 465–478 (1999)

26. Robinson, O.C., Robinson, O.C.: Sampling in interview-based qualitative research: a theoretical and practical guide. Qual. Res. Psychol. **11**, 25–41 (2016). Abstract
27. Grant, C., Osanloo, A.: Understanding, selecting, and integrating a theoretical framework in dissertation research: creating the blueprint for your "house". Adm. Issues J. Connecting Educ. Pract. Res. **4**, 12–26 (2014). https://doi.org/10.5929/2014.4.2.9
28. Bostrom, R.P., Heinen, J.S.: MIS problems and failures: a socio-technical perspective. Part I: The causes. MIS Q. **1**, 17–32 (1977). https://doi.org/10.2307/248710
29. Wilkinson, D., Birmingham, P.: Using Research Instruments a Guide for Researchers. Psychology Press, East Sussex (2003)
30. Fereday, J., Muir-Cochrane, E.: Demonstrating rigor using thematic analysis: a hybrid approach of inductive and deductive coding and theme development. Int. J. Qual. Methods **5**, 80–92 (2017)
31. Berndt, A.: Investigating the role of a cyber threat intelligence function in an organization [Unpublished manuscript]. Department of Information Systems, University of Cape Town, South Africa (2019)

# Automating the Communication of Cybersecurity Knowledge: Multi-case Study

Alireza Shojaifar[1,2](✉), Samuel A. Fricker[1,3], and Martin Gwerder[1]

[1] FHNW, IIT and IMVS, 5210 Windisch, Switzerland
{alireza.shojaifar,samuel.fricker,martin.gwerder}@fhnw.ch

[2] Department of Information and Computing Sciences, Utrecht University, Utrecht, The Netherlands
a.shojaifar@uu.nl

[3] Blekinge Institute of Technology, SERL-Sweden, 371 79 Karlskrona, Sweden
samuel.fricker@bth.se

**Abstract.** Cybersecurity is essential for the protection of companies against cyber threats. Traditionally, cybersecurity experts assess and improve a company's capabilities. However, many small and medium-sized businesses (SMBs) consider such services not to be affordable. We explore an alternative do-it-yourself (DIY) approach to bringing cybersecurity to SMBs. Our method and tool, CYSEC, implements the Self-Determination Theory (SDT) to guide and motivate SMBs to adopt good cybersecurity practices. CYSEC uses assessment questions and recommendations to communicate cybersecurity knowledge to the end-user SMBs and encourage self-motivated change. In this paper, the operationalisation of SDT in CYSEC is presented and the results of a multi-case study shown that offer insight into how SMBs adopted cybersecurity practices with CYSEC. Effective automated cybersecurity communication depended on the SMB's hands-on skills, tools adaptedness, and the users' willingness to documenting confidential information. The SMBs wanted to learn in simple, incremental steps, allowing them to understand what they do. An SMB's motivation to improve security depended on the fitness of assessment questions and recommendations with the SMB's business model and IT infrastructure. The results of this study indicate that automated counselling can help many SMBs in security adoption.

**Keywords:** Cybersecurity · Small and medium-sized businesses · Capability assessment and improvement · Do-it-yourself · Multi-case study

## 1 Introduction

Small and medium-sized businesses (SMBs) as the foundation of the EU's economy [1] are the weakest spot for cyber-attacks [2, 3]. SMBs have specific characteristics, and these characteristics separate them from large companies and make them highly vulnerable to security attacks [4–7]. The lack of financial resources, expertise, written formal security policies, and also the common wrong attitude towards security and risks are some of these characteristics. Previous studies considered these characteristics and their influences on SMBs' resilience to security threats [3, 8–10].


Published by Springer Nature Switzerland AG 2020
L. Drevin et al. (Eds.): WISE 2020, IFIP AICT 579, pp. 110–124, 2020.
https://doi.org/10.1007/978-3-030-59291-2_8

Ntouskas et al. [3] present a self-management security method which provides a consultancy environment for SMBs. Brunner et al. [9] focus on the level of automation in information security management and describe a continuous, risk-driven, and context-aware information security management system. Their framework is applicable to SMBs [9]. Furnell et al. [10] present a self-paced, flexible, and personalised security training software tool. The tool provides employees with the ability to learn some security countermeasures and desired behaviours.

In our experience of working with SMBs that were active in the IT industry, we found out that access to knowledge is not enough for motivating the SMBs to adopt appropriate behaviour. The SMBs need to understand the severity of threats and the impacts on their businesses. Moreover, providing hands-on skills that are consonant with the SMBs' capability motivates them to have security practices. We have not found any approach that considers the SMBs' motivation in the adoption of cybersecurity through self-assessment, learning, and improvement. Technical security measures form a large part of information security research [11]. Cybersecurity is more effective if the attention goes beyond the technical protecting means to the users, social, and organisational environment [11–13]. Human errors are the main cause of security failures [12] and promoting users' self-efficacy, and knowledge in information security can enhance organisation security [14].

CYSEC is a self-paced SMB-specific training and assessment method that automates elements of a counselling dialogue [15] between a security expert and employees in the SMB to ward off cyber threats. The interaction and dialogue between employees and security experts bridge the gap between them and makes the information security measures more effective [16]. Since users' resistance to accepting security tools and advice is one of the main problems for information security [17], the dialogue in CYSEC is based on theoretical foundations of motivation and the effects of employees' psychological needs on cybersecurity adoption. Persuasion is more effective than rational training strategies when the level of commitment to change is low [18].

The current study focuses on CYSEC evaluation to see whether the CYSEC is useful and effective as a method of communicating cybersecurity expertise for enabling DIY cybersecurity assessment and capability improvement for SMBs. The study purpose was approached by using an observation strategy based on the think-aloud protocol. While the previous literature mainly studies individuals' security behaviour through several interviews [16, 19, 20], the empirical findings of this study are based on observing actual usage of the tool to determine those factors which facilitate or control users' behaviour. The data was qualitatively analysed based on our theoretical model derived from Self-determination Theory (SDT) [21, 22]. Our results demonstrate that SDT can explain motivational factors for effective counselling communication, and these factors influence users' behaviour to adopt cybersecurity recommendations. Unmet psychological needs may hamper users' adoption of cybersecurity behaviours. We observed that the automated dialogue is more effective when the method offers adapted behaviour, users' self-efficacy improvement, and SMBs' confidentiality issues together.

The remainder of the paper is structured as follows. Section 2 presents the theoretical background. Section 3 describes the CYSEC method. Section 4 describes the design of the study. Section 5 presents the process of data collection in SMBs.

Section 6 analyses the results and answers the research questions. Section 7 discusses the significance of the results and the threats to validity. Section 8 summarises and concludes.

## 2 Theoretical Background

Cybersecurity studies draw on a variety of theories from different disciplines [19, 20]. Self-Determination Theory (SDT) [21] provides a rigorous theoretical framework for studying motivation and has been considered in cybersecurity [19, 20]. SDT describes and explains people's psychology of being self-motivated for adopting personal behaviours [21]. SDT was developed and evaluated with extensive research that resulted in an in-depth understanding of the conditions under which people will develop towards being a self-motivated in pursuing what they and their community consider as being desirable. The results of the research help managers and coaches to bring meaningful norms of behaviour into use and support the concerned people in adopting the conduct.

Self-motivation concerns goal-orientation, energy, and persistence – all related to producing results. If a goal is perceived to be important, the concerned person will start adapting his or her behaviour and be persistent to the extent that the behavioural change will sustain. According to SDT, a person will be self-motivated if these psychological needs have been satisfied: competence, autonomy, and relatedness. A lack of perceived competence, or self-efficacy, will lead the person to give up. Autonomy is important as the free choice determines how convinced the person is about the behaviour to be adopted. Relatedness to a person who acts as a role model for the behaviour can reinforce the self-motivation and even offer a template of how to adopt the behaviour.

Both intrinsic and extrinsic motivation leads to the adoption and internalisation of new behaviour. However, the more intrinsic the motivation is, the more effective and sustainable the adoption of the behaviour is. For each type of motivation, several forces influence how people are moved to act. People can feel motivated because they value an activity, e.g., by an abiding interest. People with such intrinsic motivation have interest, excitement, and confidence, which manifests as enhanced performance, persistence, and creativity. People under external coercion, e.g. with a bribe, fear of being surveilled, or other external pressure, are risking to be unwilling and unmotivated. Still, people can be externally motivated by a stimulating personal commitment to excel and offering role models' recognition. Table 1 shows, for the continuum from intrinsic motivation to amotivation, how behaviour may be influenced. Any method for helping users to achieve goals should operationalise these factors in the method's design.

Table 1 is pointing to the important SDT constructs that should be operationalised by a coaching method. It suggests hypotheses that can be used for evaluating whether the method supports the effectiveness of the cybersecurity knowledge communication for SMBs. The constructs concern attributes of the method user and environment with which the user interacts. The method user's attributes characterise the user's desired behaviour, self-efficacy, and autonomy. The method environment's attributes are relatedness, belonging, and connectedness offered to the user, pressure imposed through rewards, threats, and deadlines, the knowledge provided for helping the user to develop self-efficacy, and choice offered for fostering autonomy of the user.

**Table 1.** Factors for influencing desired behaviour, based on SDT.

| Motivation | How desired behaviour is influenced |
|---|---|
| **Intrinsic motivation**: a person with interested and joy in desired behaviour tends to seek out novelty and challenges, to explore, learn, and exercise one's capacities even in the absence of specific rewards | Autonomy of choice, perceived competence or self-efficacy, and a caring environment with optimal challenges and feedback of how the person's actions lead to the outcomes enhance intrinsic motivation and performance [23]. Extrinsic rewards, threats, deadlines, pressured evaluations, and imposed goals diminish intrinsic motivation |
| **Extrinsic motivation**: continuum from coercion to stimulating intrinsic motivation<br>A) **External regulation** is associated with control or alienation, and actions are perceived imposed by external regulators<br>B) **Introjected regulation** is not accepted as the one's own, but behaviours are performed to maintain a feeling of worth, e.g. to avoid guilt or anxiety or attain pride<br>C) **Regulation through identification**: conscious valuing and acceptance of rules as being personally important<br>D) **Integrated regulations:** fully assimilated as a result of evaluation and brought into congruence with one values and needs | With prescribed behaviours and values, new behaviour is internalised with meaningful rationales, autonomy, and relatedness [23]. External regulation is achieved with salient rewards or threats. Introjected regulation is achieved with the provision of belonging and connectedness, e.g. by having significant others to whom people feel attached or related prompt, model, endorse, or value the desired behaviour. Regulation through identification can only be achieved if autonomy of choice is provided. To integrate a regulation, the rules' meaning must be synthesised with respect to the person's goals and values with great autonomy in the sense of choice, volition, and freedom from excessive external pressure |
| **Amotivation**: lacking the intention to act due to coercion, leading to failed goal achievement | Amotivation is resulting from not valuing an activity, not feeling competent to do it, or not expecting the activity to yield desired outcome |

## 3 CYSEC, a DIY Cybersecurity Improvement Method

CYSEC is a method and tool allowing SMBs' Chief Information Security Officer (CISO) to improve cybersecurity in a do-it-yourself fashion. The method guides the CISO in following Deming's plan-do-check-act (PDCA) [24] cycles of selecting sensible security themes, implementing a recommended practice, checking progress, and adapting based on lessons-learned. The tool offers memory allowing the CISO to continue the PDCA work where he left off. The tool also includes design elements based on SDT that aim at offering motivation for effective results and sustainability of the improvements.

Figure 1 shows the two main interfaces offered to the user. A dashboard offers the features (1) recommendations for next improvements, (2) access to capability areas for PDCA work, (3) summary information about the company progress. Once the PDCA work for a given capability area is started, e.g. by choosing a recommendation or a capability area, the user enters the work area that offers the features (4) self-assessment, (5) access to expert knowledge, and (6) action cockpit for creating calendar entries, emails, and reminders. Table 2 describes how CYSEC operationalises SDT.

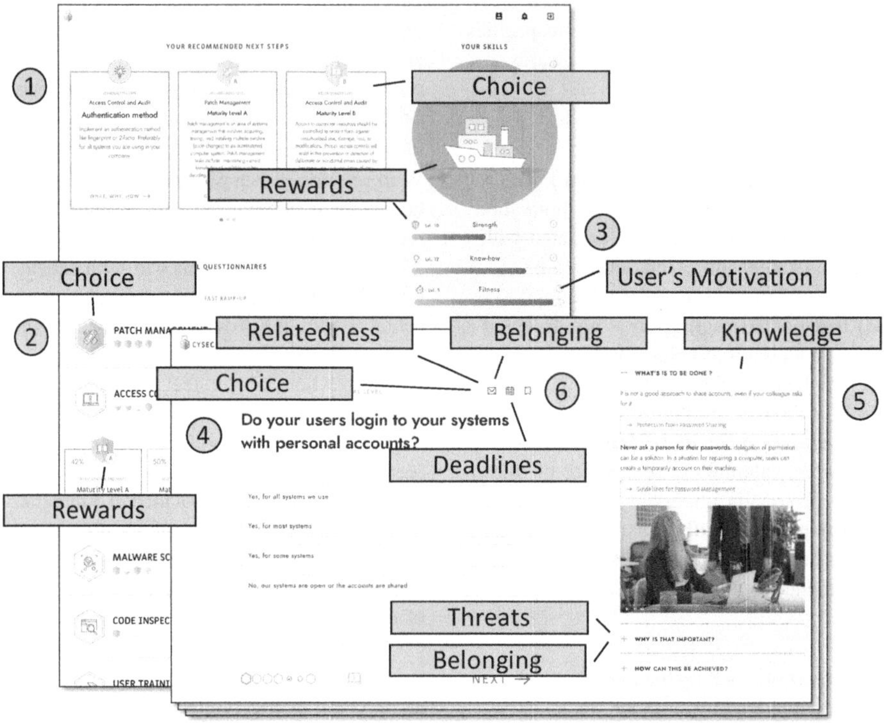


**Fig. 1.** Main user interfaces of the CYSEC tool and mapping of its features to SDT constructs.

The content has been organised into five cybersecurity themes (Patch Management, Access Control and Audit, Malware Scans, User Training, Back up). These themes allow fast ramp-up of security capabilities with minimal effort and large impact on SMBs.

Recommendations are generated based on users' answers to the self-assessment questionnaires for maturity improvement [25]. For the first time, new users will see one recommendation to fill out the company coach. As an adaptation rule, the answers to the company coach affect the questions asked in the other coaches. After completing the company coach, several coaches will be active in the dashboard. The available capabilities are defined and prioritised based on the cybersecurity expert's propositions (third author). When a user selects one coach, s(he) has access to the self-assessment questions and relevant capability training content. Providing the content was based on the research into the training material [26], technical reports provided by Symantec and Ponemon, and meeting with experts. Technical reports provide updated cybersecurity solutions and statistics. At the end of each coach, users see summary information and are redirected to the dashboard. In the dashboard, they see the progress information, achieved scores, and new recommendations for cybersecurity practices and selection of the next coach(es).

**Table 2.** Operationalisation of SDT constructs

| SDT construct | CYSEC function | Operationalisation |
|---|---|---|
| Relatedness | Dashboard: recommendations | Self-adaptation of recommendations to SMB profile and improvement progress |
| | Dashboard: progress summary | Continuous feedback about progress and motivation |
| | Work area: steps | Self-adaptation of recommended next improvements |
| | Offline | Personal workshops with SMBs for reflecting about improvement experience |
| Belonging and connectedness | Work area: action cockpit | Fostering of personal communication between CISO and employees |
| | Offline | Personal workshops with SMBs for reflecting about improvement experience |
| Rewards, threats, and deadlines | Dashboard: progress summary | Feedback about the defence strength built and knowledge acquired in the company, and persistence in working on cybersecurity ("fitness") |
| | Work area: expert knowledge | Information about the importance of improvements, e.g. by referring to cyber risks that should be mitigated |
| | Work area: action cockpit | Setting of calendar entries and emailing reminders to employees |
| Knowledge | Dashboard: access to capability areas | Access to knowledge and recommendations for building cybersecurity in the SMB |
| | Work area: expert knowledge | Presentation of knowledge and recommendations for building cybersecurity in the SMB |
| Choice | Dashboard: recommendations | Presentation of the three top recommendations, offering choice about the next important improvements |
| | Dashboard: access to capability areas | Presentation of capability areas, offering choice about the type of cybersecurity to build |
| | Work area: action cockpit | Choice of deferring improvements with a calendar entry or bookmark and of involving employees by email |

# 4 Study Design

The study aimed at evaluating whether CYSEC is useful and effective as a method of communicating cybersecurity expertise for enabling DIY cybersecurity assessment and capability improvement for SMBs. To achieve this aim, we designed a deductive multi-case study and used observation as the main method for data collection [27]. Case studies are common in information systems research and cybersecurity [20].

For planning the case study, a study protocol was developed and sent to the participating SMBs. Before conducting the case studies, a pilot workshop was performed for a start-up project that involved the second and third researchers and a developer. The pilot allowed to identify and resolve initial problems in the study design. The selection of the cases was based on the availability of the SMBs. It has been done in two steps. At first, data collection was based on four SMBs, and during the study (project lifetime), two more SMBs were included. Based on Yin [27], when using a multiple-case design, the number of case replications is essential instead of sampling logic, and the model of generalisation is analytic generalisation when we have a developed theory as a template. The selected SMBs have security resources, working in the software industry, and their CISOs have a level of expertise in security. The CISOs' behaviour was the unit of analysis. Table 3 presents our SMBs' demographics. Based on the EU Commission definition, companies with <50 employees and annual turnover $\leq$€10 million are small, and those with <250 employees and annual turnover $\leq$€50 million medium.

## 4.1 Research Questions and Case Selection

The following two research questions were analysed. RQ1 related the communication method to the user's motivation and adoption of cybersecurity recommendations. RQ2 reflects users' evaluations of the method and tool after the actual usage.

RQ1: *How do the CYSEC dashboard and work area features influence the effectiveness of communicating cybersecurity to motivate users' adoption of desired behaviour?* To improve SMBs' cybersecurity capability, they need to adopt good cybersecurity practices. Since CYSEC provides security experts' recommendations and training content, we are studying SMBs' security adoption through CYSEC communication. The factors of the study are based ont he SDT constructs and CYSEC features in Table 2. We evaluate the effectiveness of communication by observing users' behaviour, attention, comprehension, and theoretical cause-effect relationships [27]. RQ2: *Do the SMB human end-users perceive CYSEC to be acceptable and useful as a tool assisting DIY cybersecurity assessment and improvement?* Tool acceptance and perceived usefulness are significant for us since a problem for information security is the users' resistance to accepting security tools [17]. Therefore, in RQ2, we want to have the users' attitude.

**Table 3.** SMBs demographics

| ID | Step | Size | Offices | Maturity (some controls implemented) | Structure |
|---|---|---|---|---|---|
| 1 | 1 | Medium | 3 | Access control., network controls, backup, encryption | CEO, security team, employees |
| 2 | 1 | Medium | 3 | Password mgmt., patch mgmt., encryption, (training) security best practices for developers | CEO, security team, employees |
| 3 | 1 | Small | 2 | Password mgmt., Code inspection | CEO, security team, employees |
| 4 | 1 | Small | 1 | Access control, patch mgmt. | Professors, manager, Security team, users |
| 5 | 2 | Small | 1 | Using a firewall, Access control | CEO, manager, employees |
| 6 | 2 | Small | 1 | Password mgmt. | CEO, managers, developers |

### 4.2 Workshop Design and Meeting with Companies

Each workshop started with an explanation of the study, steps, and relevant objectives. To collecting honest responses [28], the researcher emphasised that the collected data would be applied anonymously for academic purposes and then obtained the subjects' consent. During the workshops, the researcher took notes about how the subjects interacted with the tool and asked them to "think aloud" [29] and explain their expectation. The workshops had four parts and four tasks for the CISO in the SMB. In part 1, the CISOs characterised their companies. In part 2, and to understand the main user's capabilities, the CISOs answered three questions about their level of education, experience in cybersecurity, and their roles. The responses to the questions were used to confirm the suitability of the selected case for the study. In part 3, the user applied the CYSEC. In part 4, the observation was supplemented with a post-observation quantitative questionnaire (Table 4). The result section presents the process of the workshops.

## 5 Results

In this section, we present the process of data collection in the 1-day workshops.

Company 1: two people (CISO) participated in the workshop, which took 26 min. This workshop took a short time since the users only provided their feedback at the end of the workshop. The researcher had the lowest degree of interaction in this workshop. It seems they were familiar with the topics and questions, so they refer to the training content only two or three times.

Company 2: Two people from a team of cybersecurity participated. The workshop took one hour and forty-three minutes. The users referred to the training content several times when they were not able to understand the actual goal of the questions. The users stated that the training content for some questions is not completely correct.

Company 3: Only one person (CISO) participated. The workshop took two hours and thirty-five minutes. The user explained that their SMB had not managed any cybersecurity training courses and security awareness issues are usually sent to the employees by email. During the workshop, the user experienced several system time-outs. So, the user required to log in several times. This issue was due to a bug in the tool, and it distracted the user's attention to some extent. So, the researcher needed to interact with the user. For this SMB, confidentiality issues were very critical.

Company 4: A team of seven IT specialist participated. The workshop took two hours and a half. The users went through the coaches the same as the first workshop. The distinctive feature of this workshop was the discussion about each question between participants to find suitable answers based on the company's requirements. The users applied training content too much to understand the questions. For this SMB dynamic, and reliable training material was significant.

Company 5: Only one person (CISO) participated. The workshop took thirty-four minutes. The user stated that their SMB has no chain of management. In this workshop, the user emphasised that some of the questions have no suitable options for the answer.

Company 6: Two people from a team of cybersecurity participated. The workshop took forty minutes. People in the workshop had a language problem, and they used Google translate to understand the content. So, the researcher needed to interact with the users. The users went through some of the coaches.

In all workshops, the mechanism of the tool usage was almost the same and the users referred to the training content mostly when they had a problem to understand questions. The meaning of some of the questions was not clear for the CISOs. Also, all of them required a summary and recommendation after finishing each coach.

## 6 Analysis

For answering the research questions, we explain the researcher's observations of the tool usage based on SDT- specific features of the CYSEC, which indicated in Table 2.

### 6.1 Factors Influencing Cybersecurity Communication (RQ1)

According to the workshop results, the CYSEC dashboard and work area features affected the users' motivation for the adoption of desired behaviour. These features together can facilitate security management and inter-organisational connection between the CISO and the employees and support self-efficacy and capability improvement in the SMBs. The participating SMBs learned about cybersecurity and adopted practices and controls when the immediate perceived learning experience was good.

**Available Expert Knowledge (CYSEC Work Area).** As suggested by SDT, we have observed that improving self-efficacy had a positive impact on the users' self-motivation. The immediate relevance of the training material provided by the CYSEC tool affected the subjects' decision to study the training material. Still, even though the participants did not have any systematic cybersecurity course so far, none of them read the full knowledge texts provided by CYSEC. Instead, the subjects studied training material when they did not understand a question or wanted to know more about a topic to select suitable answers. *Company 4: "We need practical instructions and steps to help us solve our issues and not general ideas." Company 2: "some materials are not relevant to the right topics/questions."* When responding to some of the questions, they referred to the training content occasionally and only to find a specific issue. For instance, to explore how they can measure the strength of password based on a tool.

Perceived reliability, expert support, clarity, and local language support of the content were important in the sense that the lack of these quality attributes hindered participants from accepting training input. *Company 4: "Parts of the content are not clear enough for us, and some materials (statistics) are not reliable since they are not covering many security experts and SMBs' opinions." Company 2: "Training content needs to present the severity of threats clearly." Company 2: "Since the coaches are in English, it might be possible for some SMBs to be unwilling to apply the tool." Company 6: "Can you please tell me what actually you mean* [even after using Google translate for the training content]*."* The quotes here can demonstrate the users' awareness and attention to the training content with respect to the effectiveness of the communication.

**Assessment Questions for Next Step Improvement (CYSEC Work Area).** As suggested by SDT, choice supported autonomy and self-motivation. However, the options should always be relevant and adapted to the IT infrastructure and operations of the company. The participants looked for questions that fit their interest and perceived needs. If they could not find such questions, they explained their needs by referring to their company's characteristics (assets). Moreover, they wanted the coach to adapt the questions to the SMB's characteristics specified with preceding answers. *Company 3: "here, the tool should provide a lot of questions to cover different operating systems."*

Also, the users wanted each question to be answerable with options for the response that explained the situation precisely. The researcher observed that the users did not answer some questions or selected an imprecise option due to lack of suitable choices. *Company 2 about the question* "Do your users use any other authentication method, such as fingerprint or 2-factor authentication, to control access to your sensitive systems:" *"for some systems yes, for some systems and users no. I cannot answer properly, so I select the answer* [Yes, for some systems]*." Company 5: "I need an option between yes and no."* The quality of the questions also influenced the efficiency of the users. Some of the questions were perceived to be confusing. When being confronted with such questions, the participants looked for training content, searched the Internet for the topic, or asked the researcher for clarification. *Company 4: "some of the questions are confusing and not clear enough for us." Company 2: "I could not understand if the question is related to servers or employees' computers."* The quotes here can demonstrate the users' comprehension and their ability to answer the assessment questions. Their behaviours and comments refer to the effectiveness of communication.

**Action Cockpit (CYSEC Work Area).** As suggested by SDT, we have observed that respect of the belonging within the organisation is important. While the CISOs answered most training and awareness questions, they communicated with their colleagues to find the answer for some of the questions. The CISO in Company 2 made a call to answer some questions. When he could not find his colleague, he highlighted the question for future consideration. Also, in Company 4, the IT specialist had a discussion to find the best answers for some questions based on their company requirements.

**Recommendations (CYSEC Dashboard).** As suggested by SDT, self-efficacy and relatedness had a positive impact on users' autonomous motivation. All SMBs wanted to receive feedback after finishing a coach and recommendations for next improvements. *Company 1: "we need a summary and recommendation after each coach."*

**Access to Capability Areas (CYSEC Dashboard).** As suggested by SDT, choices support users' autonomy and motivation. Still, a recommended order was appreciated by the SMBs, even though the order must not be enforced. Some of the participants selected capability areas based on reflected priorities or requirements. *Company 2 on which capability do you want to select to answer? "no preference [for the capabilities]. we can answer based on the list."* Other participants followed different orders, and one looked for a specific capability area that was not available in the list of capability areas.

**Progress Summary (CYSEC Dashboard).** None of the participants was intrinsically motivated; SDT's model of introjected regulation was best explaining the participants' adoption behaviour. The participants wanted feedback about their performance, and it was important that the feedback was credible. The gamification elements of showing progress impacted the users' motivation. All the participated CISOs in this study wanted to have a simple summary which indicated their company's progress.

## 6.2 Acceptance and Usefulness of CYSEC (RQ2)

The answer to RQ2 is based on the supplementary data collected at the end of each study about the users' attitudes. Users evaluated the usefulness of the tool by responding to a five-level Likert scale questions about the tool usefulness (low [L], rather low [RL], medium [M], rather high [RH], high [H]) and justified their evaluation. The follow-up questionnaire (Table 4) aimed at understanding users' attitudes about tool acceptance and usefulness. However, the short survey and small number of SMBs were not statistically significant for analysis. Company 1: "*CYSEC is easy to use and useful.*" Company 2: "*the severity of the threats should be more visible in the training content.*" Also, Company 2 stated "*CYSEC needed to be evaluated by our employees.*" Company 3: "*I have not referred too much to the training content, so I prefer not to evaluate the second question.*" Moreover, this company explained that "*the confidentiality issues and the lack of some relevant questions in the specific topics influence our evaluation.*" Company 4: "*although CYSEC is easy to use, the instructions in the training content are not easy to implement and practical for us.*" Company 5: "*CYSEC provides lots of training material in one place. However, the gamification elements of showing progress need to be more transparent.*" Company 6: "*the logic behind the questions needs to be improved to better support adaptation.*" CYSEC usefulness was perceived to be high by Company 1, Company 4 and Company 6, rather high by Company 2 and Company 5, and medium by Company 3. The lowest rank (medium [M]) chosen by Company 3 put a strong emphasis on a) confidentiality before and during the study and b) the lack of relevant questions in specific advanced topics. This result indicates that a tool like CYSEC that is based on self-assessment and tailored training modules was accepted as a do-it-yourself approach allowing SMBs to manage most capabilities.

**Table 4.** Questionnaire for the workshops' part 4.

| Part 4 questionnaire | ID 1 | ID 2 | ID 3 | ID 4 | ID5 | ID6 |
|---|---|---|---|---|---|---|
| Have you been aware of these threats/vulnerabilities? (Content) | RH | RH | H | RH | RH | H |
| How do you evaluate the quality of the information in the training content? | RH | RH | – | RH | RH | H |
| Does the training content send a clear message about the threat severity or your vulnerability? | RH | M | M | RH | RH | RH |
| Are the instructions of the training content doable? | H | RH | M | M | H | H |
| How easy is applying CYSEC (easy to use)? | RH | – | M | H | H | H |
| How useful is applying CYSEC to improve your security awareness and capability? | H | RH | M | H | RH | H |

## 7 Discussion

We have presented an approach for allowing SMBs to improve their cybersecurity in a DIY fashion. This result allows moving from a bespoke, consultancy-centred advisory to an automated model of communicating cybersecurity knowledge that is scalable yet individualised, hence allows to serve many SMBs with little effort. Our approach implements the self-determination theory [21], which describes the motivation for achieving outcomes and the factors influencing such motivation. SDT is not the only relevant theory, however. Protection motivation theory [19] is one of the widely used theories and would offer an alternative for method and tool design, allowing us to focus on motivating the users to protect their assets and company. We have chosen to implement SDT first as, in our understanding, the improvement of cybersecurity also concerns the creation of new capabilities in the organisation: installing and configuring tools, establishing policies, and training employees beyond just protecting an asset.

In a multi-case study, we offered insights on the actual use of our designed method and tool in real-world SMB settings. Such validation goes beyond just evaluating intentions as in [19] or theoretical relationship as in the common survey-based studies. The presented work is the first step towards operationalising SDT and using it to achieve an impact on practice. As a result, we have discovered issues for future research that would not have been discovered otherwise. The findings of the study suggest that one challenge of motivating and supporting SMBs is the choice of knowledge that is being communicated. The wrong knowledge, extraneous security awareness details, or knowledge gaps reduce motivation and influence the adoption of security recommendations. Also, we discovered a potential barrier that should be addressed by future research: confidentiality. While SDT emphasises relatedness, we observed resistance to documenting and sharing security-related information both within and among companies. Alleviating confidentiality worries is crucial for improving the method's success.

Following Yin [27], our study has the following threats to validity. **Construct validity:** are the operational measures for the concepts being studied correct? Our choice of constructs is based on SDT (Table 1) that we implemented in the CYSEC tool (Table 2) and discussed with the study participants. We described how we had implemented the constructs and offered a chain of evidence between the answers to the research questions and the data collected in the workshops. To ensure that the results reflect not only our subjective impressions, we did member checking.

**Internal Validity:** Can the cause-effect relationships in SDT be distinguished from bogus relationships? We used pattern matching and explanation-building for addressing internal validity threats. We identified relevant observations and feedback collected in the workshops and evaluated which ones spoke for a relationship, respectively against, resulting in the reported analysis. We also asked for what could have influenced the assessment, for example, whether the participants had cybersecurity training before the workshop to rule out the influence of such expertise. A longitudinal study, e.g., based on follow-up surveys, could be a research strategy for evaluating whether and how the SMBs change their practices with extended use of the CYSEC tool.

**External Validity:** Can the study be generalised? The participating SMBs were diverse but still had similarities: all were active in the digitisation, had a CISO without deep expertise in cybersecurity but several years of experience, and did not provide any training to their employees. Since they had some knowledge in cybersecurity, they were able to answer the questions without continually referring to the training content and succeeded to implement some security controls. However, this study has not covered a) SMBs with considerable expertise in the cybersecurity b) SMBs that hardly use IT, and c) SMBs without any budget and personnel for cybersecurity. The study results may change for such SMBs because of different knowledge needs and relevance of assessment questions and improvement recommendations.

**Reliability:** Can the study be replicated with the same results? We developed and piloted a case study protocol that we applied in the main study. The protocol ensured that the operational steps were clear and that each SMB had enough time to use the tool without distraction. All the steps were traced in a case study database. To strengthen the chain of evidence, we presented our findings to the participating SMBs' subjects and cybersecurity experts in a formal meeting for correction (member checking).

## 8 Summary and Conclusions

The paper has evaluated the actual usage of the CYSEC, a do-it-yourself (DIY) security assessment and improvement method for small and medium-sized businesses (SMBs), through an explanatory multi-case study. This study followed a deductive approach and tested constructs drawn on the Self-Determination Theory to evaluate the impact of the method on the effectiveness of cybersecurity communication to the SMBs. We applied observation and feedback questionnaires for data collection.

The results support the influence of the following features on communication effectiveness and users' motivation: expert knowledge, self-adaptating assessment question, action cockpit for connectedness in SMBs, self-adaptating recommendations, provided capability areas, and progress summary. They empower SMBs in adopting and adhering to cybersecurity. The content, including questionnaires and recommendations, need to be presented in an easy-to-understand manner to improve users' competency. The assessment questionnaires and recommendations need to adapt to each specific SMB to increase autonomy. Also, for users' acceptance and adherence, CYSEC needs to consider the company confidentiality seriously. Users are emotionally connected to the SMBs' data do not want to share their information, especially about vulnerabilities, with the tool or third parties outside the SMB. Thus, confidentiality, trust, and relatedness may influence security communication and tool acceptance positively.

**Acknowledgements.** This work was made possible with funding from the European Union's Horizon 2020 research and innovation programme under grant agreement No 740787 (SMESEC) and the Swiss State Secretariat for Education, Research and Innovation (SERI) under contract number 17.00067. The opinions expressed and arguments employed herein do not necessarily reflect the official views of these funding bodies.

## References

1. Muller, P., et al.: Annual report on European SMEs 2016/2017: Focus on self-employment. European Commission (2017)
2. Caldwell, T.: Securing small businesses – the weakest link in a supply chain? Comput. Fraud Secur. **2015**, 5–10 (2015)
3. Ntouskas, T., Papanikas, D., Polemi, N.: A collaborative system offering security management services for SMEs/mEs. In: Georgiadis, C.K., Jahankhani, H., Pimenidis, E., Bashroush, R., Al-Nemrat, A. (eds.) e-Democracy/ICGS3 -2011. LNICSSITE, vol. 99, pp. 220–228. Springer, Heidelberg (2012). https://doi.org/10.1007/978-3-642-33448-1_30
4. Goucher, W.: Do SMEs have the right attitude to security? Comput. Fraud Secur. **2011**, 18–20 (2011)
5. Gupta, A., Hammond, R.: Information systems security issues and decisions for small businesses: an empirical examination. Inf. Manage. Comput. Secur. **13**, 297–310 (2005)
6. Mijnhardt, F., Baars, T., Spruit, M.: Organizational characteristics influencing SME information security maturity. J. Comput. Inf. Syst. **56**(11), 106–115 (2016)
7. Kurpjuhn, T.: The SME security challenge. Comput. Fraud Secur. **2015**, 5–7 (2015)

8. Valli, C., Martinus, I.C., Johnstone, M.N.: Small to Medium Enterprise Cyber Security Awareness: an initial survey of Western Australian Business (2014)
9. Brunner, M., Sillaber, C., Breu, R.: Towards automation in information security management systems. In: 2017 IEEE International Conference on Software Quality, Reliability and Security (QRS), Prague, Czech Republic, pp. 160–167. IEEE (2017)
10. Furnell, S.M., Gennatou, M., Dowland, P.S.: A prototype tool for information security awareness and training. Logist. Inf. Manage. **15**, 352–357 (2002)
11. Dhillon, G., Torkzadeh, G.: Value-focused assessment of information system security in organizations. Inf. Syst. J. **16**, 293–314 (2006)
12. Cranor, L.F.: A framework for reasoning about the human in the loop. In: UPSEC 2008 Proceedings of the 1st Conference on Usability, Psychology, Security, Berkeley, USA (2008)
13. Pahnila, S., Siponen, M., Mahmood, A.: Employees' behavior towards IS security policy compliance. In: 40th Annual Hawaii International Conference on System Sciences (HICSS 2007), Hawaii, USA, pp. 156–166. IEEE (2007)
14. Rhee, H.-S., Kim, C., Ryu, Y.U.: Self-efficacy in information security: its influence on end users' information security practice behavior. Comput. Secur. **28**, 816–826 (2009)
15. Shojaifar, A., Fricker, S.A., Gwerder, M.: Elicitation of SME requirements for cybersecurity solutions by studying adherence to recommendations. In: REFSQ Workshops (2018)
16. Albrechtsen, E., Hovden, J.: The information security digital divide between information security managers and users. Comput. Secur. **28**, 476–490 (2009)
17. West, R.: The psychology of security. Commun. ACM **51**(4), 34–40 (2008)
18. Hayes, J.: The Theory and Practice of Change Management. Palgrave, New York (2002)
19. Menard, P., Bott, G.J., Crossler, R.E.: User motivations in protecting information security: protection motivation theory versus self-determination theory. J. Manage. Inf. Syst. **34**(4), 1203–1230 (2017)
20. Pham, H.C., Pham, D.D., Brennan, L., Richardson, J.: Information security and people: a conundrum for compliance. AJIS **21**, 1–16 (2017)
21. Ryan, R.M., Deci, E.L.: Self-determination theory and the facilitation of intrinsic motivation, social development, and well-being. Am. Psychol. **55**, 68–78 (2000)
22. Deci, E.L., Ryan, R.M.: Self-determination theory: a macrotheory of human motivation, development, and health. Can. Psychol. **49**(3), 182–185 (2008)
23. Deci, E.L., Ryan, R.M.: The general causality orientations scale: self-determination in personality. J. Res. Pers. **19**(2), 109–134 (1985)
24. Deming, W.E.: Elementary principles of the statistical control of quality. Nippon Kagaku Gigutsu Remmei: Japanese Union of Science and Engineering (JUSE) (1951)
25. Yigit Ozkan, B., Spruit, M.: A questionnaire model for cybersecurity maturity assessment of critical infrastructures. In: Fournaris, A.P., Lampropoulos, K., Marín Tordera, E. (eds.) IOSec 2018. LNCS, vol. 11398, pp. 49–60. Springer, Cham (2019). https://doi.org/10.1007/978-3-030-12085-6_5
26. Gardner, B., Thomas, V.: Building an Information Security Awareness Program: Defending Against Social Engineering and Technical Threats. Elsevier/Syngress, Amsterdam (2014)
27. Yin, R.K.: Case Study Research: Design and Methods, 4th edn. Sage, Thousand Oaks (2009)
28. Bennett, R.J., Robinson, S.L.: Development of a measure of workplace deviance. J. Appl. Psychol. **85**(3), 349–360 (2000)
29. Runeson, P., Höst, M., Rainer, A., Regnell, B.: Case Study Research in Software Engineering: Guidelines and Examples. Wiley, Hoboken (2012)

# Gaming for Cybersecurity Training

# A Serious Game-Based Peer-Instruction Digital Forensics Workshop

Ludwig Englbrecht(✉) and Günther Pernul

Department of Information Systems, University of Regensburg, Regensburg, Germany
{ludwig.englbrecht,guenther.pernul}@wiwi.uni-regensburg.de

**Abstract.** Increasing threats in the area of information security raise the necessity for companies to be prepared for a digital forensic investigation. However, even the best investments in technology and infrastructure will fail if employees are not adequately trained. In this paper we propose a workshop concept combining the peer instruction method and elements from the field of serious games. The goal of the combined methods is to enable the participants to investigate a use case in an interactive and playful way. Our concept guides the participants step by step into an increasingly independent way of performing a digital forensic investigation.

**Keywords:** Digital Forensics · Workshop · Peer instruction · Serious games · Capture the Flag

## 1 Introduction

Over the past few years, threats exposed by cybercrime has increased significantly around the world. Due to the increasing threat of cybercrime, many companies are implementing ambitious technical measures to ensure information security. In doing so, they often rely mainly on defensive IT security measures instead of benefiting from methods from the field of Digital Forensics (DF). Digital traces collected during forensic investigations allow a comprehensive clarification of an IT security incident and can also be used as conclusive evidence in court [1].

However, the best security system is useless if cybercriminals can obtain confidential information by manipulating targets. People are often underestimated and seen as one of the biggest risk factors for information security. Inadvertent actions, a lack of security culture and insufficiently trained personnel are a popular target for attackers in most companies.

Consequently, raising employee awareness for computer crime and the use of DF techniques in companies contribute to a holistic information security. In this context the human has been recognized as an important information security factor. Von Solms and Warren [2] proposes a risk framework that can be used to understand human security issues originating from a lack of security awareness.


Published by Springer Nature Switzerland AG 2020
L. Drevin et al. (Eds.): WISE 2020, IFIP AICT 579, pp. 127–141, 2020.
https://doi.org/10.1007/978-3-030-59291-2_9

A human can make a valuable contribution to the detection of an IT security incident if he or she detects and reports suspicious activities [3].

An enterprise can be prepared for a possible investigation of an IT security incident. Besides the technical and organizational measures, employees play a central part in DF. A well-planned training course for employees can make a massive contribution to being prepared for a DF investigation. The awareness for DF can significantly increase the maturity level of a company for Digital Forensic Readiness (DFR). However, this aspect is one of the most difficult challenges to reach a company-wide maturity level in DFR [4].

The aim of our workshop concept is to provide the participants with the skills of a DF investigation. The participants are put into the role of a DF expert, collect data and analyze traces in order to be able to understand procedures of a DF investigation. Furthermore, their awareness of cybercrime should be increased.

The paper is structured as follows. In the following section we present basics in DF, peer instruction, and serious game concepts. The development approach for a workshop concept is presented in Sect. 3. In Sect. 4 a possible implementation of the workshop is described. Section 5 provides a summary and an outlook on future work.

## 2 Background and Related Work

### 2.1 Digital Forensics

The forensic science deals with the application of scientific methods for investigations in legal cases [5]. Forensic scientists have to adapt questions of a legal case into scientific questions and answer these by using appropriate and scientifically validated methods [6]. This means, that DF has to provide profound methods to preserve and process digital evidence to guarantee the highest possible objectivity in DF investigations [7].

The collection and analysis of digital evidence must be based on a defined procedure. The model of Kent et al. [8] is a common procedure for forensic investigations. The investigation process is divided into four phases: *Collection, Examination, Analysis and Reporting.* This model has been used as a baseline for our workshop.

### 2.2 Peer Instruction Learning

Peer instruction (PI) was developed by the physicist Eric Mazur as part of his lectures at Harvard University [9]. Studies have shown the improvement of learning success through the use of the method [9,10]. This led to an increased application of PI in the teaching of scientific subjects.

DF combines concepts from three different disciplines: computer science, criminology and law. The use of PI is intended to facilitate the understanding of DF and the interaction of the three subject areas [9].

**Objectives Pursued Through PI.** One goal is the activation of the participants by toggling between professional input and PI comprehension questions. With this the participants are actively involved in the lecture and are encouraged to cooperate. They are also encouraged to not only passively learn the material, but to independently reflect and interpret the learning content and to link it to their previous knowledge [9].

**Deepening the Understanding of the Concept.** PI focuses on promoting a basic understanding of concepts. Questions concerning the understanding help to internalize and adapt what has been learned. The greatest learning effect is achieved through the discussion phase. The participants are asked to convince others of their own solution to the question by using technical arguments. In this way, cognitive learning processes are initiated and the participants benefit from the form of learning through teaching. In addition, ambiguities, misunderstandings and misconceptions are identified and can be solved in a targeted manner [9].

**Instant Feedback to the Teacher.** This teaching method enables the teacher to verify knowledge already during the lecture and receives direct feedback about how much the participants have understood. The teacher can then adapt the design of the course to the needs of the learners. This can be done, for example, to specifically address uncovered ambiguities or knowledge gaps [9].

However, the above-mentioned objectives can only be achieved if the method is implemented correctly. The procedure of a PI sequence and the formation of effective comprehension questions are explained in detail in the following section.

### 2.3 Serious Game Concepts

Games can provide an interacting and motivational environment for learning [11]. Entertainment can be seen as the main motivation for traditional games. However, in the last decade, serious games that combine both computer and video games for non-entertaining purposes have become popular [12]. For this work we use Marsh's definition [12].

We also focus on digital game-based learning in an experiential environment. This is one aspect of the serious games continuum. In experiential environments, an *inductive learning* approach is used. In comparison to that, traditional instructional design usually includes methods to encourage *deductive learning*.

Inductive learning empowers students to deepen their understanding of content and develop their inference and evidence-gathering skills. This concept has been successfully applied in privacy-related areas to increase the awareness of shared information via social networks [13]. Inductive learning also provides a powerful setting to let students discover and verify hypotheses during a DF investigation. Adapted to our workshop digital evidence are meant to be found and verified to reconstruct a malicious action.

## 3 A Serious Game-Based Peer-Instruction Digital Forensics Workshop

By combining PI with a competitive serious game, we pursue three main goals in our workshop concept. After a motivational lecture under the guidance of the lecturer, the students are supposed to switch to an independent processing mode. The lecturer guides the students and checks their understanding of the task at regular intervals. The second goal is to gradually reduce the workload of the lecturer. This is achieved by systematically reducing the amount of assistance. And the third goal is that the students solve the challenges of a Capture the Flag (CTF) as independently as possible and thereby experience a game-based and competitive-like character of the workshop. In Fig. 1 our workshop concept is illustrated and grouped into five phases. In the following the different phases and the relation to the workload of the lecturer *(light grey)* and the workload of the students *(dark grey)* over the time will be described:

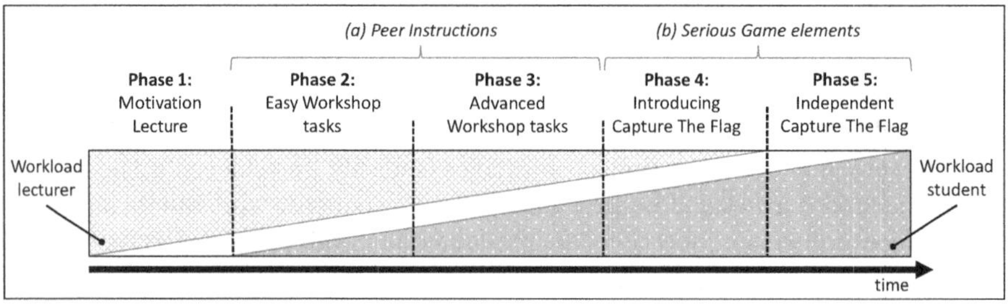


**Fig. 1.** Illustration of our workshop concept

**Phase 1: Motivation Lecture.** In this phase a motivating lecture on the topic of DF will be held. This will show the basics and general procedures of DF. In addition, the special features of digital evidence and the investigation process will be explained. The teaching content has its origin in a Europe-wide decentralized cybersecurity curriculum [14]. This source enables the usage and exchange of clear content, module and delivery structure, and the appropriate tool support to facilitate collaboration and content reuse. In this phase the students only have to listen attentively and do not have to perform any activities.

**Phase 2: Easy Workshop Tasks.** At the beginning of the actual workshop unit the case of the examination is briefly presented. A story frame will be created which will continue through the next phases.

In this phase the students are introduced to the techniques for the clarification of an IT security incident. The lecturer must still provide considerable support in the use of the forensics tools and the explanation of case-specific characteristics. By using peer-instruction, students can be given small tasks to find traces and to deduce the cause of the incident. In phase 2 and 3 PI is used several times as a short sequence during the lecture.

In a PI sequence, the participants are asked a multiple-choice format question about the content of the course. They are given two to three minutes to answer the question by hand signals, voting slips, clickers or mobile devices [10]. The aim of this first vote is to obtain a spontaneous and individual answer to the question asked by the instructor [9].

Depending on the results, the continuation of the lecture will be adjusted accordingly. If the participants answer the question correctly between 30% and 80%, a peer discussion and a second vote is held [10,15]. In the discussion, the participants are given three to five minutes to convince their neighbors of their own solution with arguments. By explaining the problem to each other, conceptual thinking processes are set in motion and the understanding is deepened. Consequently, the rate of correct answers is usually higher in the second vote [10].

If the rate of correct answers is less than 30%, the teacher needs to provide further explanations and then repeat the vote. However, if more than 80% of the answers are correct after the first vote, the question can be resolved by one participant and the discussion phase can be skipped [15].

The success of the PI method is therefore primarily dependent on the questions of understanding. The intention is not to ask for knowledge, but to facilitate the processing and internalization of the contents.

The formulation of questions of understanding is crucial for the learning success of the participants when using PI. The aim of the multiple-choice questions is to promote the transfer of knowledge, to motivate discussion among the participants and to check the understanding of the presented content. Answering the questions should require the application of concepts and the transfer of previously learned knowledge. In this way the greatest learning effect is achieved [10]. In this paper the process of developing comprehension-oriented questions is applied and illustrated in Fig. 2.

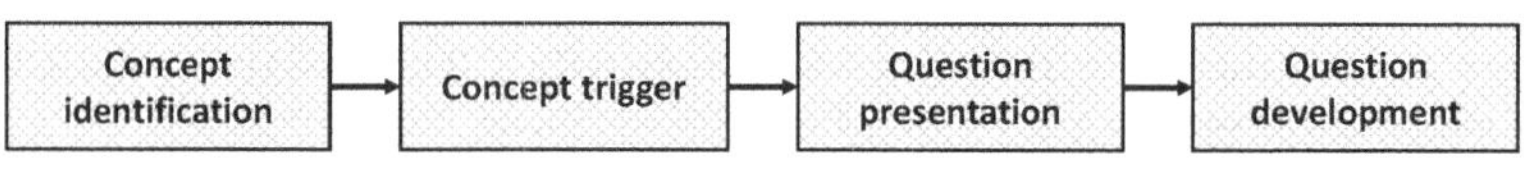


**Fig. 2.** Process for developing peer instruction conceptual questions (based on [10])

**Concept Identification.** The concept is determined, which needs to be conveyed to the participants through the PI question [10,16].

**Concept Trigger.** Suitable "concept triggers" are selected to be included in the question. These are hidden elements that cause conceptual thought processes in the participants and should stimulate discussion [16]. An example is "Compare and contrast", in which the participants have to compare different situations with each other and conclude on the correct solution [10].

With the concept trigger *Use "none of the above"* the participants are given the opportunity to reject the remaining answer options and to think about alternatives [10].

**Question Presentation.** The next step is to determine how the question should be formulated and presented. There are various possibilities: In the scenario question, a scenario is described to which the question of understanding refers. The participants have to check the described situation for its clearly formulated and implied characteristics and decide on the correct answer. Example-Questions, however, are limited to giving an example (e.g. an excerpt of a code). This variant leaves less room for interpretation than the scenario question. In a Definition Question, a definition is given, so that in order to answer the question, it is necessary to differentiate from other concepts. In the Diagram Question, a corresponding graph must be interpreted correctly in order to solve the question of understanding. In feature-questions, certain features of a concept must be correctly identified and assigned [10].

**Question Development.** The multiple-choice comprehension question is then formulated and completed on the basis of the previous process steps [10].

**Phase 3: Advanced Workshop Tasks.** In this phase, the degree of difficulty with regard to finding and interpreting digital traces is systematically increased. Tools such as *file carvers* and elements from the field of *open source intelligence* will be used. Since the lecturer has already introduced the analysis environment and tools in the previous phase, a low level of support from the lecturer is expected in this phase. The students will also learn to answer the questions of the lecturer more independently. By means of peer-instruction, the lecturer can monitor the learning progress and repeat teaching content if necessary.

**Phase 4: Development of a Subsequent Capture the Flag.** In the previous phase the students have already learned to use and work with the forensics tools. Now the participants move into a competition. This means that the participants can now form teams and a CTF to the presented case is carried out. In this phase the instructor must explain the procedure and the rules of the CTF. A CTF is a good concept to introduce students to a variety of technical concepts within the computer science curriculum [17].

Through the previous phases the students have a common level of knowledge in DF and are already familiar with the case that needs to be analyzed. With this, the story has already been imparted for a serious game. Especially the use of a CTF ensures at that point of time an active and playful participation in the investigation of the incident. The main goal of this serious game situation is to encourage a competitive atmosphere between the groups.

The individual stages of the CTF can now be solved by the student with the methods learned before. By submitting the solution the students can find out if the solution was correct. In this phase, the lecturer steps more and more into the background in order not to disturb the competitive spirit. However, he offers assistance in case of unexpected complications.

**Phase 5: Independent Capture the Flag.** The last phase of the workshop is mainly focused on the independent solution of given challenges within the CTF. The procedure is similar to the previous phase. However, it is important that the lecturer is only marginally available for questions. The goal for the participants is to work out a dynamic and independent solution for practical questions in the field of DF. This can even go so far that the lecturer is no longer physically present and can only be reached by email. This phase can be extended to a period of several days as the students can solve the questions independently of their location.

## 4 Instantiating of the Workshop Concept

The basic course architecture is designed to be a more generalized concept within the cybersecurity discipline. This enables a broad adaption in DF and related areas (e.g. incident response or malware analysis). We focus within our instantiating of the workshop concept on business-related crime to attract the attention of managers and decision-makers of an organization.

### 4.1 Conception of the Workshop

Based on the theoretical foundations of digital forensics described in Sect. 2 and the proven teaching method of PI, the workshop on the investigation of white-collar crime using Mobile Forensics Analysis was designed in four successive steps. The development process is based on a top-down approach. The methodology describes a procedure in which the planning stages are concretized step by step from top to bottom and finally a connection is established.

The first step was to define the objectives and target group of the workshop. The next step was to determine the practical and theoretical knowledge, taking into account the characteristics of the participants, which is necessary to achieve the previously defined goals. The contents are to be worked out by the workshop participants themselves in a use case and internalized by PI and a CTF. In the third step, a fictitious white-collar crime case was developed with the decisive roles and scenes that are used for forensic clarification. At the same time, the PI comprehension questions and CTF challenges were formulated to deepen the presented contents. Based on this, the schedule of the workshop was determined.

### 4.2 The Goal of the Workshop

For a successful workshop concept it is essential to define the objectives and the target group. Both points have a significant influence on the subsequent elaboration. The definition of the objectives and target group of the workshop is described below.

Companies are increasingly becoming victims of cybercrime and the digital attacks are also costing companies a significant amount of money. Given this increasing threat, organizations are making a high technical effort to protect themselves from attacks. However, people are regularly underestimated and seen as one of the biggest risk factors for information security. Besides technology, the consideration of the human factor as a security measure is also decisive. The aim of our workshop is to sensitize the participants to the topic of cybercrime and thus to minimize the dangers caused by employees in this area in companies and organizations.

The use of DF enables companies not only to detect cyber attacks but also to prosecute the perpetrators. However, many organizations have not yet been aware of the benefits of DF in this context. For this reason, the workshop aims to use Mobile Forensics Analysis to clarify a fictitious white-collar crime case in order to strengthen the understanding of the importance of information security in companies and to illustrate the role of DF in securing evidence that can be used in court and in solving the crime.

**Target Group.** The technical measures and the associated IT experts are only one part of a security system. The workshop focuses on managers since they are responsible for personnel management tasks and thus have a significant influence on the behavior of other employees in the company. In addition, young professionals and graduates, i.e. young employees who are about to start their careers are among the target groups of the workshop. They are highly motivated to put their knowledge into practice. This can contribute to the rapid spread of a security-aware culture within a company.

Based on the defined objectives and the characteristics of the defined target group, the content of the workshop is determined in the next section.

### 4.3 Definition of the Content of the Workshop

The aim of the workshop is to sensitize the participants to the tactics of cybercriminals and to create an awareness for responsible security actions in everyday life. When determining the content of the workshop, it must be taken into account that the participants do not necessarily have in-depth IT knowledge. The presented contents and all connections must be coherent, understandable and interesting. In this way, the attention of the participants can be maintained throughout the entire presentation and thus the best learning effect can be achieved.

In our workshop the participants should first be informed about current threats of cybercrime in general to get motivated. They will also learn current cases, causes of threats, (resulting) damages and factors that promote cyber attacks in companies. They will also learn the characteristics of the most common manifestations: phishing (identity theft), malware, ransomware (digital blackmail), social engineering, botnets, DDoS attacks and CaaS.

After an introduction to a fictitious white-collar crime case to be dealt with, the workshop participants are thereafter introduced to the forensic process according to Kent et al. [8] as an essential component of DF. The interaction between employees and IT experts is crucial in forensic investigations and will be highlighted in the lecture.

Using a fictitious case study, the tasks of the four phases of the investigation process Collection, Examination, Analysis and Reporting are demonstrated. The focus is particularly on understanding the volatility of digital evidence. Knowledge about this shows that evidence can be inadvertently destroyed in the event of an IT security incident. In this context, the participants will be familiarized with the characteristics of persistent, semi-persistent and volatile traces. They will learn that traces must be captured according to a specific sequence of preservation, depending on their volatility, and that they must be collected and processed by means of post-mortem or live analysis.

Through the live analysis of digital traces using examples, the participants are given the opportunity to put themselves in the role of an IT forensic scientist and apply the basic principles of forensic science. For this purpose, hypotheses are established during the clarification of the fictitious white-collar crime case and verified or falsified during the forensic investigation process. The digital traces found are identified, classified and individualized according to Inman and Rudin [18]. Subsequently, the associations are established and based on this the course of events is reconstructed. Finally, the participants receive recommendations for behavior with regard to cyber attacks and preventive measures for companies are explained.

The practical and theoretical contents and interrelationships are better demonstrated within the workshop by working through the use case. This will be explained in detail in the next section.

### 4.4 Development of a Use Case

By processing a use case, the participants of the workshop are expected to understand cybercrime and DF techniques. The workshop will use realistic case descriptions to demonstrate cybercrime and the procedure of a DF investigation.

The reasons for espionage have remained unchanged to this day. However, the methods and possibilities have evolved over time. Nowadays, for example, services for committing or supporting computer-based crimes (e.g. CaaS) can be easily purchased over the internet [19]. The illegal services offered include the sale of commercial malware such as spyware, which enables to spy on the infected system and thus obtain confidential information.

The use case is a core component of the workshop and, in view of this new threat potential, addresses the use of the popular manifestations of computer crime. Especially CaaS and social engineering in the context of espionage will be addressed.

The participants will be introduced to the case study with the presentation of two fictitious companies in the lighting industry. Hyperlight AG is the current market leader with a turnover of approximately 4 billion EUR and would like to secure its competitive position in the future. Luxia AG (approx. 2 million EUR turnover), on the other hand, has only a small market share so far. By installing a commercial spyware on the smartphone of a sales representative of the competitor company, Luxia AG can gain considerable competitive advantages through espionage. As a result, Hyperlight AG suffers high material and immaterial damages.

The task of the participants is to put themselves in the role of an IT forensic scientist and to clarify and reconstruct this course of events through forensic investigation. The four phases of the investigation - collection, examination, analysis and reporting - are explained step by step and illustrated using examples. In the collection phase they learn about the characteristics of persistent, semi-persistent and volatile data and the differences between post-mortem and live analysis are explained. On the basis of the knowledge acquired, the participants decide to perform a live analysis on the infected smartphone. The examination of the application memory, network traffic and browser cache will be illustrated as realistically as possible by providing a modified smartphone. The digital traces found are identified, classified and individualized according to Inman and Rudin [18]. Based on the derived associations and verified hypotheses the course of events can be reconstructed step by step:

Luxia AG has made use of the illegal business model CaaS. CaaS generally offers a comprehensive range of tools and technologies as services to support or carry out cyber attacks. The participants can be made aware of the fact that nowadays no extensive IT knowledge is necessary to carry out cyber attacks. In this way, commercial spyware is installed on the smartphone of the Hyperlight AG sales employee by the competitor company. This is initially noticeable through conspicuous features such as slow reaction times, program crashes and disturbances during telephone calls. In this way, the workshop participants learn about the signs of an infected mobile phone. They also discover that the spyware collects a variety of confidential information such as GPS data, messages and images unnoticed and without the system user's consent, and forward it to the attacker's server. To install commercial spyware, usually physical access to the smartphone is required.

This is intended to sensitize workshop participants to the fact that social engineering can be used to obtain safety-relevant data comparatively easily by exploiting human components. After the clarification and reconstruction of the course of events, the material and immaterial damages following a cyber attack will be discussed using Hyperlight AG as an example. During the processing of the use case, the knowledge transfer is checked and deepened several times by PI comprehension questions. The next section deals with the development of the corresponding questions.

### 4.5 Formulation of Peer Instruction Comprehension Questions

Peer instruction comprehension questions are not intended to test knowledge, but rather to facilitate the participants' understanding and internalization of the contents presented. In addition, the discussion potential of the question is particularly important in order to initiate thought processes and thus achieve the greatest learning success. Five PI sequences will be used in the workshop. In the following, the development of the comprehension-oriented questions used in the lecture will be explained.

The first PI comprehension question is based on the development of cybercrime as presented earlier in this paper. For this purpose, current cases are presented on the one hand and diagrams are shown on the other hand on the increase in the number of cyber attacks and the costs of companies in connection with computer crime (Example/Diagram-Question). In order to answer the question, it is necessary to interpret and reason the diagrams (Concept Triggers: Interpret representations, Analysis and reasoning). In this way, the participants learn about the factors that promote cyber attacks (Concept Triggers: Extend the context). In the use case, features of a smartphone infected with spyware are listed (Feature-Question).

In order to answer the second question of understanding, these signs must be compared with the characteristics of the various manifestations of cybercrime that have been identified previously (Concept Trigger: Compare and contrast). It is necessary to select those types of cyber attacks that can cause the described abnormalities. By answering the question, the participants are also given the option of rejecting the remaining answers (Concept Trigger: Use "none of the above"). This should motivate them to think about alternative solutions.

The workshop covers the properties and effects of spywares and fileless malware (scenario question). Participants have previously learned how to use post-mortem and live analysis. In the context of the third PI comprehension question, they have to decide on the appropriate approach for obtaining and processing digital traces in the respective situation (Concept Trigger: Qualitative question). In order to answer the question, it is necessary to compare the two approaches (Concept Trigger: Compare and contrast). Based on this, the correct solution can be concluded after the analysis of the described scenario (Concept Trigger: Analysis and reasoning).

After the incident has been reconstructed (Scenario-Question), the workshop participants should identify the damage caused by the cyber attack in the context of the fourth comprehension-oriented question (Concept Trigger: Qualitative questions). To answer the question, assumptions must be made (Concept Trigger: Require unstated assumptions). This is intended to sensitize the participants to potential material and immaterial damage.

Based on the content presented within the workshop, especially the characteristics of DF investigations, the final question of understanding will address possible problems of criminal prosecution of cyber attacks (feature-question) (Concept Trigger: Extend the context). For this purpose, the respective answer options of the multiple-choice question must be evaluated and justified by the participants (Concept Trigger: Qualitative question, Analysis and reasoning).

Through these five PI comprehension questions, the teacher can verify the participants' knowledge and receive feedback on how much the participants have understood. The distribution of questions during the workshop is illustrated in the next section.

### 4.6 Time Schedule of the Workshop

After determining the theoretical foundations of DF to be taught, developing the use case and formulating the PI comprehension questions, the workshop was developed. As a final result of the conception, the corresponding time schedule and procedure will be described in detail in this section.

A total of three and a half hours are scheduled for the workshop (break/s are not included). This allows the workshop to be held as a half-day teaching module. The lecture will be divided into the following sections:

**Phase 1: Introduction and Motivation.** First, the participants are introduced to the topic. Current cases of cybercrime will be highlighted and the increasing threats of cyber attacks for companies will be illustrated with adequate diagrams. Then the potential material and immaterial damages are discussed. The participants will also learn about the manifestations of phishing, malware, ransomware (digital blackmail), social engineering, botnets, DDoS attacks and CaaS. This section will take about 30 minutes to motivate the students and to frame the context.

**Phase 2: Presentation of the Use Case.** Next, the use case is presented. Subsequently, the participants are asked to relate the described signs of an infected smartphone to the corresponding manifestations of cybercrime they have previously learned. This is performed by means of a PI comprehension question. Furthermore, a first hypothesis is put forward and spyware as a specific form of malware is explained. This section will take about 30 min to bring up ideas and discuss the input of the participants followed by performing easy workshop tasks.

**Phase 3: Forensic Investigation 1/2.** The third section begins with a short presentation of the forensic investigation process. The tasks of the first process step *collection* are explained. In particular, the volatility of digital traces and the backup sequence based on them are illustrated. In addition, the participants will learn the characteristics and use of the basic approaches of post-mortem and live analysis. The understanding will be tested with a PI comprehension question. Next, the *examination phase* of an investigation will be introduced. It is necessary to analyze application memory, network traffic and browser cache of the smartphone for digital traces. For this section about 30 min are planned to find a good balance between the explanation of the tools and the interpretation of the results.

**Phase 4: Forensic Investigation 2/2.** This section introduces the core of the workshop, the *analysis phase*. Participants will learn how to apply the basic principles of forensic science to the Inman and Rudin forensic process [18]. The digital traces found by the participants are identified, classified and individualized. Subsequently, associations are made and previously established hypotheses are verified. In phase 4 the CTF is introduced first and the participants solve different challenges under guidance. Finally, the case will be reconstructed and the extent of damage caused by the cyber attack will be discussed.

The last step of the forensic investigation process, the reporting, is described. A cyber kill chain will then be drawn and the course of events will be summarized once again using the seven points Reconnaissance, Weaponization, Delivery, Exploitation, Installation, Command and Control, and Actions on Objectives [20].

The presentation of preventive measures is important to bridge the gap between the fictitious case and possible future situations. The workshop concludes with the presentation of measures to prevent cyber attacks. The participants will receive recommendations for behavior and preventive measures for companies and organizations will be explained. Approximately 15 min are scheduled for the presentation of preventive measures.

The lecture contains a total of five PI comprehension questions to review and deepen the presented contents. For each question 5–9 min are planned (these are already included in the duration of the respective section). For the whole phase 4, about 90 min are scheduled.

**Phase 5: Capture the Flag.** The last phase of the workshop is mainly focused on the independent solution of given CTF questions. The concept of a CTF is applied. For this phase the remaining time as well as time after the workshop can be used. This means that the participants can solve the challenges after the workshop.

The workshop should also be prepared and followed up. The preparation includes the planning of a sufficiently large room. Furthermore, the technology required for the presentation should be checked beforehand. The schedule and agenda of the workshop can be sent electronically to the participants a few days before. In the follow-up, a protocol of the results should be provided together with feedback forms. The time planned for the CTF is very individual and can range from a minimum of 30 min to a period of days. This allows the students to pursue and deepen the content outside of the workshop.

## 5 Conclusion and Future Work

Companies are increasingly becoming victims of cybercrime and the digital attacks are also costing companies more and more money. For this reason, a workshop was designed to clarify white-collar crime using Mobile Forensics Analysis. The aim is to sensitize employees of companies and to create an awareness for responsible security actions in everyday life. In addition, the advantages of methods from DF to be able to react quickly and purposefully to cyber attacks need to be illustrated. The workshop was conceived in four successive steps. First, the objectives and target group were defined in detail. Based on this, the theoretical and practical knowledge about cybercrime and DF has been defined. This has been incorporated in a use case and enriched with PI comprehension questions. The use of the teaching method PI supports the processing and internalization of the presented contents during the entire workshop. For this purpose five comprehension-oriented multiple-choice questions and a CTF were formulated. As a final result of the design, a time and sequence plan was then drawn up, linking the previous planning stages.

However, the question of the success of this security awareness measure remains open. To improve and strengthen the security culture is also an important component of a holistic information security. Therefore, the measurement of employee awareness and the effectiveness of an interactive workshop based on the concept of this paper will be addressed in future work.

**Acknowledgment.** This work is partly performed under the BMBF TRIO project which is supported by the German Federal Ministry of Education and Research. (https://www.innovative-hochschule.de/de/innovative-hochschulen/trio).

## References

1. Meier, S.: Digitale Forensik in Unternehmen. Ph.D. thesis, University of Regensburg (2017)
2. von Solms, R., Warren, M.: Towards the human information security firewall. Int. J. Cyber Warfare Terrorism (IJCWT) **1**(2), 10–17 (2011)
3. Vielberth, M., Menges, F., Pernul, G.: Human-as-a-security-sensor for harvesting threat intelligence. Cybersecurity **2**(1), 23 (2019)
4. Englbrecht, L., Meier, S., Pernul, G.: Towards a capability maturity model for digital forensic readiness. Wireless Netw. **26**(7), 4895–4907 (2020). https://doi.org/10.1007/s11276-018-01920-5
5. Cohen, F.: Toward a science of digital forensic evidence examination. In: Chow, K.-P., Shenoi, S. (eds.) DigitalForensics 2010. IAICT, vol. 337, pp. 17–35. Springer, Heidelberg (2010). https://doi.org/10.1007/978-3-642-15506-2_2
6. Elyas, M., Ahmad, A., Maynard, S.B., Lonie, A.: Digital forensic readiness: expert perspectives on a theoretical framework. Comput. Secur. **52**, 70–89 (2015)
7. Grobler, T., Louwrens, C.P., von Solms, S.H.: A framework to guide the implementation of proactive digital forensics in organisations. In: ARES 2010, Fifth International Conference on Availability, Reliability and Security, Krakow, Poland, 15–18 February 2010, pp. 677–682. IEEE Computer Society (2010)
8. Kent, K., Chevalier, S., Grance, T., Dang, H.: Guide to integrating forensic techniques into incident response. NIST Special Publication 10(14), 800–86 (2006)
9. Crouch, C.H., Mazur, E.: Peer instruction: ten years of experience and results. Am. J. Phys. **69**(9), 970–977 (2001)
10. Johnson, W.E., Luzader, A., Ahmed, I., Roussev, V., Richard III, G.G., Lee, C.B.: Development of peer instruction questions for cybersecurity education. In: 2016 USENIX Workshop on Advances in Security Education (ASE 2016). USENIX Association, Austin, TX (2016)
11. Kiili, K.: Digital game-based learning: towards an experiential gaming model. Internet High. Educ. **8**(1), 13–24 (2005)
12. Marsh, T.: Serious games continuum: between games for purpose and experiential environments for purpose. Entertain. Comput. **2**(2), 61–68 (2011)
13. Cetto, A., et al.: Friend inspector: a serious game to enhance privacy awareness in social networks. CoRR abs/1402.5878 (2014)
14. Tokola, T.J., et al.: A collaborative cybersecurity education program. In: Cybersecurity Education for Awareness and Compliance, pp. 181–200. IGI Global (2019)

15. Lasry, N., Mazur, E., Watkins, J.: Peer instruction: from Harvard to the two-year college. Am. J. Phys. **76**(11), 1066–1069 (2008)
16. Ahmed, I., Roussev, V.: Peer instruction teaching methodology for cybersecurity education. IEEE Secur. Priv. **16**(4), 88–91 (2018)
17. McDaniel, L., Talvi, E., Hay, B.: Capture the flag as cyber security introduction. In: 2016 49th Hawaii International Conference on System Sciences (HICSS), pp. 5479–5486, January 2016
18. Inman, K., Rudin, N.: The origin of evidence. Forensic Sci. Int. **126**(1), 11–16 (2002)
19. Manky, D.: Cybercrime as a service: a very modern business. Comput. Fraud Secur. **2013**(6), 9–13 (2013)
20. Yadav, T., Rao, A.M.: Technical aspects of cyber kill chain. In: Abawajy, J.H., Mukherjea, S., Thampi, S.M., Ruiz-Martínez, A. (eds.) SSCC 2015. CCIS, vol. 536, pp. 438–452. Springer, Cham (2015). https://doi.org/10.1007/978-3-319-22915-7_40

# Threat Poker: Gamification of Secure Agile

Audun Jøsang[1(✉)], Viktoria Stray[1], and Hanne Rygge[2]

[1] University of Oslo, Oslo, Norway
{josang,stray}@ifi.uio.no
[2] Norsk Tid AS, Oslo, Norway
hanne.rygge@gmail.com

**Abstract.** Agile software development is practiced in most software development projects around the world. To explicitly consider and include security requirements as part of agile software development is referred to as 'secure agile'. To include security will naturally require additional time and effort, with potentially reduced agility as a consequence. To maintain agility, it is important to have efficient methods to include security in the development process. In this study, we describe enhancements to Threat Poker, which is a game designed for the software development team to deal with security threats identified during the agile development project. Games can be valuable educational tools for actively engaging students and practitioners alike. An experiment with students indicates that playing Threat Poker increases security awareness and that it is a fun and simple way to discuss identified security threats and how to remove security vulnerabilities during the software development process.

## 1 Introduction

Agile software development, currently the most common approach to software development, was not originally conceived with security in mind. As such, many agile projects do not have built-in steps for dealing with security issues. However, with the introduction of new laws and regulations for security, such as GDPR in the EU, design principles for 'security by design' and 'privacy by design' must be followed in order for the developed systems to be legally compliant [1].

'Security by design' and 'privacy by design' are relatively general concepts for describing the integration of security and privacy considerations throughout the life-cycle of ICT systems. The term 'by design' simply means that threat, vulnerability and risk assessment related to information security and privacy must be included in the requirements specification, architecture design, coding, testing, deployment and management of all systems, products and services that involve ICT components. This paper focuses on using gamification to strengthen security and privacy by design during the steps of architecture design and coding.

Gamification [2] is defined as *"The application of typical elements of game playing (e.g., point scoring, competition, rules of play) to other areas of activity,*


Published by Springer Nature Switzerland AG 2020
L. Drevin et al. (Eds.): WISE 2020, IFIP AICT 579, pp. 142–155, 2020.
https://doi.org/10.1007/978-3-030-59291-2_10

*typically as an online marketing technique to encourage engagement with a product or service"*. The principle of gamification is to use various aspects of games to engage the 'players' in the task at hand. Students of software engineering are generally positive to using games to stimulate learning [3]. A recent systematic literature review concluded that gamification in software engineering education is still in its infancy [4]. The authors encourage researchers to explore this topic further since gamification is shown to motivate students and stimulate learning.

Several researchers have introduced games to increase awareness of security in software development projects. For example, Denning *et al.* proposed a tabletop card game called Control-Alt-Hack to generate awareness of security issues and increase the accuracy of people's perceptions of computer security as a discipline [5]. They found that students enjoy playing the game and that it increases their security awareness. Another game called [d0x3d!] is an open-source content-license game (allowing free distribution and adaptation) that provides an artificial context for discussing real ideas in network security [6]. The Security Requirements Educational Game (SREG) is a card-based game that is intended to be used for security-requirements education and that has shown to increase the understanding of security issues and vulnerabilities [7].

Williams *et al.* introduced Protection Poker as a game for estimating security risk during software development projects [8,9]. Protection Poker is inspired by Planning Poker (see Sect. 3.3 below) and uses special cards to express levels of risk resulting from a specific threat. The effect and usability of Protection Poker were further studied in [10,11] where it was found that challenges for its adoption are the overhead in terms of time spent on playing Protection Poker, as well as the difficulty of transforming results from playing Protection Poker into more secure code. This calls for the need to make the game light-weight and to focus on solutions that have a positive impact on making the code more secure.

Threat Poker introduced in 2018 by Rygge and Jøsang [12] is inspired by Protection Poker in the sense that it also focuses on estimating risks related to threats, similarly to Protection Poker. In addition, Threat Poker also focuses on estimating the effort of implementing security solutions during agile software development. An important goal of Threat Poker is to make the game easy to learn and play for students, and for that reason it only uses standard playing cards. Using a deck of familiar playing cards (instead of unfamiliar specialized cards) is a good way of giving an intuitive feeling of playing a game during learning, and during practice in a software development team.

This study proposes ways to improve Threat Poker and investigates how it fits into an agile development process. For this purpose we investigated the following research questions:

RQ1: How can threat modelling and risk assessment be included in agile software development?

RQ2: How can Threat Poker be adapted and utilized in agile projects?

The remainder of the paper is organized as follows: Risk management and threat modelling are briefly described in Sect. 2, then the principles of agile software development are described in Sect. 3. In Sect. 4, we describe our research method and results of adapting Threat Poker. In Sect. 5, we discuss our findings, conclusion and suggest future work.

## 2 Risk Management

### 2.1 Threat Modelling

Threat modelling is to identify how systems can be attacked, which is an essential step in identifying vulnerabilities and risks. *"Threat modelling works to identify, communicate, and understand threats and mitigations within the context of protecting something of value."* [13].

The main purpose of doing threat modelling is to identify relevant threat scenarios with the aim of understanding how they can be mitigated or blocked.

Threat modelling is a component of risk management. The steps of risk management are typically to define the target scope of the risk management, identify the threat agents and possible threat/attack scenarios, understand existing countermeasures and their limitations, identify remaining exploitable vulnerabilities, estimate and prioritize identified risks, and last to propose and implement countermeasures to mitigate and remove vulnerabilities which in turn results in strengthened security, and hence in reduced risk.

### 2.2 Threat Actors and Threat Scenarios

It is important to distinguish between the concepts of 'threat actor' and 'threat scenario', where the former denotes active agents (e.g., persons or organisations), and the latter denotes what they do as a series of steps during an attack. When simply using the term 'threat' in this paper, it should be understood as a 'threat scenario'.

Many threat actors have the motivation and capacity to attack digital systems and ICT infrastructures. It is crucial to understand and attempt to predict how threat actors will attack, which is done by threat modelling. Identifying threat scenarios is a prerequisite for knowing how to stop them. It is, of course, impossible to identify all relevant threat scenarios. However, the designers and developers of software products must use the security skills and experience they have to do the best they can. Additional training or the inclusion of more experienced persons can be required if the software development team members feel that they have insufficient security skills and experience.

The identification of threat scenarios requires the team members to think like an attacker, and try to come up with a method to attack the system. Whenever the team sees an opportunity to successfully attack the system they have identified a threat scenario. The difference between 'threat scenario' and 'attack' is that an attack can be seen as the instantiation of an abstract threat scenario. There can be an infinity of different threat scenarios, but only those that are practical and realistic should be considered. When a threat scenario has been identified which realistically could be executed, it means that there are vulnerabilities in the system or in the surrounding infrastructure that can be exploited by potential attackers to execute the threat scenario. Blocking or mitigating a threat scenario is equivalent to removing the corresponding security vulnerabilities, and this is precisely what has to be done by the design team during software development.

## 3 Agile Software Development

Agile software development is an umbrella term which covers different frameworks and practices which can be applied by software developers to deal with a continuous changing environment, based on specific principles that were outlined in the Agile Manifesto [14]. The main principles consist of early and continuous delivery, welcoming changes, frequent delivery of working software, business people and developers working together, building projects around motivated people, and giving them the resources to succeed [15].

Agile focuses on face-to-face meetings, seeing working software as the measurement of progress and also on promoting sustainable development. Agile also gives attention to technical excellence and good design, simplicity, and assumes that self-organizing teams help develop good architectures, requirements and design. It also has a focus on reflection and on adjusting the process accordingly.

### 3.1 Scrum

Scrum is the most widely used agile development methodology [16] and is set up by fixed rules and roles for the team members [17].

The Scrum process consists of several different components such as the product backlog, sprint planning, daily Scrum meetings, review meetings and retrospective meetings. Like most development methodologies, Scrum originally was not designed with a specific integrated way to deal with security and privacy concerns, and because of this it does not contain a guide on how to best implement security in the method. There have been developed several methods to try and solve this problem like 'Secure Scrum', and 'Security Backlog' in Scrum. Authors have also developed games that can be useful for dealing with the security shortcomings of Scrum. Examples of games are Protection Poker [9], Microsoft's Elevation of Privilege [18], as well as Threat Poker described here.

### 3.2 Secure Scrum

The Secure Scrum Model [19] is an example of how to consider security in Scrum. Its four main components are: 1) the Identification component, 2) the Implementation component, 3) the Verification component, and 4) the Definition-of-Done component. These components have the effect of influencing the different stages in the Scrum process. Security concerns are identified and marked in the Product Backlog as a result of the Identification component. The Implementation component is used in Sprint Planning and the Daily Scrum meetings and is focused on the awareness of the security concerns. The possibility of testing with focus on security is done in the Verification component. Finally, the Definition-of-Done component defines what Definition-of-Done for security related issues are.

When dealing with the security backlog of Scrum in Secure Scrum, a new backlog can be added to deal with all the new security concerns the occurs in the software or due to new features added to the software solution [19]. The purpose of the security backlog is to implement different design principles based on security and privacy to limit the numbers of vulnerabilities and to reduce the risk to the software that is being developed. In addition to the new backlog, another role can be added, called the Security Master, whose role is to manage the security backlog and also decide which security or privacy features require the most attention, and then add it to the sprint backlog which is then completed by the developers.

### 3.3 Planning Poker

Planning Poker [20] is a card-based method for time estimation and planning, often used when following the Scrum process. Planning is started by reading a user story or description of the feature to be developed. Each of the team members will have a deck of special cards, Planning Poker cards, which are cards with increasing values, often the sequence: 0, 1, 2, 3, 5, 8, 13, 20, 40 and 100. The team members are then able to ask questions of the product owner and discuss the feature internally. When the team finishes the discussion, each member will use the cards for estimation, and if the team members are in agreement, the estimate becomes the estimate for the feature. If there are discrepancies in the estimation, a second round will commence, with new discussions and estimations, and this pattern will continue until a relative consensus is reached.

### 3.4 Kanban

Kanban was developed for Toyota's Lean Production System as a specific approach to agile software development and is inspired by the requirements for just-in-time production systems. Kanban focuses on visualizing the 'what', the 'when' and the 'how' of the production process, or development process when talking about software development. There are four major principles that make up the Kanban framework. These consists of visualizing work to increase communication and collaboration, avoiding an unmanageable amount of non-prioritized open tasks, measure and optimize the flow, gather information, and predict future problems, and lastly, to aim for continuous improvement by analysis [21]. Teams that employ Kanban often use practices such as daily meetings and retrospective meetings, but rarely Planning Poker as they do not have to estimate the backlog items the same way as is needed in Scrum (when planning the next iteration).

## 4 Threat Poker

Threat Poker is an efficient method for discussing threats in agile software projects and how to remove or mitigate vulnerabilities in the developed software [12]. Two essential elements of security by design are that the designers identify relevant threat scenarios, and then take the necessary steps to block or mitigate the said threat scenarios, i.e., to solve the threats. In this paper we focus on Threat Poker as a form of 'gamification' of the process for dealing with threats and vulnerabilities during agile software development.

### 4.1 Equipment

In Threat Poker, the team members use regular decks of playing cards. Most people are familiar with traditional playing cards, and sitting around a table with playing cards in the hand typically triggers the positive feeling of playing a game. People's familiarity with playing cards also gives an intuitive interpretation of the cards' face values with regard to threats and their solutions. Low cards intuitively represent low threats or effort estimations, and picture cards intuitively represent high threats and effort estimations for solving the threat scenarios.

### 4.2 Adaptation to Agile Methods

Depending on the development method, there are several stages in the used methodology where Threat Poker can be implemented. When using Scrum, several specified meetings are used for different purposes. There are daily Scrum meetings, planning meetings, and also retrospective meetings. When using Scrum, Threat Poker is most useful in the planning stages of the process where the sprint iteration is planned out, what feature to work on, where security and privacy risks can be assessed and evaluated and where the solution can be discussed, found and solved, if needed, during each sprint.

Kanban, on the other hand, does not have specified meetings set up in the methodology, but a common practice is to use retrospective meetings to improve the team's way of working, and participants often discuss past challenges and how to overcome them to work better together in the future. We suggest that a retrospective in agile software development could be a good meeting to play Threat Poker in since it is meant to be a positive team meeting which would fit with playing a game.

We suggest that Threat Poker can be used as a means to identify and discuss threats to be worked on, and that the next step would be to make these threats visible to the whole project, for example by introducing a separate 'Security board' or 'Threat board' or as tasks added to the backlog or the 'todo'-column. The idea is that when, during the development process, a security or privacy concern is discovered, it could be added directly to the security board and then, during either the planning meeting or the retrospective meeting, could be discussed and made into a features and added to the 'To-Do' column of the Kanban board.

Agile teams also rely on daily meetings to coordinate their work and make decisions [22], we therefore suggest that identification of threats could be part of the daily meetings. If a person has identified a threat, this can be discussed in the daily team meeting. It could be added to the board or backlog. Either as a security item to be investigated or the team could have a designated Security or threat board were they could collect possible threats and discuss these when playing Threat Poker. Discussing security threats would then be an iterative process, which fits well with agile methods.

### 4.3 User Stories and Use Cases vs. Attacker Stories and Threat Scenarios

A user story describes the user, what the user is supposed to do as well as what the user wants to achieve. A user story typically is in the format: *"As a* **user**, *I want* **action** *so that* **effect***"*. This approach can also be applied to the attacker which can be expressed as an 'attacker story' e.g. expressed as *"As an* **attacker**, *I want* **to execute the threat scenario** *so that* **I reach my attack goals***"*.

A use case is a more detailed description of a function or application than a user story. A use case includes actions or event steps typically defining the interactions between roles (actors) and system components to accomplish a goal. The negative version of a use case is a 'threat scenario' which includes actions or event steps typically executed by the threat actor (attacker) who misuses system and network components and interactions between them to accomplish the attack goal. A threat scenario can thus be seen as a 'misuse case'.

The features to be discussed during Threat Poker can be presented either as an attacker story, as a threat scenario, or as a specific vulnerability without any specific attacker story or threat scenario associated with it.

### 4.4 Vulnerability Management

The Open Web Application Security Project (OWASP) describes the 'Top 10 Security Risks' [23]. These risks involve well-known security threats and corresponding vulnerabilities that (unfortunately) are typically found in web application software. Similarly, the Common Weakness Enumeration (CWE[1]) is a community-developed list of common software security weaknesses (vulnerabilities). CWE serves as a common language, a measuring stick for software security tools, and as a baseline for weakness identification, mitigation, and prevention efforts. CWE and OWASP Top 10 are a good starting point for discussions around threats and vulnerabilities during software development. Security vulnerabilities in software can also be identified and assessed without reference to specific threat scenarios. For example, CVSS (Common Vulnerability Scoring System) provides a method for estimating the severity of specific security vulnerabilities. The severity level can be translated into a qualitative representation (such as low, medium, high, and critical) for prioritization in vulnerability management.

### 4.5 Estimation of Risk and Effort

Threat Poker focuses on evaluating the risks from relevant threat scenarios or other vulnerabilities that the team is able to identify, and on estimating the

[1] https://cwe.mitre.org/.

efforts needed to solve those threats and vulnerabilities. The face values of the playing cards are thus used to represent these two things:

- the estimated risk level of a specific threat scenario or vulnerability,
- the estimated effort level to solve the specific threat scenario or vulnerability.

**Risk-Level Estimation.** There is a distinction between security risk as seen from the point of view of the organisation, and the privacy risk as seen from the user (data subject in the terminology of GDPR). Threat Poker considers both types of risk together.

Two main factors or principles are considered for estimating security/privacy risk levels. The first principle states that risk increases as a function of the probability of attack, i.e. the ease with which the attacker can successfully execute the threat scenario. The second principle states that risk increases as a function of the negative security/privacy impact resulting from an attacker's successful execution of the threat scenario.

Security risk is the negative impact affecting the owner of the information assets that are being attacked. Privacy risk is the negative impact affecting a person whose personal information has been misused with reference to relevant data protection principles such as those of GDPR. This can be expressed as:

$$\begin{cases} \text{Security risk} = (\text{ease of executing threat}) \times (\text{potential security impact}) \\ \text{Privacy risk} \;\; = (\text{ease of executing threat}) \times (\text{potential privacy impact}) \end{cases} \tag{1}$$

Given the different victims of security risk and privacy risk respectively, there can be different threat scenarios causing these different risks. To consider these two types of risks separately might help the team analyze and prioritize the most important and pressing features to implement and how to best deal with the security and privacy concerns regarding the features. Note that the system owner can represent a privacy threat actor in case it collects and processes personal information in breach of data protection principles.

Identifying and estimating these risks can be difficult, especially when the team consists of developers who may not have much experience with software development that focuses on security. There are several standards that can aid the team in finding risks or give an indication of where the most common security and privacy risks occur and also how to deal with them.

In software and system development, the principle of 'security by design' means to adequately consider security during every step of the development process, and when working with this, it can be helpful to consider common design principles. Several principles are defined by OWASP (Open Web Application Security Project) in its ASVS (Application Security Verification Standard) [24], and these can give an indication of most common vulnerabilities, and also guidelines on how to prevent these risks.

**Effort-Level Estimation.** The estimation of the effort needed to solve the threat or vulnerability is similar to the estimation of effort levels in Planning Poker described in Sect. 3.3 above. The solution to the identified threat can be seen as a new item to be added to the backlog in Scrum, or to the board in Kanban. This item can be taken into the current development sprint, or be delayed to a subsequent sprint. In any case, the effort to implement the idem should be estimated by the members playing Threat Poker.

### 4.6 Card Values

Figure 1 illustrates suits of cards used for playing Threat Poker. Each player (member of the Scrum or Kanban team) gets an entire suite from the deck, i.e. of Hearts, Spades, Diamonds or Clubs. With four suits one deck is sufficient for four players. For more than four players, two or more card decks are needed. The suit colour has no meaning other than separating the players from each other.

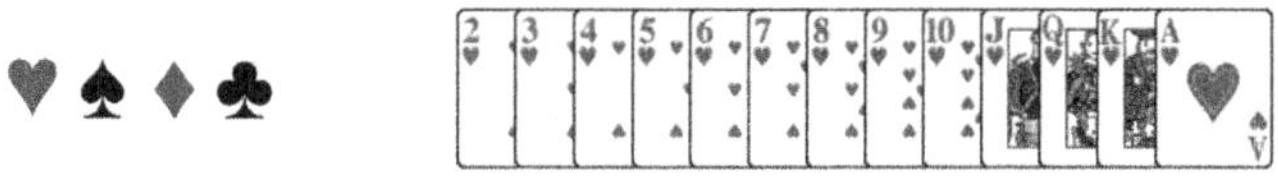

**Fig. 1.** Card suits

Each player sorts out the cards, odd-numbered cards and even-numbered cards. The security and/or privacy risk is represented by odd values: 3, 5, 7, 9, Jack (11), King (13) and A (Ace). The solution-effort level is represented by even values: 2, 4, 6, 8, 10 and Queen (12). As a mnemonic, players of Threat Poker can see risk as an 'oddity' (represented by an odd-value card) which must be 'evened out', i.e. fixed (represented by an even-value card).

Table 1 gives the interpretation of each card value in terms of security/privacy risk and effort level to solve the threat.

Threat Poker described in [12] used a different interpretation of card values, and had two different types of rounds for playing a game. First there was a risk estimation round which was followed by a solution-effort estimation round. We found that the relative complexity of this scheme in itself was a barrier to learning and for successfully practicing secure agile.

We simplified the original Threat Poker from [12] so that participants are playing integrated risk and solution rounds instead of separate rounds for the risk level and the effort level respectively. In the integrated version, odd-numbered cards now indicate the (security and privacy) risk level associated with the threat, while the even-numbered cards indicate the estimated effort required to solve the threat, i.e. to remove or mitigate the corresponding vulnerability.

**Table 1.** Risk and effort levels

| Odd values: risk levels | | Even values: effort levels | |
|---|---|---|---|
| 3 | Insignificant risk, can be ignored unless the effort is minimal | 2 | Minimal effort, can be solved quickly and easily |
| 5 | Very low security and/or privacy risk, only solve if the effort is (very) low | 4 | Very low effort, very easy and quick to solve |
| 7 | Low security and/or privacy risk, should be solved if the effort is low/moderate | 6 | Low effort, relatively easy to solve |
| 9 | Moderately high risk, should be solved even if (moderately) high effort needed | 8 | Moderately high effort, solve threat in this sprint if time, or else in other sprint |
| J | High risk, should be solved even when high or very high effort needed | 10 | High effort, the solution to this threat will be a major part of this/other sprint |
| K | Very high risk, with potentially very severe consequences. Must be solved | Q | Very high effort, a separate sprint might be needed to focus on solving this threat |
| A (Ace) – Extreme risk. Must be solved, or else reconsider the viability of user story | | | |

## 4.7 Playing Threat Poker

For each user story to be implemented the team must do threat modelling as described in Sect. 2.1. Threat modelling is a prerequisite for secure agile, and for applying Threat Poker.

A game of Threat Poker starts by discussing a specific threat scenario or vulnerability which has been identified. This discussion can continue during the repeated rounds of the same game.

For each threat or vulnerability that the team has identified and wants to consider, they play a game of Threat Poker as illustrated in Fig. 2.

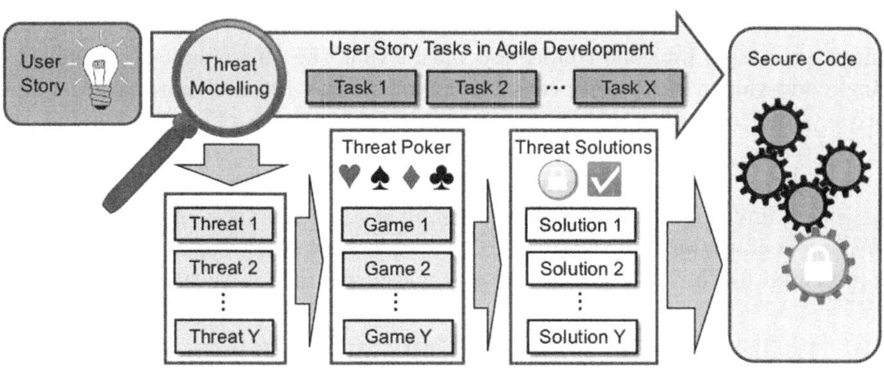


**Fig. 2.** Integration of Threat Poker in secure agile

The game starts by discussing the security and privacy risks involved with the threat, as well as the best solution to solve the threat, i.e. to remove the vulnerability. When the preliminary discussion is completed, each player must make two subjective estimations; one for security/privacy risk and one for the effort/time needed to solve it. Then they play out cards for the first round.

Each player puts down two cards facing down; an odd-value card for the risk level and an even-value card for the solution effort level. Low cards express low risk/effort, and high cards express high risk/effort. Then the cards are turned to show their values. In the case of significant deviations between card values, a discussion follows where each player explains the reasoning behind the risk and/or effort assessment. During the discussions, the players typically influence each other's estimations. Then a new round is played.

Repeated rounds are played, with discussions in between, until an approximate consensus is achieved, for both risk and effort levels. After a consensus is reached, the estimated risk and solution effort levels are used as parameters in the simple decision rule of Eq. (2) as an approximate guideline to decide whether the team should spend time and effort to solve the threat.

$$\begin{array}{ll} \textbf{IF} & \textbf{Risk level} - \textbf{Effort level} > 0 \\ \textbf{THEN} & \textbf{Solve threat} \\ \textbf{ELSE} & \textbf{Ignore threat} \end{array} \tag{2}$$

Threat Poker is thus also an instrument to assist the team in making the decision whether a threat should be solved. The team must decide if the solution shall be implemented in the current iteration or be put into the backlog, or even if it is better to reconsider the viability of the whole user story.

We had students at the University of Oslo trying out Threat Poker. The course was a 20 ECTS course involving a major project in software engineering. During a project period of 13 weeks, students were assigned to develop an app and using agile methods and practices. We had student teams play Threat Poker and report how they experienced it. The teams participating were comprised of between 2–6 students.

The simplification of Threat Poker by integrating separate rounds of risk and effort estimation into one round also meant that the participants just played a single odd-valued card to represent a combined risk level for both security and privacy, and a single even-valued card to represent the effort for solving the risk. At this point in the game, the specific type of risk (security or privacy) is considered irrelevant. The important point is that threats and risks should be solved anyway, regardless of whether it is a security risk or a privacy risk. When revealing the card values, each developer explained whether the risk value represented by the odd-valued card was a security risk, a privacy risk, or both.

### 4.8 Traditional Playing Cards vs. Planning-Poker Cards

There are several different games used for development purposes, and many of them card games. Common among them is that they often require or encourage the use of specially developed cards to play the game. Planning poker use planning poker cards with values based on a Fibonacci sequence, Microsoft's Elevation of Privilege also use specific cards to describe the risk to be played about, Threat Poker, on the other hand, when under development, it was decided to use regular playing cards.

There exists several different reasons why this was thought the best tool to use for estimation in this game, but reasons that could also be applied to other games intended for development teams.

By using playing cards, the team members are provided with cards they are already familiar with, and with face values that are intuitive to the players because they already know how the cards are used for playing. The use of regular playing cards with familiar face values give better intuitive meaning than just a set of values in a number sequence. Based on the intrinsic value of the different types of cards, the risk severity expressed by the value of a king which is a high value card in a regular card deck, might be easier to understand than the value 50 in a number sequence, because familiar playing cards provide more of a context to the values than what unfamiliar cards would provide.

Using regular playing cards also helps creating an association between traditional card games and Threat Poker, and as such can help make the relatively abstract tasks of risk evaluation and effort estimation into something fun and tangible. Gamification around the discussion and estimation of threats and solutions will also stimulate learning among the members of an agile software team.

Another reason for using regular playing cards is their availability. While specially designed cards, such as the Planning Poker cards, and the cards used in Microsoft's Elevation of Privilege can be difficult and time consuming to get hold of, normal playing cards are easy and cheap to buy anywhere. Getting regular playing cards does not require special ordering or manufacturing, and most offices will have at least one deck lying around, ready to be used.

## 4.9 Variations of Threat Poker

Another way of playing Threat Poker is as a board game. Some modifications are required to the method on how to play, but not on the fundamental principles of the game. The team will still use the same user stories and discussion techniques, but will forgo the deck of cards in favor of a created $2 \times 2$ grid that can easily be drawn up before the game is stared. The grid is drawn up and each sector will represent a different level of risk and effort. One sector will be high risk and difficult to solve/long time to solve, another will be high risk but easy to solve/short time to solve, the third will be low risk and difficult to solve/long time to solve and the last is low risk and easy to solve/short time to solve. Each player will use some form of tokens, to place on the board, and after each discussion or round, will move their tokens to represent their opinions on the feature that is discussed. When all players are in agreement with tokens in the same section of the grid, the team has reached consensus and can move on.

## 5 Discussion and Conclusion

Threat Poker is a card-based method to help development teams focus on security and privacy by design which is becoming a standard requirement for software development, as e.g.. required by law in the EU due to GDPR. Threat Poker helps guide developers into considering security and privacy threats and vulnerabilities during the entire development process and also in producing documentations for privacy and security audit.

Using Threat Poker helps estimating the severity of security risks and/or privacy risks identified during software development, as well as estimating the effort to solve those risks. This can be seen as an important element of privacy-by-design and security-by-design which are now required for the development of computer software.

We had student teams in a software engineering course at the University of Oslo play an adapted version of Threat Poker. Our results show that even though the students shared a lot of the same general knowledge, and none of them were security experts, Threat Poker helped articulate thoughts and opinions about possible threats to the system. During the session in which Threat Poker was played and practiced, all the participants took part in the discussion, asking questions, sharing knowledge, trying to think what could go wrong with the user story in case of an attack, how this could be exploited and how best to protect against the threat scenario.

The general feedback from all the student teams was that Threat Poker is a useful technique, and helpful to generate a discussion about security that should be a mandatory part of the development process. Using Threat Poker forced the teams to consider different threat scenarios and how to deal with them. We believe that the simplified version of Threat Poker described in this paper, a threat and its solution are discussed and evaluated in the same round, is better than the original version of Threat Poker where threats and solutions were discussed in separate rounds.

Future research should investigate how Threat Poker encourages and supports teams to solve security threats, compared to other games that exist such as the Security Requirements Education Game [7], [d0x3d!] [6] and Control-Alt-Hack [5]. Furthermore, since we have only tested Threat Poker on students, future research should investigate how agile software development projects in companies would benefit from Threat Poker, and in what way the developed software becomes more secure as a result of playing the game.

## References

1. Tankard, C.: What the GDPR means for businesses. Netw. Secur. **2016**(6), 5–8 (2016)
2. Definition of gamification. https://en.oxforddictionaries.com/definition/gamification
3. Ivanova, G., Kozov, V., Zlatarov, P.: Gamification in software engineering education. In: 42nd International Convention on Information and Communication Technology, Electronics and Microelectronics (MIPRO), pp. 1445–1450. IEEE (2019)

4. Alhammad, M.M., Moreno, A.M.: Gamification in software engineering education: a systematic mapping. J. Syst. Softw. **141**, 131–150 (2018)
5. Denning, T., Lerner, A., Shostack, A., Kohno, T.: Control-Alt-Hack: the design and evaluation of a card game for computer security awareness and education. In: Proceedings of the 2013 ACM SIGSAC Conference on Computer & Communications Security, pp. 915–928. ACM (2013)
6. Gondree, M., Peterson, Z.N.J., Denning, T.: Security through play. IEEE Secur. Priv. **11**(3), 64–67 (2013)
7. Yasin, A., Liu, L., Li, T., Wang, J., Zowghi, D.: Design and preliminary evaluation of a Cyber Security Requirements Education Game (SREG). Inf. Softw. Technol. **95**, 179–200 (2018)
8. Williams, L., Gegick, M., Meneely, A.: Protection poker: structuring software security risk assessment and knowledge transfer. In: Massacci, F., Redwine, S.T., Zannone, N. (eds.) ESSoS 2009. LNCS, vol. 5429, pp. 122–134. Springer, Heidelberg (2009). https://doi.org/10.1007/978-3-642-00199-4_11
9. Williams, L., Meneely, A., Shipley, G.: Protection poker: the new software security "game". IEEE Secur. Priv. **8**(3), 14–20 (2010)
10. Tøndel, I.A., Jaatun, M.G., Cruzes, D.S.: Collaborative security risk estimation in agile software development. Inf. Comput. Secur. 27 (2019)
11. Lopez, J., Zhou, J., Soriano, M. (eds.): ESORICS 2018. LNCS, vol. 11099. Springer, Cham (2018). https://doi.org/10.1007/978-3-319-98989-1
12. Gruschka, N. (ed.): NordSec 2018. LNCS, vol. 11252. Springer, Cham (2018). https://doi.org/10.1007/978-3-030-03638-6
13. Shostack, A.: Threat Modeling: Designing for Security. Wiley, Hoboken (2014)
14. Beck, K., et al.: Manifesto for agile software development, Andrew Hunt (2001)
15. Beck, K., et al.: Principles behind the Agile Manifesto (2001). http://agilemanifesto.org/iso/en/principles.html
16. VersionOne: 12th state of agile report. https://www.infoq.com/news/2018/04/state-of-agile-published
17. Schwaber, K., Beedle, M.: Agile Software Development with Scrum, vol. 1. Prentice Hall, Upper Saddle River (2002)
18. Shostack., A.: Elevation of privilege: drawing developers into threat modeling. In: 2014 {USENIX} Summit on Gaming, Games, and Gamification in Security Education (3GSE 2014) (2014)
19. Törpe, S., Poller, A.: Managing security work in Scrum: tensions and challenges. In: Jaatun, M.G. (eds.) International Workshop on Secure Software Engineering in DevOps and Agile Development (SecSE 2017), Oslo (2017)
20. Grenning, J.: Planning Poker or How to avoid analysis paralysis while release planning. Technical report, Wingman Software (2002)
21. Kniberg, H., Skarin, M.: Kanban and Scrum making the most of both (2010). http://www.infoq.com/minibooks/kanban-scrum-minibook
22. Stray, V., Moe, N.B., Sjøberg, D.I.K.: Daily start breaking the rules. IEEE Softw. (2018). Daily Stand-Up Meetings
23. OWASP (Open Web Application Security Project). Threat modeling (2020). https://owasp.org/www-community/Threat_Modeling
24. OWASP. ASVS - Application Security Verification Standard v.4.0 (2019)

# Teaching of Detection and Forensics

# How to Teach the Undecidability of Malware Detection Problem and Halting Problem

Matthieu Journault[1], Pascal Lafourcade[2], Malika More[2], Rémy Poulain[1], and Léo Robert[2](✉)

[1] Sorbonne Université, LIP6, Paris, France
[2] Université Clermont Auvergne, LIMOS, IREM, Aubière, France
leo.robert@uca.fr

**Abstract.** Malware detection is a term that is often associated to Computer Science Security. The underlying main problem is called *Virus detection* and consists in answering the following question: Is there a program that can always decide if a program is a virus or not? On the other hand, the undecidability of some problems is an important notion in Computer Science: an undecidable problem is a problem for which no algorithm exists to solve it. We propose an activity that demonstrates that virus detection is an undecidable problem. Hence we prove that the answer to the above question is no. We follow the proof given by Cohen in his PhD in 1983. The proof is close to the proof given by Turing in 1936 of the undecidability of the Halting problem. We also give an activity to prove the undecidability of the Halting problem. These proofs allow us to introduce two important ways of proving theorems in Computer Science: proof by contradiction and proof by case disjunction. We propose a simple way to present these notions to students using a maze. Our activity is unplugged, i.e. we use only a paper based model of computer, and is designed for high-school students. This is the reason why we use Scratch to write our "programs".

**Keywords:** Virus detection problem · Halting problem · Undecidability · Computer science unplugged

## 1 Introduction

After Alan Turing gave birth to Computer Science in 1936 [1,2] and the technological advances that ensued, nowadays computers are ubiquitous. The original main concerns of Computer Science were to design hardwares and softwares that can solve some problems. Afterwards, the main challenge became to establish communications between computers. This was the goal of the project ARPANET (Advanced Research Projects Agency Network) initiated by the DARPA (Defense Advanced Research Projects Agency) in the USA in 1962,


Published by Springer Nature Switzerland AG 2020
L. Drevin et al. (Eds.): WISE 2020, IFIP AICT 579, pp. 159–169, 2020.
https://doi.org/10.1007/978-3-030-59291-2_11

but really born in 1969, with a first demonstration in 1972. Finally in 1986, the Kenbak-1 was the first Personal Computer (PC), according to the Computer Museum of Boston. Unfortunately, all these projects were designed for an ideal world where everyone is honest and there is no malicious participant.

However, as soon as a system is working, it is unavoidable that some people try to hack or attack it. This is the reason why security is one of the main issues in Computer Science. Some of the most popular terms associated to Computer Science are malware and antivirus. Following the definitions given by F. Cohen in his PhD and in [3], let us clarify some related notions:

- a *malware* is a set of instructions that runs on a computer and makes a system do something that an attacker wants it to do.
- a *virus*[1] is a program that can infect other programs by modifying them to include a, possibly evolved, version of itself.
- a *worm* is a similar program, which has in addition an automatic propagation mechanism without human assistance. In contrast, a virus needs human actions such as opening an email attachment.
- a *ransomware* is a malware, that encrypts the victim's data unless a ransom is paid.
- a *trojan* is a program that seems harmless but performs malicious action.

History shows that the evolution of malwares closely follows the evolution of computers. In 1982, the high-school student Rich Skrenta wrote the first virus ever released in the wild, called *Elk Cloner*. It was a boot sector virus. Then the virus called *Brain*, designed by Basit and Amjood Farooq Alvi in 1986, was the first virus to infect some PCs. It affected IBM PCs by replacing the boot sector of a floppy disk with a copy of the virus. The first internet worm was the *Morris Worm*, written in 1988 by the Cornell student Robert Tappan Morris. The first ransomware was designed by Joseph L. Popp in 1989. It was called *AIDS/PC Cyborg*, was sent by postmail on a floppy disk and requested 189 US$.

On the other hand, an important part of the research in Computer Science consists in drawing the frontier between undecidable and decidable problems. A problem is said to be *decidable* if there is an algorithm that can solve it, and *undecidable* otherwise. In spite of the existence of many well known undecidable problems (e.g., [2,4–8]), this very notion is often unknown to Computer Science students. However, we think that it is an important notion all programmers should know about, in order not to loose their time trying to solve undecidable problems whenever they encounter one. One of the most simple examples is the undecidability of the resolution of a system of diophantine equations [6]. It is a problem that can naively pass as an easy exercise for an unknowing teacher. For instance, she might consider that designing a software to solve systems of equations where coefficients and solutions are real numbers might be too difficult, because computers are not designed to manipulate real numbers. Hence this

[1] The term of virus was first used in 1972 in a science fiction novel written by the American David Gerrold and called "When HARLIE Was One", where a program called VIRUS that reproduces itself appears.

teacher might want to simplify the problem by replacing real numbers by positive natural integers, which is exactly solving a system of diophantine equations. Thus, we believe that the notion of undecidability is an important concept that we should teach to students (and teachers) as soon as possible. Teaching them this notion also helps us to stop let them think that a computer can already solve any problem, or that it is just a matter of time until an AI solves it in the next years.

In this article, we show that there cannot exist an algorithm that always decides if a program is a virus or not, which is indeed an undecidability proof.

*Contributions:* We present a pedagogical activity for high school students in order to prove that a perfect antivirus does not exist. For this, we follow the approach presented in the PhD of F. Cohen in [3]. This activity is unplugged, it means it does not require any computer, but only some printed papers, following the line of thought proposed in [9]. In order to prepare students to this proof, we also designed an activity that proves that it is not possible to determine if a program terminates or not on a given input. This activity follows Turing's proof of the undecidability of the Halting problem [1,2]. These two proofs use some essential techniques in Computer Science: proof by case disjunction and proof by contradiction. In order to present these two proof techniques to students, we use a simple situation, where Alice aims at escaping from a maze. Moreover, our material uses some programs written in Scratch [10], but of course other languages can be used instead, such as Snap! [11], Python, C, Java, etc.

*Outline:* In Sect. 2, we give a few simple programs that help the students to understand how our computer model works. In Sect. 3, we explain how a proof by contradiction and a proof by case disjunction work, using a simple example based on a maze. In Sect. 4, we present the proof of undecidability of the Halting problem and in Sect. 5 we prove that a perfect antivirus cannot exist.

## 2 Preliminary Work

We first introduce the material used for this activity. Then we describe each "Scratch" program used to prove the two undecidability results.

### 2.1 Material

In order to simulate the execution of our programs on a computer, we use a simplified model. The computer is viewed as a "*slate*" (or a sheet of paper) on which is drawn the diagram of Fig. 1.

This simplified computer has two inputs, denoted by I1 and I2, two outputs denoted by O1 and O2, and three register boxes denoted by A, B and C. The goal of the next section is to get used to operating this simplified computer by handling small programs. In addition, students get acquainted with an abstract model of computation. In this activity, the computer model is closed to a three registers machine.

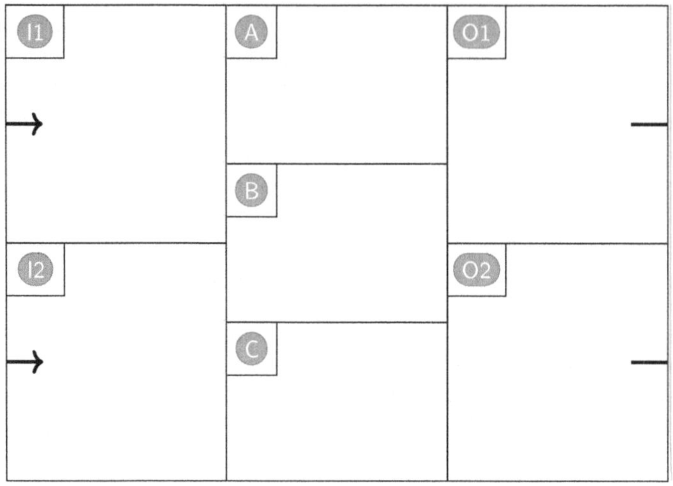


**Fig. 1.** Computer model.

### 2.2 Simple "Scratch" Programs

The word *machine* denotes a group of three participants, equipped with a slate on which is drawn the diagram of Fig. 1. The slate is used to help representing the states of the computer during the execution of a program.

Thanks to the simple examples given in Figs. 2, 3, 4 and 5, we explain how programs are executed in our computer model. For each case, a copy of the program is given to the students. The programs are presented with a pedagogical progression, which we believe helps to understand how our computer model works.

For example, the program *Increment*, given in Fig. 2, is the simplest one. Each student picks an integer and uses it as the input of the program *Increment*. This program just adds one to its input and outputs the result. The goal of this program is to get used to the material.

The next program is *Minus*, given in Fig. 3, which, as its name explains, just makes the subtraction of its two inputs and outputs the result. It uses a loop and contains internal variables.

The next program, *Minus*$^\star$, given in Fig. 4, is similar to the previous one but does not terminate. For the students, it is often the first time they encounter a program that does not terminate. The students must realize that this program *Minus*$^\star$ is obtained from the program *Minus* just by "forgetting" one instruction. Thus they should realize that it is generally hard to determine whether a program halts or not just by examining its source code.

For the program *Super*, given in Fig. 5, each student picks an input and runs the program. Some executions do not terminate, depending on the inputs, while others terminate. The goal for the students is to find under which conditions the program terminates or not.

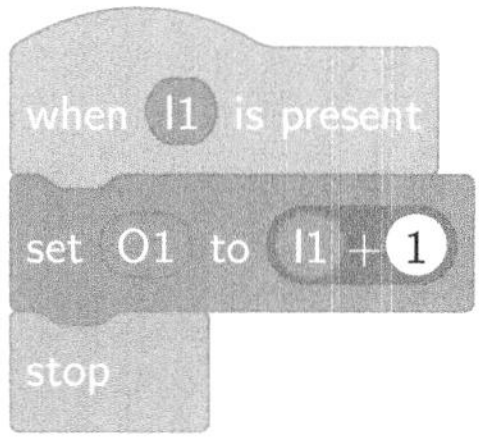


**Fig. 2.** Program INCREMENT

# 3 Proof by Case Disjunction and Proof by Contradiction

In order to introduce the notions of proof by case disjunction, which is widely used in Computer Science, as well as proof by contradiction, we consider a situation where no mathematical background is required. We propose the simple maze given in Fig. 6, with two deadly obstacles, a precipice noted $P$ and a monster noted $M$. If Alice meets the monster, she dies as well as if she falls into the precipice. Alice starts at point $A$ and our goal is to prove that she cannot escape alive from the maze.

We prove this result by contradiction. Assume that Alice can escape from the maze alive. She has only two options from her starting point $A$: going down or going right.

We consider the two cases above and show that they are both impossible.

1. **Going right:** If Alice goes right, then she is going to fall into the precipice $P$, and die. Since she does not leave the maze alive this case is impossible.
2. **Going down:** If Alice goes down then she is going to be eaten by the monster $M$, and die. This case is also impossible.

Finally we conclude that the assumption "Alice can leave the maze alive" is false. Hence we have shown that Alice cannot escape the maze alive.

This part of the activity can be conducted as an interactive discussion with the students. Its goal is to explain step by step how to use those two proof variants on a simple example.

# 4 Proof of Undecidability of the Halting Problem

This section is assigned to present a proof by contradiction of the Halting problem (*i.e.*, always determine whether a given program terminates or not on a given input).

## 4.1 Three Programs

We present three programs used in the proof: PHOTOCOPY, NEGATION and HALT.

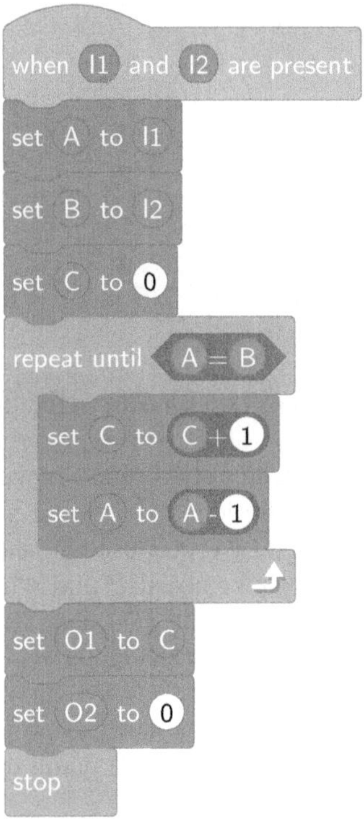


**Fig. 3.** Program MINUS, under condition $E1 > E2$.

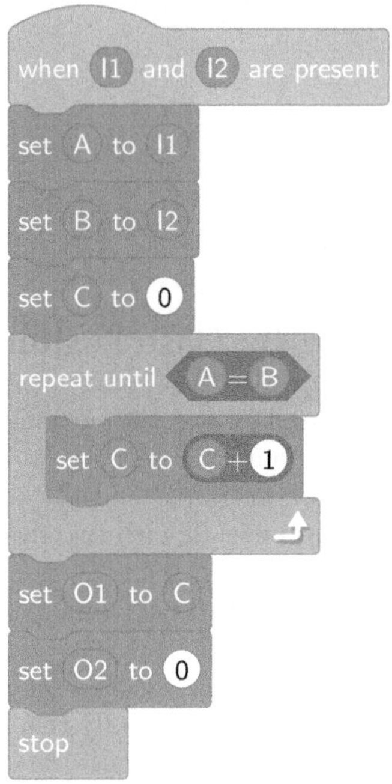


**Fig. 4.** Program MINUS*, under condition $E1 > E2$.

The program PHOTOCOPY, given in Fig. 8, copies its input given in I1 to outputs O1 and O2. This program can be tested by the students by choosing numerical inputs at first. They discover that the input is just copied in the two outputs as a photocopier would do. Then we ask the students to use a program such as *Increment* as input. It is a bit perturbing for them at first, but they finally accept without too much difficulty that the input of the program PHOTOCOPY may be a program as well as a number.

The program NEGATION, given in Fig. 9, can be tested on inputs *HALTS* and *DOES NOT HALT*. Students try both inputs and discover that the program NEGATION behaves the exact opposite of what its input says.

The program HALT, given in Fig. 7, takes as input I1 and I2 and returns *HALTS* if the execution of the program I1 on the input I2 terminates; otherwise it outputs *DOES NOT HALT*. This program, HALT, cannot actually exist because of the following line:

execution of program I1 halts on input I2

The purpose of this activity is too prove this result.

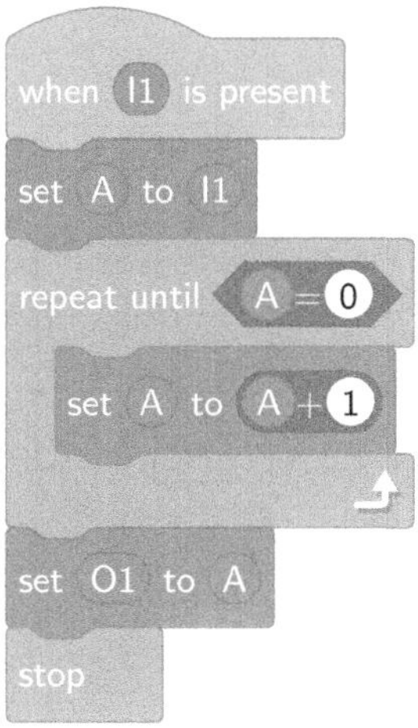


**Fig. 5.** Program SUPER

### 4.2 Undecidability Proof

The aim of this section is to prove that the program HALT, given in Fig. 7, cannot exist. We assume that this program exists and show that this assumption leads to a contradiction.

The proof is constructive in the sense that we build a program, denoted by X, composed of three programs one after the other. The first one is PHOTOCOPY, the second is HALT and the third is NEGATION. The idea is now to use the program X as its own input, and show that a contradiction ensues.

We have two possibilities concerning the behavior of the program X on the input X:

1. The execution of HALT on the inputs X and X outputs *HALTS*. In this case, the program NEGATION receives *HALTS* as its input, so its execution never terminates. Finally, the execution of the program X with X as its input never terminates which contradicts the output given by HALT. The latter being assumed to never be wrong, this case is not possible.
2. The execution of HALT on the inputs X and X outputs *DOES NOT HALT*. In this case, the program NEGATION receives *DOES NOT HALT* as its input, hence its execution terminates. Finally, the execution of the program X with X as its input terminates, which contradicts the output given by HALT. The latter being assumed to never be wrong, this case is also not possible.

Both cases are impossible, which proves that the initial assumption is false. In other words, it means that the program HALT cannot exist.

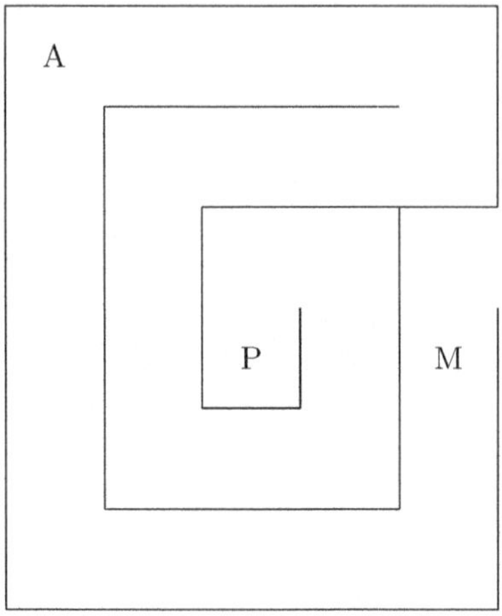


**Fig. 6.** Maze.

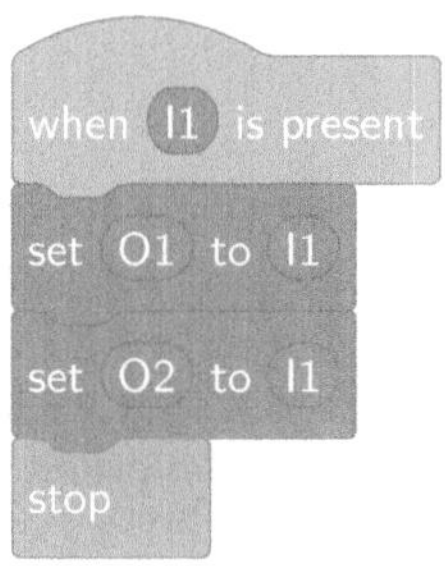


**Fig. 7.** Program PHOTOCOPY.

## 5 Proof of Undecidability of isVirus

We prove by contradiction that it is not possible to have a perfect antivirus. Hence, we assume the existence of such a program, called ISVIRUS and given in Fig. 10. This program takes as input a program $P$ and determines whether $P$ is a virus or not. The program ISVIRUS *never fails* to determine if $P$ is a virus or not.

We begin by manipulating this program ISVIRUS with students before showing that such a program cannot exist.

### 5.1 The Program isVirus

Let us consider the program called ISVIRUS with input I1 and output TRUE in O1 if I1 is a virus and FALSE in O1 otherwise (see Fig. 10).

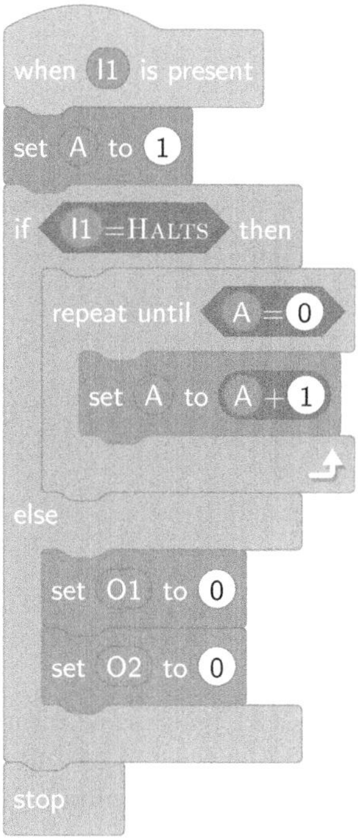


**Fig. 8.** Program NEGATION.

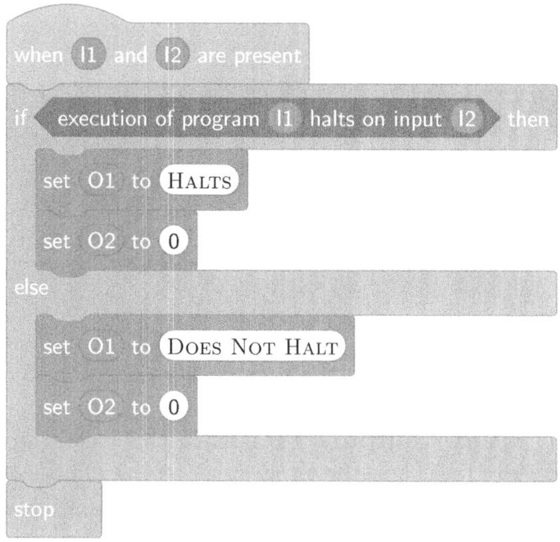


**Fig. 9.** Program HALT.

### 5.2 The Program Test

Let us consider the program called TEST with one boolean input I1 and output O1. If I1 is TRUE then the output is set to 0 meaning that the program stops its execution. If the input I1 is FALSE then the program behaves like a virus and thus infects.

### 5.3 Undecidability Proof

The proof is constructive in the sense that we construct a new program, called Y formed by the program ISVIRUS followed by the program TEST, given in Fig. 11.

The program Y works as follows: if the input of Y is a virus according to the program ISVIRUS, then the program Y terminates by outputting 0 in O1, and otherwise it infects the computer.

We now observe the behavior of Y when it is called with itself as its own input. We have two possibilities concerning the behavior of the program ISVIRUS on the input Y:

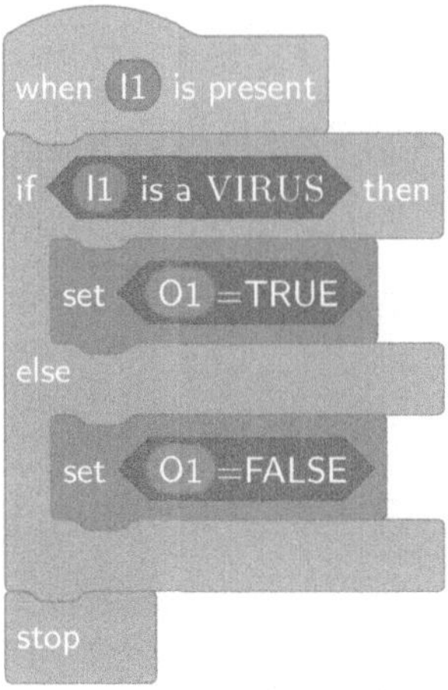


**Fig. 10.** Program isVirus.

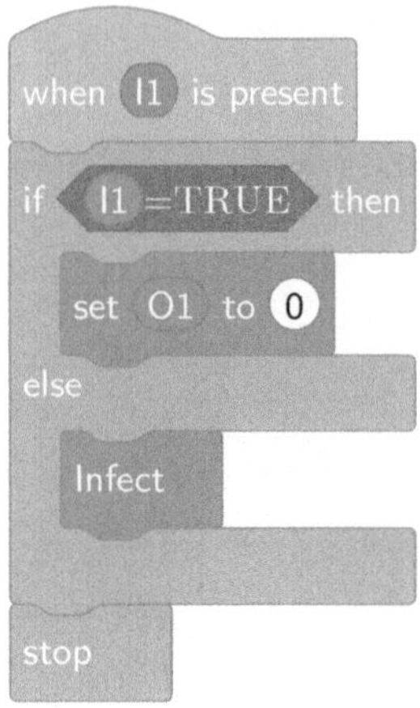


**Fig. 11.** Program Test.

1. **isVirus outputs TRUE.** In this case, the program Test receives as input TRUE. Thus the program Y stops. This contradicts the answer of isVirus that said that Y was a virus (and consequently should infect the computer). This leads to a contradiction and makes this case impossible.
2. **isVirus outputs FALSE.** In this case, the program Test receives as input FALSE. Thus the program Y infects the computer. This contradicts the answer of isVirus that said that Y was not a virus (and consequently should not infect the computer). This leads to a contradiction and also makes this case impossible.

Both cases are impossible, which proves that the assumption is false. In other words, it means that the program isVirus cannot exist.

## 6 Conclusion

In this paper, we presented a pedagogical activity demonstrating that a perfect antivirus will never exist. We also propose another activity for proving the undecidability of the Halting problem. For this, we introduced a simple computer model that only uses paper. Moreover, using a simplified maze, we present two fundamental notions that are often used in Computer Science: proof by contradiction and proof by case disjunction.

We have two main goals in this activity. First we aim at showing that Computer Science security is not an easy task and that it also has some undecidable problems. Second, we want to suggest to teachers an activity around the notion of undecidability.

This activity has been tried with high-school students but also with Master students. In both cases, the students have been surprised to discover these two undecidability results. For high-school students, the proof technique is not so easy to follow and even for university students, the principles of the proof are often new. We believe that this activity demystifies several misconceptions that students can have about the power of computers and antivirus.

Of course, it does not mean that it is useless to install an antivirus on your computer. One of the important security principles is to have an up to date system, as Bruce Schneier said “Security is a process, not a product”.

## References


1. Turing, A.M.: I.–Computing machinery and intelligence. Mind **(LIX)**(236), 433–460 (1950)
2. Turing, A.M.: On computable numbers, with an application to the entscheidungsproblem. Proc. Lond. Math. Soc. **42**(2), 230–265 (1936)
3. Cohen, F.: Computer viruses. Comput. Secur. **6**(1), 22–35 (1987)
4. Bodlaender, H.L., Downey, R., Fomin, F.V., Marx, D. (eds.): The Multivariate Algorithmic Revolution and Beyond. LNCS, vol. 7370. Springer, Heidelberg (2012). https://doi.org/10.1007/978-3-642-30891-8
5. Cassaigne, J., Halava, V., Harju, T., Nicolas, F.: Tighter undecidability bounds for matrix mortality, zero-in-the-corner problems, and more. CoRR (abs/1404.0644) (2014)
6. Matiyasevich, Y.V.: Hilbert's Tenth Problem. MIT Press, Cambridge (1993)
7. Rice, H.G.: Classes of recursively enumerable sets and their decision problems. Trans. Am. Math. Soc. **74**(2), 358–366 (1953)
8. Robinson, R.M.: Undecidability and nonperiodicity for tilings of the plane. Inventiones Mathematicae **12**(3), 177–209 (1971)
9. Bell, T., Rosamond, F., Casey, N.: Computer science unplugged and related projects in math and computer science popularization. In: Bodlaender, H.L., Downey, R., Fomin, F.V., Marx, D. (eds.) The Multivariate Algorithmic Revolution and Beyond. LNCS, vol. 7370, pp. 398–456. Springer, Heidelberg (2012). https://doi.org/10.1007/978-3-642-30891-8_18
10. MIT (2019). https://scratch.mit.edu
11. Berkley. Snap! (2011). https://snap.berkeley.edu

# Enlivening Port Scanning Exercises with Capture the Flag and Deduction

Frans F. Blauw(✉)

University of Johannesburg, Johannesburg, South Africa
fblauw@uj.ac.za

**Abstract.** Designing engaging exercises when students do not yet possess a lot of knowledge can be difficult. We show how we draw on students' prior knowledge, along with basic introductory concepts, to design an elemental (but fun) port scan exercise in an introductory security testing module. While "capture the flag" is a security industry standard for exercises, it can require a lot of in-depth knowledge to properly implement and complete. Using basic computer science concepts such as ports and ASCII values, we design a simplified capture the flag exercise where students can make use of deductive reasoning to complete the game. Overall, the exercise was received favourably by the students who found it challenging but enriching.

**Keywords:** Security testing · Experiential learning · Deductive learning · Port scanning · Capture the flag

## 1 Introduction

Hands-on practical experience is important for students to absorb theoretical knowledge [1]. This is especially true when learning the art and science of computer security testing. However, designing exercises that adequately tests specific outcomes while staying interesting (or fun) can be difficult. Where this is particularly hard is during the beginning stages of a security module where not a lot of content has been covered and the students do not yet possess a lot of knowledge that can be applied.

The basic learning concept of experiential learning [2] comes to play when designing activities for a module. Theory should be reinforced by practical experience in a setting that allows the student to not only better understand said theory, but blend it with knowledge and experiences they already possess.

In this paper, we will be discussing how we enlivened a port scanning exercise [3,4] that does not require a lot of penetration testing prior knowledge, but relies on basic prior computer science concepts and deductive learning [5]. We start by briefly discussing what a basic port scanning exercise might consist

I would like to thank my *Information Security in the WWW* class of 2019 for braving this exercise!.


Published by Springer Nature Switzerland AG 2020
L. Drevin et al. (Eds.): WISE 2020, IFIP AICT 579, pp. 170–183, 2020.
https://doi.org/10.1007/978-3-030-59291-2_12

of in Sect. 2. We introduce the concept of "Capture the Flag" in Sect. 3 while discussing how we plant our flag in Sect. 4 and our setup in Sect. 4.3. We discuss how we envisioned our students to work through the exercise in Sect. 5 by giving a guided walk through the problem. Finally, we take our students' feedback and present our observations in Sect. 6. We conclude and discuss future work in Sect. 7.

## 2 The Basic Port Scanning Exercise

A course discussing fundamental ethical hacking procedures, at some point introduces the concept of "port scanning". Port scanning, as part of information gathering, has the aim of locating live hosts on a network that could potentially contain vulnerabilities by detecting which ports are open on these hosts and which services they offer [6].

When discussing port scanning, the most common tool in the industry, *nmap* [7] (Network Mapper), is also introduced. It is at this point where students will need to gain some practical experience of the theory of port scanning as well as the tools involved. The most common approach would be to have a set of hosts on a network and have the students perform a port scan on these hosts. They will then need to write a report detailing their scanning steps and which ports were detected to be open, closed, or filtered. However, we found that simple exercises such as these could often leave students bored and wanting.

For an introduction to security testing course, at the point of discussing port scanning, we decided to create an exercise that will be a bit more exciting by having a simple introductory **Capture the Flag** game.

## 3 Capture the Flag

**Capture the Flag** is a common children's game where two teams battle it out attempting to capture the opponent's flag. Many variations of this game have been played on playgrounds around the world, and is also often used as the basis of other games such as paintball, computer games [8], and even military exercises [9].

Most importantly, the security industry regularly makes use of capture the flag exercises [10, 11]. Participants normally have to use a wide array of techniques and expertise to do so. Techniques include port scanning, host enumeration, vulnerability exploitation, and more. Once the player has successfully "captured the flag" they have won the exercise [12].

Using the **Capture the Flag** game concept early on in an introductory course proved to be difficult, especially since not a lot of content had been covered up to this point. However, we decided that we could manipulate a basic port scan to be more than a simple means to discover hosts.

# 4 Planting the Port Flag

At this point during the module, we had only covered basic port scanning and enumeration techniques. As such, the exercise should not include any advanced security testing techniques. However, we did not want to create a "boring" assignment by only having students perform a basic **nmap** port scan and give us a report. By adding a some peculiar elements to the assignment, we could give the students a bit more excitement for this assignment.

We decided to turn a port scan assignment into a "capture the flag" game. As this was their first assignment of the type, we had to make a simple, easy to discover, flag. The exercise should also only make use of existing knowledge such as Network Basics and HTTP Basics. Not only would this reinforce prior knowledge, but will also demonstrate how this knowledge can be linked to new concepts. How the flag was hidden should also be related to port scanning.

## 4.1 The Flag

The flag planted was a faked balance sheet for a fictional company named *ASCII Inc.* and was hidden behind a password protected page. The flag must be obvious to the students, so they know that they had found it. We also made it obvious that the students were nearing the flag by spotlighting the secure area. The name of the company itself serves as a clue, as we will see later.

## 4.2 Concealing the Flag

The flag (the balance sheet) was hidden behind a Basic HTTP Authorisation page. Since this was a port scanning assignment, we were going to hide the password in the ports. The best way to do so would be to use ASCII numbers to represent characters of the password. Each port would then somehow represent a character in the password. Our chosen password was **HAPPENCHANCE**. Interestingly, each character in this password occurs exactly twice. This would help us later to reinforce that the port number represents something meaningful. The ASCII mapping for each letter is shown in Table 1.

The flag itself was served on Port 443 for two reasons: firstly, 443 does not map to a normal ASCII character; and secondly, since 443 is normally reserved for HTTPS, it should signal that something secure is hidden here.

Once the flag was hidden, we now had to hide the password in the ports.

## 4.3 Setting Up the Hunting Grounds

We started by spinning up a virtual instance of Ubuntu Linux 18.04 LTS containing only the basic components to serve content to the Internet. A number of ports were then opened to serve content. The ports were 65, 67, 69, 72, 78, and 80 representing the ASCII characters. All the EVEN ports served HTTP content backed by *nginx* [13]. The ODD ports served RAW content, backed by a custom *python* script. We also opened ports 83 and 443 using *nginx*.[1]

**Table 1.** Character to ASCII

| Character | ASCII value |
|---|---|
| A | 65 |
| C | 67 |
| E | 69 |
| H | 72 |
| N | 78 |
| P | 80 |

Table 2 shows precisely what each port served. After setting up all the above ports, we blocked Port 22, which is used to remotely connect (via SSH) to the server, to ensure that students do not confuse it as part of the exercise.

**Table 2.** Port services and responses

| Port | | |
|---|---|---|
| 72 | **Server type** | HTTP |
| | **Response HTTP code** | 200 |
| | **Response body** | Content-Length: 35 Content-Position |
| | **Additional HTTP header** | Content-Position: 1,8 |
| 78 | **Server type** | HTTP |
| | **Response HTTP code** | 200 |
| | **Response body** | N |
| | **Additional HTTP header** | Content-Position: 6,10 |
| 80 | **Server type** | HTTP |
| | **Response HTTP code** | 200 |
| | **Response body** | Welcome to ASCII Inc. Finance Department. This section is restricted to authorised personnel only |
| | **Additional HTTP header** | Content-Position: 3,4 |
| 83 | **Server type** | HTTP |
| | **Response HTTP code** | 403 |
| | **Response body** | 13 |

(*continued*)

[1] The *nginx* configurations and *python* scripts are available for download from: https://blauw.link/wise13.

**Table 2.** (*continued*)

| Port | | |
|---|---|---|
| 65 | **Server type** | RAW |
| | **Response body** | Content-Position: 2,9 |
| 67 | **Server type** | RAW |
| | **Response body** | ASCII Inc. Letter |
| | **Correct input expected** | C |
| | **Correct response body** | Content-Position: 7,11 |
| 69 | **Server type** | RAW |
| | **Response body** | Content-Position: 5,12 |
| 443 | **Server type** | HTTP (not HTTPS) |
| | **Response HTTP code** | 401 |
| | **Response body** | 13 |

# 5 Finding the Flag

Now that the flag had been planted, it was up to the students to try and capture it. In this section, we describe the way in which we envisioned the students would have approached the exercise. This is by no means the only method the students could have used, but the one we found to be the simplest to explain.

## 5.1 The Exercise

Students were given this exercise directly after a lecture on portscanning as part of their assignments. The assignment document given to the students was as follows:

**ASCII Inc.** has been receiving reports that their financial information might have been leaked. The CIO suspects that the Finance Department uses non-standard security techniques to secure their confidential documentation. They have asked you to perform a penetration and security test on their network and the Finance Department computer system.
The CIO has requested that you provide a report on your results and process.
**Instructions:**
- The only host you are allowed to target is *[IP Address]*, you may **NOT** attempt to scan or enumerate any other host.
- Attempt to capture the Company Financial documents from the host.

- You may only use **scanning** techniques.
- You may **NOT** use any destructive techniques.
- Be creative. Think outside of the box.
- Write a report describing your process and results.
- Keep the details of your report confidential.

The possible points that can be accumulated for the exercise are shown in Table 3. All the criteria are self-explanatory and based on the procedure (discussed in the following section). We made **Bonus Points** available if students did something ingenious or we did not expect.

**Table 3.** Points assigned to the exercise

| Criteria | Points |
|---|---|
| Captured the flag | 30 |
| Identified password | 10 |
| Identified port to ASCII mapping | 20 |
| Identified all services | 10 |
| Found all ports | 5 |
| Performed port scan | 5 |
| Produced detailed report | 20 |
| **Total** | **100** |
| Bonus | (20) |

Students had a week to complete the exercise and could complete it from home or from the university campus.

### 5.2 The Procedure

Now that the students have been given the assignment they can start. Since this is a port scanning exercise, the first step would be to run *nmap* on the given host. The output from *nmap* would show which ports are open on the host as well as the potential services based on those ports. A sample output from *nmap* using the "nmap -v -T5 -p 1-1024 *[IP Address]*" is shown in Fig. 1 and is summarised in Table 4.

Looking at the open ports, the students might be overwhelmed by the number of "strange" ports that are open. However, they should notice that two more commonly known ports are open: Ports 80 and 443.

The student now has to attempt to reveal the service hosted on each particular port. Since the ports suggested by nmap, as in Table 4, are only the "common" services, it is up to the security tester to confirm the case.

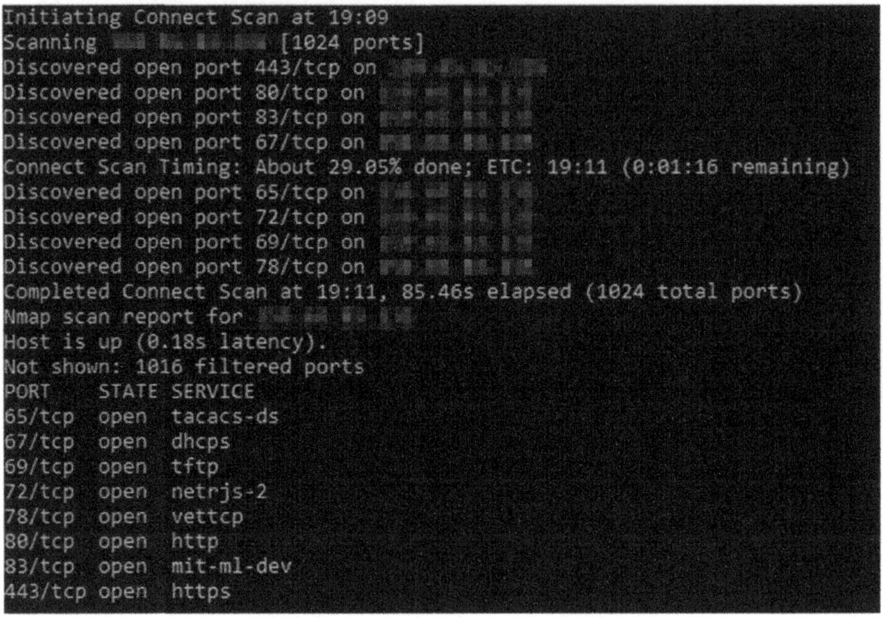


**Fig. 1.** Output from *nmap*

**Table 4.** Open Ports found by *nmap*

| Port | State | Service |
|---|---|---|
| 65/tcp | open | tacacs-ds |
| 67/tcp | open | dhcps |
| 69/tcp | open | tftp |
| 72/tcp | open | netrjs-2 |
| 78/tcp | open | vettcp |
| 80/tcp | open | http |
| 83/tcp | open | mit-ml-dev |
| 443/tcp | open | https |

Students are free to use whatever means they want to confirm the service, either by connecting to the port via a telnet-like session and obtaining the header or by eliciting further output from nmap. For simplicity of demonstration, we will demonstrate the HTTP services using a web browser and the RAW services using a console.

The first, most common, port is Port 80, which might reveal some additional information about the organisation or the use of the server. Once connected, a browser output should be similar to Fig. 2. It should come as no surprise to them that the information is not readily available here. At this point, as well, we did not expect them to realise that information was hidden HTTP headers.

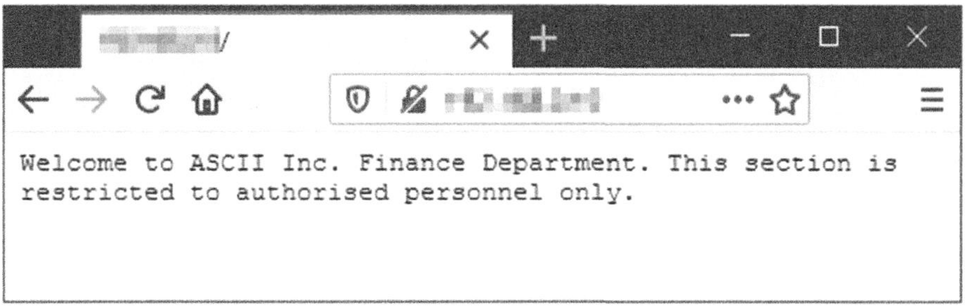


**Fig. 2.** Browser output from Port 80

Next, the student might try to connect to 443 using HTTPS. However, since the service running on Port 443 is not truly HTTPS, their browser should give them an error. They can manually force their browser to connect to Port 443 using normal HTTP, upon which they will be met with a **401 Authorization Required** dialog, as shown in Fig. 7. They do not yet have the password and so cannot continue.

Students can now cast their attention to the rest of the available ports. As none of the "standard" services running on those ports are known to the students, it was expected that they will now conduct some research on the services. This was a purposefully a red-herring to reinforce that services running on certain ports might not always be the "standard" service as expected on the particular port.

Failing to connect to the ports using conventional means, students can now start experimenting with these ports. The best way would be to attempt to capture a banner for each service in order to determine what is really running on that particular port. To do so, students can attempt to make a RAW connection to each port to determine the service and see if they can extract some information. The order in which students can connect is arbitrary, but the ideal order is as follows:

**Fig. 3.** Browser output from Port 72

Connecting to Port 72, it should be obvious that it is running a normal HTTP service. When connecting to this port using a browser (or manually using HTTP commands), students are met with the output as shown in Fig. 3. In the response body **Content-Length** is shown along with another word **Content-Position**. Knowing that **Content-Length** is an HTTP header, this should lead the student to look at the HTTP Headers as was sent by the server. **Content-Length** then matches what was shown in the HTTP Body and **Content-Position** has the value of **1,8**. Students can now start connecting to the other HTTP services.

Connecting to Port 78 using a browser (or manually again), will only show the response body of **N**, as shown in Fig. 4. Looking at the HTTP headers, **Content-Position** has the value of **"6,10"**. The **N** in the Response Body maps the ASCII value of 78 (the port). However, if the student did not pick up on this clue yet, it should become clear later.

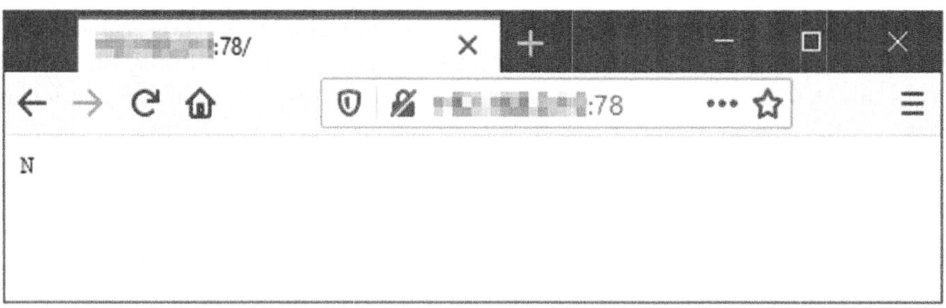


**Fig. 4.** Browser output from Port 78

Port 80, as shown earlier is a basic landing page, but in the HTTP header **"Content-Position"** has the value of **"3,4"**.

The next ports are not HTTP services, but RAW services and should ideally be connected using a TELNET client.

When connecting to Port 65, the service will only return **"Content-Position: 2,9"** and then disconnect. The same with Port 69 that will return **"Content-Position: 5,12"** and disconnect. An example is shown in Fig. 5.

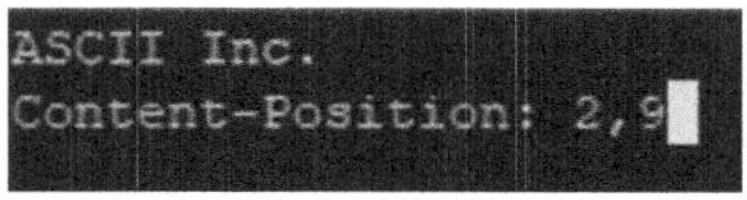


**Fig. 5.** RAW output from Port 65

However, connecting to Port 67 the service will output **"ASCII Inc."** followed by **"Letter:"**. The service will not disconnect and wait for input. If the student figured out the ASCII clue from earlier, they should find out which character 67 maps to in ASCII. However, the service will also allow them to attempt multiple times. Once the student enters the correct letter, **"C"**, the service will output **"Content-Position: 7,11"**. A sample exchange is shown in Fig. 6.

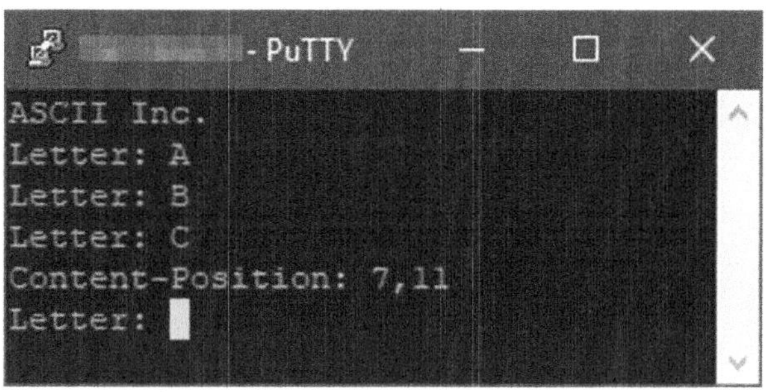


**Fig. 6.** RAW output from Port 67

Once the student has deduced that the port numbers map to ASCII and that each of the services running on the ports output **"Content-Position"**, they should start putting the clues together. Mapping all the port numbers to the ASCII equivalent character, and placing them in the correct position, the word **HAPPENCHANCE** should be revealed as shown in Table 5.

**Table 5.** Final position to character mapping

| Content-Position | 1 | 2 | 3 | 4 | 5 | 6 | 7 | 8 | 9 | 10 | 11 | 12 |
|---|---|---|---|---|---|---|---|---|---|---|---|---|
| Port/ASCII value | 72 | 65 | 80 | 80 | 69 | 78 | 67 | 72 | 65 | 78 | 67 | 69 |
| Character | H | A | P | P | E | N | C | H | A | N | C | E |

**The Red Herring.** The keen observer might have noticed that there was one last port, Port 83, open that is not used. This port was opened as a red herring and there were several clues left to indicate that it should not form part of the password.

First, the HTTP response code was **403 Forbidden** as opposed to 200 OK as with the rest of the HTTP clues.

Secondly, even though the body contains the number **"13"**, which could be a position, there was no direct reference to "Content-Position".

Finally, in the password "**HAPPENCHANCE**" each letter appears twice, the letter 'S' that corresponds to the ASCII value of 83 would only have appeared once.

## 5.3 Capturing the Financials

Now that the students have put together the password, it is time to use it. Previously they should have discovered that the HTTP service running on Port 443 was a password-protected area. They should now navigate to that page and will be presented by the login as shown in Fig. 7. The login popup shows "login admin". Though it was slightly obscure, the student should have assumed that the **User Name** for the authorized area should be "admin". The **Password** that they deduced is **"HAPPENCHANCE"**, although lowercase "happenchance" was also accepted.

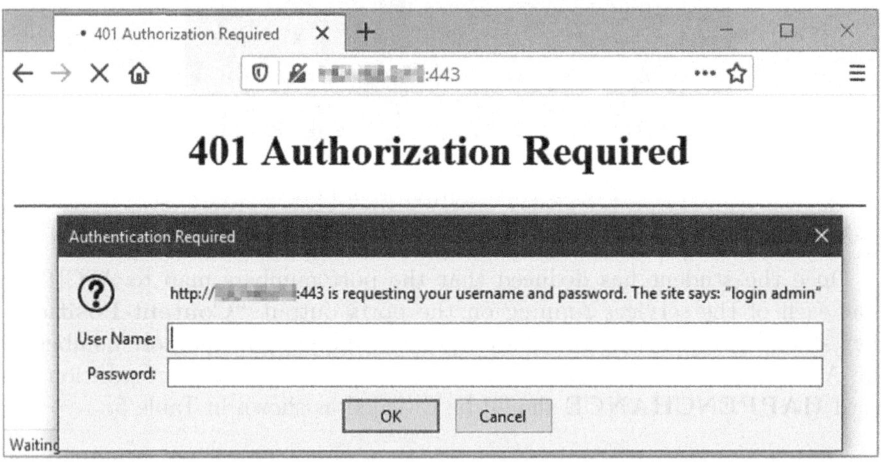


**Fig. 7.** Browser output from Port 443

Once entering the restricted area, the student will be met with a screen as shown in Fig. 8 from where they can download the Balance Sheet! Congratulations.

**Fig. 8.** Browser output from authorised area

After the week given to the students to complete this exercise, we explained the scenario to them and the procedure we envisioned them to follow. In the following section we will share some observations regarding this exercise.

## 6 Our Observations

When the exercise above was given, 18 students were registered for the module. Of those, 15 students completed the exercise with 9 students finding the solution completely or partially.

Overall, informal feedback found that the students were quite excited about this first exercise in that they were able to use "professional" tools. They found the lack of guidance to be difficult at first but did discover the excitement when figuring out a peculiar puzzle. Common feedback was the solution was "very straight forward once you know what to look for". Regardless of their outcome, the majority of students described the experience as "fun" and "interesting".

There were a couple of mistakes and different routes that we did not expect:

**Not All Ports.** The most common reason for not completing the exercise was that the students did not run a thorough port scan. They scanned the host using only the default nmap ports, which are the most common 1000 ports. As such their scans did not detect the lesser-used ports (65, 67, 69, 72, and 78).

**Thinking Too Far Ahead.** Another common mistake that we found was that students attempted and got stuck on other enumeration and vulnerability exploitation techniques. The most common of these was the use of "SQL Injection" for the *401 Authorization Required* prompt, as shown in Fig. 7. As we had not covered SQL Injection at this point, students were going in blind and attempting to follow tutorials they found online. They also did not realise that eliciting output using SQL Injection during a *401 Authorization Required* prompt is nearly impossible.

**Conspiracy Theories.** One student informed us that they thought the exercise was "too straightforward" and that there "must be more than meets the eye". As such, the student in question attempted to find the (non-existent) deeper meaning in all of the clues. This caused the student to spend too much time on a wild goose chase, while the tame geese were just sitting and waiting.

**Web Look-Ups.** Although we do not necessarily find this to be a mistake, we do note that some students got carried away with trying to find additional information surrounding the host on which the exercise was hosted. As we had only given them an IP address to scan, they, for example, reported back on who the owner of the IP address was and whether the IP address had appeared on the blacklists. While this information could be very useful during a normal security test, it did not contribute to the assignment. Students were awarded for this additional effort, however.

**ISP Blocks.** We had a single student who could not complete the exercise because their personal Internet Service Provider had blocked users from accessing non-standards ports. Since most students completed the exercise from home, we questioned the group of students and discovered that it was this single ISP who prevented scanning and connecting to non-standard ports.

## 7 Conclusion

This paper showed how we made a basic port scanning exercise more exciting without requiring too much new knowledge. In the exercise, students were able to use prior knowledge of computer science and the newly introduced information gathering techniques. They were then reliant on the deductive reasoning skills to complete the task. We showed that students will take part in and enjoy a task that allows them to use industry-level tools and skills as quickly as possible.

We also showed that students will intuitively start using their reasoning skills if they are not provided with too much information, allowing them to approach the problem in an unconventional manner. Not only does this improve their reasoning skills, but allows students to think independently and creatively. Based on the participation and feedback, we deemed this exercise to be a success and will begin moulding future exercises using the same premise.

As indicated in education theory, experiential learning can reinforce the theory taught in classes and should be applied as quickly and systematically as possible. In the future, in order to allow students to get hands-on experience in the shortest practical time, we will be making use of more simple exercises that rely on prior knowledge and deduction skills. Future studies will include examining the role deduction plays in improving the use of tools as well as the understanding of security testing as a whole.

## References

1. Senge, P.M.: The Fifth Discipline: The Art & Practice of The Learning Organization. Doubleday, New York (2006)
2. Kolb, D.A.: Experiential Learning: Experience as the Source of Learning and Development. Pearson Education, Upper Saddle River (2015)
3. Huotari, K., Hamari, J.: Defining gamification - a service marketing perspective. In: Proceeding of the 16th International Academic MindTrek Conference, pp. 17–22, October 2012. https://doi.org/10.1145/2393132.2393137
4. Lee, N., Manners, D.: Gamification of penetration testing. Counterterrorism and Cybersecurity, pp. 343–347. Springer, Cham (2015). https://doi.org/10.1007/978-3-319-17244-6_14
5. Felder, R.M., Silverman, L.K., et al.: Learning and teaching styles in engineering education. Eng. Educ. **78**(7), 674–681 (1988)
6. Wilhelm, T.: Professional Penetration Testing: Creating and Learning in a Hacking Lab. Syngress, Waltham (2013)
7. NMAP: Nmap: the Network Mapper - Free Security Scanner (2020). https://nmap.org/
8. Rocha, J.B., Mascarenhas, S., Prada, R.: Game mechanics for cooperative games. ZON Digit. Games **2008**, 72–80 (2008)
9. Atkin, M.S., Westbrook, D.L., Cohen, P.R.: Capture the flag: military simulation meets computer games. In: Proceedings of AAAI Spring Symposium Series on AI and Computer Games, pp. 1–5 (1999)
10. Bishop, M.: A design for a collaborative make-the-flag exercise. In: Drevin, L., Theocharidou, M. (eds.) WISE 2018. IAICT, vol. 531, pp. 3–14. Springer, Cham (2018). https://doi.org/10.1007/978-3-319-99734-6_1
11. Cowan, C., Arnold, S., Beattie, S., Wright, C., Viega, J.: Defcon capture the flag: defending vulnerable code from intense attack. In: Proceedings DARPA Information Survivability Conference and Exposition, vol. 1, pp. 120–129. IEEE (2003)
12. Vigna, G.: Teaching network security through live exercises. In: Irvine, C., Armstrong, H. (eds.) WISE 2003. IAICT, vol. 125, pp. 3–18. Springer, New York (2003). https://doi.org/10.1007/978-0-387-35694-5_2
13. nginx: Server block examples — NGINX (2020). https://www.nginx.com/resources/wiki/start/topics/examples/server_blocks/

# Encouraging Equivocal Forensic Analysis Through the Use of Red Herrings

Wai Sze Leung(✉)

University of Johannesburg, Johannesburg, South Africa
wsleung@uj.ac.za

**Abstract.** A core concept taught to forensic investigators is the practice of equivocal forensic analysis which is strongly advocated by researchers and practitioners to limit investigators from reaching incorrect conclusions, either due to their own bias, or as a result of subjectivity from others. The process is however a time-consuming one and students may not see the value in doing so amidst a busy academic schedule. This paper examines how the use of the red herring plot mechanism in a game-based storytelling environment can be used in a computer forensics semester module to effectively highlight the importance of evaluating the available evidence objectively and thus encourage students to avoid falling into the trap of developing and following preconceived theories.

**Keywords:** Confirmation bias · Digital forensics · Equivocal forensic analysis · Game-based storytelling

## 1 Introduction

Objectivity and a healthy dose of skepticism are essential skills that all professional forensic investigators must demonstrate [1]. Unfortunately, the goal of concluding an investigation in a scientific manner that is free from bias, can be extremely difficult to achieve, with preconceived theories representing one of the greatest root causes of errors in such complex problem-solving scenarios [2,3]. Considering that such findings are effectively expert opinions that legal proceedings may accept when reaching a decision in a court of law, expressing an incorrect view of what might have occurred in an incident can lead to serious consequences ranging from the loss of life to irreparable damage to one's reputation [4,5]. As such, lecturers tasked with teaching students in forensic investigation-related subjects should ensure that awareness of bias is raised so that students conscientiously avoid such a pitfall.

Teaching students this lesson is not simple–a lecturer can educate students on the concept of 'equivocal forensic analysis', telling the students how the process entails conducting objective and independent evaluations of the available

This research benefitted, in part, from support from the Faculty of Science at the University of Johannesburg.


Published by Springer Nature Switzerland AG 2020
L. Drevin et al. (Eds.): WISE 2020, IFIP AICT 579, pp. 184–197, 2020.
https://doi.org/10.1007/978-3-030-59291-2_13

evidence to establish the true (most likely) meaning behind that evidence [5]. Further, a lecturer may insist on the importance of equivocal forensic analysis. However, failure on the part of the lecturer in integrating this theory with practice can lead to students who struggle to apply the lessons in the real world [6].

Such an observation by education researchers highlights the need for a digital forensics classroom that affords its students with opportunities to integrate theory with practice [6]. In this paper, we describe how we designed and implemented an ongoing exercise where students were able to develop their reasoning and analytical skills while applying appropriate digital forensic techniques in uncovering the next act in a story-driven game.

The rest of this paper is structured as follows: Sect. 2 provides background on how mistakes in forensic investigations can be attributed to a lack of objectivity for both the investigator and colleagues. Next, Sect. 3 examines how storytelling is used as an epistemological approach in guiding this knowledge discovery process. As the stories are meant to push students along, they need to contain a degree of momentum that encourages its audience to remain engaged as the story unfolds. Section 4 will thus look at how stories can be propelled forward using various plot mechanisms. Based on the various elements introduced in the previous sections, Sect. 5 will detail the resultant game that was developed to increase objective investigative practices amongst digital forensics students. Finally, Sect. 6 will conclude the paper with points identified for improving future offerings of this particular learning exercise.

## 2 Challenges to Objectivity in Investigations

Under the correct conditions, a forensic investigation involves following a rational, systematic approach to identifying relevant evidence, preserving this evidence, analyzing the evidence, and interpreting its results in order to construct a balanced and plausible account of events for presentation to others [7,8].

Although evidence itself cannot be wrong, different persons examining it may view it differently, opening up the possibility of multiple interpretations of what the evidence represents [9]. The truthful outcome of the investigation thus hinges on the ability of the forensic examiner to discern the correct interpretation of said evidence [1,9].

Unfortunately, this task of selecting the correct interpretation does not appear to be an easy one with a report produced by the President's Council of Advisors on Science and Technology in 2016 suggesting a considerable degree of flawed conclusions that have led to the potential miscarriage of justice [10]. Such inaccuracies paint a very grim view for the justice system when courts rely on the expert testimonies of forensic examiners to make its critical decisions [4,11,12]. This apparent weakness in forensic examinations has led researchers from multiple disciplinary areas to identify factors contributing to these unacceptable errors, some of which include: (i) Competency; (ii) External influences; and (iii) Bias.

### 2.1 Insufficient Knowledge and Technical Competence

Perhaps the most obvious issue relates to the forensic examiner being capable of acting competently during an investigation [3]. An expectation exists that everyone involved in an investigation is familiar with the techniques, standards, and protocols, following them correctly and appropriately.

While further discussion on this factor lies beyond the scope of the research, it is important to note the researchers have attributed the technical competence shortcoming to gaps in training, citing the need for additional education initiatives to address the concern [12]. Further to this, it was also noted that teaching forensic investigators must extend to ensuring that forensic investigators also know how to sustain adherence to guidelines once they are practicing in the field [13]. Such arguments support our initiative to incorporate greater awareness of potential fallacies of forensic investigations in our digital forensics classroom.

### 2.2 External Influences

Linked closely to the aforementioned factor of sufficient technical competency is the issue of having multiple individuals involved in any given investigation - with one party handling the evidence acquisition and another its examination, there needs to be the assurance that all parties involved carried out their tasks correctly since each individual's findings are contributing some part to piecing together a greater puzzle [14].

Investigators may also produce erroneous results due to external influences insisting that an investigation be hurried along, or for the investigator to either focus or neglect a particular aspect of an investigation so that outcomes favourable to the external parties are ensured [15]. As experts in a court of law, [15] has indicated investigators must resist such influences and ensure that they behave ethically and legally.

Unfortunately, while one may successfully reject apparent attempts to influence an investigation's outcome, the human element in each of us can still lead to our third identified source of error, namely bias.

### 2.3 Bias

The topic of bias as the source of considerable error in forensic investigations has been covered rather extensively by researchers [16–19].

Bias can manifest in two categories, most of which apply to all forensic investigations in general: (i) motivational bias where the investigator may unintentionally be inclined to look for incriminating evidence rather than exculpatory ones (evidence that will demonstrate the lack of criminal intent on the part of an accused person) in a bid to build up a case against an identified suspect [20]; and (ii) cognitive bias where the person behaves in a biased manner without realizing that they are being biased [14, 18]. Each of the three cognitive biases is summarised as follows:

- **Contextual bias** – although forensic scientists may require context to carry out their job properly [14,17] notes that many forensic experts are exposed to irrelevant contextual information which can also have a detrimental effect, influencing how the forensic expert conducts their work.
- **Confirmation bias** – a decision-maker may tend to seek out or interpret evidence in such a way that it favors their existing beliefs or hypotheses while ignoring or devaluing any evidence that would contradict them [20,21]. Reaching incorrect conclusions because of confirmation bias is thus not necessarily the result of a lack of capability, but rather, due to poor reasoning and an "overall human tendency for laziness" [3].
- **Expectation bias** – similarly to confirmation bias, this form of bias is the result of reaching conclusions prematurely without having examined all the facts or having conducted the examination thoroughly [20]. Experienced investigators, who have many years of working on similar cases, are seen to be particularly susceptible to expectation bias as they see it as "yet another one of those cases" [5].

### 2.4 Equivocal Forensic Analysis

The previous section on bias highlights a particularly problematic issue for forensic investigators who are tasked to carry out their duties scientifically, approaching each discovery or evidence with objectivity and skepticism [1]. To tackle this problem, [5] propose the process of equivocal forensic analysis as a means of combating bias effectively.

When working with evidence that could be interpreted in more than one way, it would be responsible to treat it as open-ended without settling on a particular conclusion based on the assertions of others without further review. With the possibility that several people with varying degrees of expertise may have contributed to the various conclusions, it is not inconceivable, given the discussion on how errors in analyzing evidence can be introduced, that some of these findings may be flawed. With equivocal forensic analysis, a forensic examiner will examine said evidence items again, objectively and independently of findings from others. This allows them to familiarize themselves with the entire case, ascertain that the investigations were conducted correctly, verify that a crime has indeed taken place, and possibly identify new evidence or clues that may have been previously overlooked [5].

Choosing to conduct equivocal forensic analysis can be time-consuming as carrying out the process typically equates to a repetition of the investigative process itself. However, this not only ensures that fundamental issues relating to the investigation are addressed, but that every assertion made is correct [5]. Furthermore, going through the investigative process will not only allow the investigator to become familiar with the overall case, but it also protects their careers as they are effectively staking their professional reputation on the veracity of their findings [15].

These reasons should present students with a compelling reason to undertake equivocal forensic analysis to minimize bias while examining the evidence as objectively as possible. However, this may continue to be a challenge due to how classrooms have traditionally been set up.

### 2.5 Cognitive Bias in the Classroom

It can be argued that universities do not adequately prepare students to deal with bias during the course of their education. In particular, students are not presented with the appropriate learning opportunities to develop their ability to mitigate bias.

Firstly, students tasked with writing an argumentative essay will tend to misrepresent the strength of any counter-arguments they may find, undervaluing their importance so that their original assertion would appear to be the more plausible state of affairs. This apparent cognitive bias, however, cannot be wholly blamed on the student. If the success of an argumentative essay is linked to the strength of their argument, why would a student sabotage their work by acknowledging any counter-arguments as credible points? When one is induced to advocate for a particular stance, any efforts to find and organize evidence will naturally be made in favour of advancing that particular argument. Simply, the reasons for avoiding confirmation bias would be contrary to the student achieving their goal [22].

Secondly, the topic of cognitive biases does not seem to be a common topic in academic materials on research methods. [23] argues that this is shortsighted of academia considering the significant influence that cognitive biases can have on a research study's outcomes. Given how many experts have failed to recognize their own biases in a field that relies much on objectivity such as forensic science [19], it would not be surprising for novice researchers to find themselves failing to realize the subjectively-flawed choices in their research design.

The approach to getting students to tackle their cognitive biases will therefore require a different approach–[23] points out that simple didactic teaching or awareness-raising will not suffice, given that cognitive biases have already taken hold in most young adults. Rather, students should be exposed to repeated learning opportunities that encourage them to approach problems that do away with closed solutions, focusing on open-minded decision-making strategies instead.

## 3 Teaching Through Stories

One manner of promoting engaged student learning is through the approach of storytelling [24]. Considered a powerful pedagogical tool, storytelling has gained a reputation for successfully delivering messages that are both educational and entertaining [25]. The use of storytelling as a mechanism for teaching has yielded positive results such as higher student involvement (including emotional) and increased critical thinking in subjects where more traditional pedagogical choices have led to students perceiving the subject matter to be "dull" [24,25].

Infused with an element of adventure, stories arm lecturers with the ability to contextualize knowledge, making it more accessible to students who can relate to the content and achieve greater learning gains as a result [25,26]. Through context, the stories encourage students in developing several skills that include exercising their cognitive skills, establishing the meaning behind events, and retaining key points better [26].

Besides, the suitability of using storytelling in the classroom is further supported by its ability to allow lecturers to weave different technical topics together [24]. By demonstrating to students how each topic fits in the overall scheme of forensic investigations, students have the additional benefit of gaining a greater appreciation for the aforementioned topics.

Storytelling is thus a very attractive pedagogical approach for teaching computer forensics–the opportunity exists for lecturers to shape learning experiences that foster cognitive skills while exposing students to cognitive bias and presenting them with the opportunity to manage this bias. With the right elements, storytelling can deliver an overarching experience that allows students to test their competence of various computer forensics tasks (such as identifying evidence at a search and seizure scene, creating a forensically sound image of a suspect's disk drive, and recovering files that the suspect may have attempted to delete) throughout the course of the story.

Storytelling in the classroom, however, does come with a warning–the choice to tell stories requires considerable planning as they are complex and indirect, requiring preparation that allows the lecturer to rapidly adapt the story in response to however students respond. This is necessary to ensure that both the story and the underlying educational message is retained in its delivery [27].

## 4 Introducing the Red Herring

Since one of the purposes of using storytelling as a pedagogical approach to teaching and testing students on the flaws of cognitive biases, there will need to be elements of the story that present the student with scenarios that include the opportunity for students to work with evidence items that are purposely riddled with ambiguity. As indicated earlier, errors in investigations typically arise due to the evidence being in a state that is open to multiple interpretations. Other than ensuring that any ambiguity remains logical, their inclusion throughout the story needs to be done with moderation to ensure that students are not overwhelmed or discouraged by poor storytelling that does not move the plot along.

This can be achieved utilizing plot mechanisms such as red herrings in the story. Red herrings refer to a common plot device often used in mysteries and are clues that are either false or misleading. When written well, red herrings are meant to reveal useful information along the way [28]. The purpose of red herrings in our context is to create distractions that incite student interest, purposely baiting them into making decisions about the interpretation of a particular evidence item. To encourage individual work in this regard, the ambiguous possibilities will have varying levels of a likelihood that may or may not correspond strongly with the student's existing knowledge of the story thus far.

The intention is to encourage students to not allow their cognitive biases to take shortcuts without considering the alternatives that exist.

## 5 A Gamification Approach

Traditionally, our Computer Forensics module has been a primarily theoretical one with the theory conveyed in a series of lectures. While there has been a move to incorporate an increasing amount of the practical exercises into various exercises over the years, coverage on the topic of bias and equivocal forensic analysis remained topics that were briefly discussed in passing. Assessment on either topic typically involved asking students to describe the process of equivocal forensic analysis, referring to how doing so would address potential inaccuracies introduced by bias. Such an approach is considered rather elementary according to Bloom's Taxonomy and thus lacks the depth As desired of digital forensics professionals, resulting in individuals poorly-prepared for applying the theory in the real world.

To improve this shortcoming and deliver the topics in a more practical manner, a story-driven adventure was set up to span the majority of the semester (lasting 13 to 14 weeks). While this storytelling approach has been implemented to some degree in four different offerings, the inclusion of red herrings to educated students on managing their biases has only been presented twice, in 2018 and 2019 to class sizes of 18 and 21 students respectively. In our offerings, students assumed the role of a recent recruit who has been accepted into the local police department's cybercrimes division. Throughout the story, students engage in several computer forensics-related tasks, most of which contributed to a part of the primary plot and mystery of that year.

To introduce the potential for bias from out students, each primary plot borrowed heavily from major news events that had occurred that year–the motivation for doing so was to see if students allowed events that were happening in the real world to influence how they viewed the in-game characters that were caricatures of their real-life inspirations. In some cases, these similarities were deliberately intentional to see if students would make the mistake of allowing their bias to influence their decision-making.

For use to assess the students' decisions that were made to reach their various conclusions, students were taught how to prepare written detailed reports that describe the tools used and methods followed. Great emphasis is placed on how their reports must be sufficiently rigorous to stand up to scrutiny. Each student is then required to submit a report in which they detail their particular path of investigation so that their findings can be verified through the reproduction of their processes. These detailed reports allowed for us as the assessor to follow the thought processes of each individual to establish how they reached the conclusions that they did.

### 5.1 2018: The Accounting Fraud Scandal

In 2018, students were introduced through a series of news bulletins reporting on an international corporation recently accused of questionable accounting practices. The resultant fallout is that millions of hardworking people, a portion of which are about to retire, have had their retirement savings wiped out. The setup of this particular story borrowed heavily from the Steinhoff International Holdings accounting scandal that had been reported on extensively at the beginning of the year.

The investigation into the story is launched with students asked to identify and gather evidence from a crime scene where a businessman has been found dead at the bottom of his staircase in his home. The students are tasked with answering the following: was it an accident, or had someone pushed the businessman? If so, what was the motive for doing so?

In the weeks leading up to this crime scene exercise, news bulletins are made available to students to establish the background of the investigation, with each bulletin introducing a new character who would serve as a potential suspect in the investigation. The four suspects introduced were:

- **The CEO**–head of the Stonehill Investments Network (SIN) Corporation, he comes across as a businessman who continues to enjoy the finer things in life while less fortunate individuals now struggle to make ends meet in the wake of his alleged dishonesty. The victim was a business partner of the CEO and had been threatening to expose him. To some degree, the victim had been established as a vigilante type who was looking to seek justice on behalf of those whose lives had been negatively affected in the scandal.
- **The CEO's Son**–the rich, spoilt only child of the CEO, he stands to lose the privileges he is so used to if his father is indeed guilty of accounting fraud.
- **The IT Staffer**–the skilled head of IT development at SIN, he had helped the victim in creating malware to steal damning information from the SIN servers. He however does not want to engage in illegal activities any longer. The victim had resorted to threatening to report him to the police unless he continued.
- **The Security Guard**–a security guard who is about to retire. He can ill-afford for SIN to drop further in value. However, SIN's values will be wiped out completely if the CEO is exposed.

**Trapping for bias** – during the crime scene search and seizure exercise, students were split into smaller groups and allowed to work with the same crime scene. While the number and nature of the evidence items to be discovered were essentially the same, minor differences were made for each group. For example, a different laptop prop was used or the placement of the evidence was in a different location. Ultimately, each group had to identify and locate a laptop, two USB storage devices, a note, and a mobile phone. Both laptop and mobile phone could either be on, off, or locked with a passcode.

In addition to this, each student was assigned specific variables 'found' on the evidence items that would be discovered. For example, while everyone would have found the USB as evidence, the contents on the USB device would be made available to the students electronically. The delivery of the image 'made' of the USB drive would then contain content that would implicate or exonerate a particular suspect. In this way, one student's evidence could very well be another student's red herring. The outcomes were divided up in such a way that five outcomes were possible: the murderer was one of the four suspects, or, it was merely an accident as the victim had slipped and fallen to his death.

**Students' responses** – perhaps similarly to the work done by [19] where different scenario debriefings presented to students (either murder or suicide) led to vastly different types and amount of evidence found, the 2018 mystery game showed that none of the students concluded that it was likely an accident. Most students believed that the murderer was none other than the CEO, despite the lack of evidence to back this up. Even evidence of the incident being an accident was ignored, despite all four suspects having alibis in place. The tendency for students to opt for foul play would appear closely linked to their expectations for a story with an 'exciting ending'. This is a common expectation that is repeatedly mentioned in feedback provided from students over the years, with students forgoing the more plausible options in favour of endings that go out with a bang.

Specifically, one report documented how each of the suspects had their alibi at the time, demonstrating that they had correctly interpreted the relevant evidence. However, rather than write that there are no clues to suggest that the victim had been pushed off the stairs.

Overall, the results were therefore of poor quality when it came to applying logic appropriately. It further confirmed that students at the Institution were not only biased but did not appear to be aware that they were being biased either. This suggested a lack of understanding of the concept of bias in the first place.

### 5.2 2019: A Case of City Capture

In the following year, the central plot of the story moved to another news topic that was gaining much media coverage, that of 'state capture'. First coined in 2000, this term was used by World Bank researchers to describe how predatory parties exert influence over government to extract favourable outcomes for particular private actors at the expense of society [29].

Due to the shortened lecturing period in 2019, there was a need to establish certain settings earlier. This was done by providing students with some background into the history of the city in which the student worked in their module introduction guide (all modules are accompanied by a guide which provides them with the details of the module). In addition to providing guidelines on how to request important documentation such as search warrants and vehicle registration queries from the relevant personnel at the police department, the guide introduced the wealthy family boasting numerous highly profitable dealings with the city.

In the first few weeks, students are introduced to several characters, including a few interactions with the chief of police. In the fourth week, after a fair portion of the theory has been covered, students are called to apply what they have learnt (and also, studied up on their own) on one of two different crime scenes with a particular objective:

- **Murder in the Evidence Room**–the grumpy evidence officer has been found murdered in the evidence room, bludgeoned in the head. As a member of the digital forensics team, students must gather all relevant (digital) evidence in hopes of finding the murderer.
- **Signs of City Capture**–with news that grumpy evidence officer has been found killed in the evidence room, students in the teams sent to investigate the chief of police's office are tasked with finding evidence that the chief might be working to advance the wealthy family's businesses.

Students were split into four groups, two of which investigated the murder while the other two looked into the police chief's dealings. As with the 2018 offering, each crime scene had a similar set of evidence items that were to be identified, bagged, and tagged for further processing. At least one evidence item hinted towards a connection with the other scene. Ultimately, students had to establish whether the chief of police was allowing a wealthy family to influence and control the city police.

Ultimately, the question that must be answered was: 'Is the chief of police captured by a wealthy family which seemingly have their influence everywhere?'. In the case of those investigating the murder, did the police chief have the evidence officer killed?

**Trapping for bias** – to make the concept of cognitive bias more apparent, the police chief was made to look like the sort of person one would likely dislike. Depending on the group, physical notes found would suggest that the chief is not only corrupt but a racist and having an affair with the police department's finance officer. Additional evidence found at both crime scenes would further suggest that the evidence officer had been blackmailing the chief and that there is a 'Mr. Australia' who is mentioned in several correspondences.

As in 2018, each student was required to analyze the content on the evidence items that they identified. By delivering a custom set of digital content that is on the evidence items (the USB drives and laptop – while mobile phones were discovered in the crime scenes themselves, the analysis on the content of the mobile phone is beyond the scope of the learning outcomes of the module), each student is presented with evidence that works towards either establishing the chief as an innocent or guilty member of the police station. Therefore, for some, the evidence will implicate the chief while others will indicate his innocence.

Based on the evidence delivered, the outcome of the investigation would have been:

- **Captured**–the police chief is indeed corrupt, using the finance officer to assist with signing improper deals that benefited the wealthy family. In exchange, the police chief received a lucrative amount of money in exchange. Because the evidence officer had uncovered this corruption, the chief had either personally killed the officer, or the wealth family sent a hit-man to get rid of the evidence officer.

- **All Above Board**–the police chief has been a beneficiary of the wealthy family's generous bursaries funding program. While he is extremely grateful to the family for allowing him to study further, he maintains a strictly professional relationship.
- **The Mystery of Mr Australia**–Mr Australia is either a hit-man (who murdered the evidence officer) from Down Under or, a guest of the police department who wants to learn more about how police officers work in the city. He is a former bodybuilder who is now doing motivational speeches across the country.

**An exercise on cognitive bias** – In light of the poor performance of students in 2018, students were given a research assignment in the first week of the semester in which they were asked to search predatory conferences. The exercise included the students getting briefed on the topic of heuristic searches and confirmation bias. While some reports still yielded bias in their results, approximately 60% of the class delivered reports that suggested attempts to avoid confirmation bias altogether.

Feedback was given back to the students promptly (within a week) to ensure that they were equipped with this knowledge before their search and seizure exercise.

**Students' responses** – unfortunately, it would appear that for most students, the lessons learnt from the early cognitive bias exercise were quickly forgotten with numerous students jumping to conclusions at every possible opportunity. In one example, a student discovering a love message with a name on a Post-It note loudly remarked to their team members that the chief had a mistress. Although this was the intention behind planting the evidence in the first place, it is telling that the student had mentioned mistress as at no point in time, had the team been informed of the chief being married (the intention was for this piece of information to be introduced at a later stage). For the exercise, the note for this particular group was supposed to be ambiguous–through the digital delivery of the content on the evidence the students receive later, students would then discover that the message was either from the chief's wife or his mistress, the police's finance officer.

Despite the setback, the results of 2019 could still be regarded as being an improvement on the bias mitigation front. At least two reports were more careful in their wording, demonstrating caution when it came to making claims. This could be seen in their four teams' group reports in which they documented their findings based on the search and seizure of evidence items alone.

### 5.3 Planned Revisions

With the feedback and consultations with colleagues taken into consideration, the following changes are planned in our next or future offerings:

- Incorporate more regular mentions of bias and the need to manage it throughout the course of the story. This is in line with the findings by [23] who recommended that repeated learning opportunities be exploited to turn it into a habit
- Model suspects on real-life polarizing personalities. Depending on the role, create characters that are based either on an existing individual that the public largely dislikes or adores. This allows us to test students to see if they are either directed towards or away from the suspect as a result.
- Have the teams that conducted crime scene investigations at different sites discuss their findings with each other. It may be helpful to have peers assess each other in terms of whether a particular evidence item should have been interpreted the way it was by the discovery team. Such a setup will lead to part of the student's findings being sourced by another investigator, making the need for equivocal forensic analysis more obvious.
- Break up the detailed report into iterative submissions. One of our findings is that students did not always provide sufficiently detailed reports, leading to some difficulty in assessing the their process of reaching their findings. Although our 2018 offering allowed us the opportunity to interrogate students in the form of a question and answer session at the end of the presentation of their findings, the exercise can be time-consuming and impractical with greater class sizes. As an alternative, students will be asked to submit detailed reports after a particular staging of events, allowing for earlier feedback, and allowing the students to revise and work on their final reports in iteratively.
- Consider the introduction of a courtroom setting as the concluding part of the game. During this phase, students will be able to play the roles of different expert witnesses who have been called to testify, either for the prosecution or the defending party. The aim of introducing this addition is to allow students to experience the full incident resolution from discovery to the presentation. By allowing students to represent either side of the court case, it is anticipated that the students will be able to interact with each other, identifying potential counterarguments in response to claims made by the opposition.

It should be however noted that the final item planned may take some time to introduce as initial discussions with members of the legal community have raised concerns over how time-consuming running a moot court hearing can become.

## 6 Conclusion

The problem of cognitive bias in forensic investigations has proven to be a significant one that has garnered considerable attention from researchers in various disciplines over the years. Since the domain of digital forensics is no different, attention too, must be paid to ensuring that students in this specialization receive training on how best to minimize their bias.

Through a storytelling approach that deliberately uses red herrings to distract students, we were able to provide a learning environment that promoted an increase in awareness of cognitive biases amongst our computer forensics students to some small degree, leading to reports that expressed less wild speculation and more conclusions that were better founded. However, we noticed that additional reminders would be beneficial to the students, along with a shorter feedback cycle in place.

Specifically, we will need to restructure the game and storytelling so that students can receive feedback sooner and more regularly so that any biased decision-making can be rectified. This will allow students to submit final reports that are built on mostly correct findings, as opposed to only finding out in the end how far from the true state of affairs they have been. It is anticipated that early feedback will serve as a more regular reminder of bias at play and that students will recognise the importance of conducting equivocal forensic analysis in mitigating the effects of that bias, allowing them to reach what should be a more correct conclusion at the end of the day.

## References

1. Turvey, B.E.: Criminal Profiling: An Introduction to Behavioral Evidence Analysis, 4th edn. Academic Press, Oxford (2012)
2. Piper, C.E.: Investigator and Fraud Fighter Guidebook: Operation War Stories. Wiley, Hoboken (2014)
3. Turvey, B.E., Crowder, S.: Forensic Investigations: An Introduction. Academic Press, London (2017)
4. Camilleri, A., Abarno, D., Bird, C., Coxon, A., Mitchell, N., Redman, K., Sly, N., Wills, S., Silenieks, E., Simpson, E., Lindsay, H.: A risk-based approach to cognitive bias in forensic science. Sci. Justice **59**(5), 533–543 (2019)
5. Casey, E., Turvey, B.E.: Investigative reconstruction with digital evidence. In: Digital Evidence and Computer Crime: Forensic Science, Computers and the Internet, 3rd edn., pp. 255–284. Academic Press, Cambridge (2011)
6. Wrenn, J., Wrenn, B.: Enhancing learning by integrating: theory and practice. Int. J. Teach. Learn. High. Educ. **21**(2), 258–265 (2009)
7. Gardner, B.O., Kelley, S., Murrie, D.C., Dror, I.E.: What do forensic analysts consider relevant to their decision making? Sci. Justice **59**, 516–523 (2019)
8. Hopkins, S., Wilson, A., Silva, A., Forsythe, C.: Facilitation of forensic analysis using a narrative template. Procedia Manuf. **3**, 5022–5027 (2015)
9. Cooley, C.M., Turvey, B.E.: Observer effects and examiner bias: psychological influences on the forensic examiner. In: Crime Reconstruction, 2nd edn., pp. 61–90. Academic Press, Cambridge (2011)
10. Lander, E., Press, W., Gates Jr., S.J., Graham, S.L., McQuade, J.M., Schrag, D.: Report to the president: forensic science in criminal courts: ensuring scientific validity of feature-comparison methods (2016)
11. Almazrouei, M.A., Dror, I.E., Morgan, R.M.: The forensic disclosure model: what should be disclosed to, and by, forensic experts? Int. J. Law Crime Justice **59**, 100330 (2019)

12. Biedermann, A., et al.: E-learning initiatives in forensic interpretation: report on experiences from current projects and outlook. Forensic Sci. Int. **230**, 2–7 (2013)
13. Powell, M.B.: Designing effective training programs for investigative interviewers of children. Curr. Issues Crime Justice **20**(2), 189–208 (2008)
14. Thompson, W.C.: Developing effective methods for addressing contextual bias in forensic science. Office of Justice Programs' National Criminal Justice Reference Service (2018)
15. Casey, E.: Digital evidence in the courtroom. In: Digital Evidence and Computer Crime: Forensic Science, Computers and the Internet, 3rd edn., pp. 49–84. Academic Press, Cambridge (2011)
16. Cooper, G.S., Meterko, V.: Cognitive bias research in forensic science: a systematic review. Forensic Sci. Int. **297**, 35–46 (2019)
17. Dror, I.E.: Biases in forensic experts. Science **360**(6386), 243 (2018)
18. Kukucka, J., Kassin, S.M., Zapf, P.A., Dror, I.E.: Cognitive bias and blindness: a global survey of forensic science examiners. J. Appl. Res. Mem. Cogn. **6**(4), 452–459 (2017)
19. van den Eeden, C.A.J., de Poot, C.J., van Koppen, P.J.: The forensic confirmation bias: a comparison between experts and novices. J. Forensic Sci. **64**(1), 120–126 (2018)
20. Forensics. www.forensicbasics.org. Accessed 15 Mar 2019
21. Nickerson, R.S.: Confirmation bias: a ubiquitous phenomenon in many guises. Rev. Gen. Psychol. **2**(2), 175–220 (1998)
22. Helping Students Overcome Confirmation Bias. https://nobaproject.com/blog/2018-12-05-helping-students-overcome-confirmation-bias. Accessed 15 Mar 2019
23. Stapleton, P.: Avoiding cognitive biases: promoting good decision making in research methods courses. Teach. High. Educ. Crit. Perspect. **24**(4), 578–586 (2018)
24. Suwardy, T., Pan, G., Seow, P.: Using digital storytelling to engage student learning. Account. Educ. **22**(2), 109–124 (2019)
25. Herreid, C.F.: Start with a Story: The Case Study Method of Teaching College Science. National Science Teachers Association, Virginia (2006)
26. Storytelling as a Pedagogical Tool. http://teachingthroughthearts.blogspot.com/2012/07/storytelling-as-pedagogical-tool.html. Accessed 15 Mar 2019
27. Storytelling: an Important Pedagogical Approach. https://www.westpoint.edu/sites/default/files/inline-images/centers_research/center_for_teching_excellence/PDFs/mtp_project_papers/DzwonczykJ_18.pdf. Accessed 15 Mar 2019
28. What Is a Red Herring in Writing? Definition of Red Herring with Examples - 2020. https://www.masterclass.com/articles/what-is-a-red-herring-in-writing-definition-of-red-herring-with-examples. Accessed 15 Mar 2019
29. Rothstein, B., Varraich, A.: Making Sense of Corruption. Cambridge University Press, Cambridge (2017)

# Author Index

The manufacturer's authorised representative in the EU is Springer Nature Customer Service Centre GmbH, Europaplatz 3, 69115 Heidelberg, Germany. If you have any concerns regarding our products, please contact ProductSafety@springernature.com

Printed and bound by CPI Group (UK) Ltd, Croydon, CR0 4YY
30/09/2026
02225505-0005